A CAT'S TALE

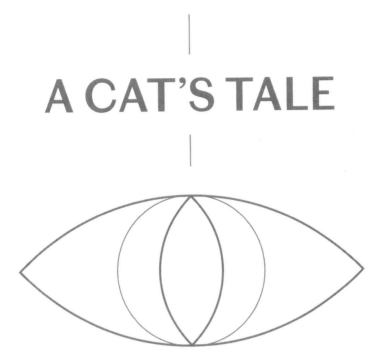

A CAT'S TALE

A JOURNEY THROUGH FELINE HISTORY

Baba the Cat

as dictated to Paul Koudounaris

Henry Holt and Company
New York

Henry Holt and Company
Publishers since 1866

120 Broadway, New York, New York 10271
www.henryholt.com

Henry Holt ® and 🅗® are registered trademarks of Macmillan Publishing Group, LLC.

Distributed in Canada by Raincoast Book Distribution Limited

LIBRARY OF CONGRESS CATALOGING-IN-PUBLICATION DATA

Names: Koudounaris, Paul, author.

Title: A cat's tale: a journey through feline history / Paul Koudounaris.

Description: First edition. | New York, New York: Henry Holt and Company, 2020. | Includes bibliographical references and index.

Identifiers: LCCN 2019032333 (print) | LCCN 2019032334 (ebook) | ISBN 9781250217721 (hardcover) | ISBN 9781250217714 (ebook)

Subjects: LCSH: Cats–History. | Domestic animals–History.

Classification: LCC SF442.6 .K68 2020 (print) | LCC SF442.6 (ebook) | DDC 636.8–dc23

LC record available at https://lccn.loc.gov/2019032333
LC ebook record available at https://lccn.loc.gov/2019032334

ISBN: 9781250217721

Our books may be purchased in bulk for promotional, educational, or business use. Please contact your local bookseller or the Macmillan Corporate and Premium Sales Department at (800) 221-7945, extension 5442, or by email at MacmillanSpecialMarkets@macmillan.com.

FIRST EDITION 2020
Design by Simona Materazzini at Barnbrook
Printed in the United States of America

10 9 8 7 6 5 4 3 2 1

This book is dedicated to all those
indomitable cats who made history,
and to the humans who had the wisdom
to stay out of their way and let them do so.

CONTENTS

INTRODUCTION: INVITATION FOR A GRAND ADVENTURE FROM A VERY LEARNED TABBY CAT

Humans are ever so fond of remarking on how difficult it is for them to understand cats. As this has proven to be a vexing issue for your species, permit me to set the record straight: we cats are eminently understandable to one another, therefore any challenge in understanding us is entirely on your end. Furthermore, if I may be frank, it is more than a bit presumptuous of humankind to believe it should be their prerogative to know our business.

I must concede, however, that there is never any harm in a bit of understanding. You have shown yourself to be of commendable intention and ample curiosity by beginning these pages, so I will therefore offer my services in supplementing your meager store of knowledge. And dare I say that if you wish to know about cats, you have come to the right place, as none among us has so dedicated herself to our study as I!

Ah—but what is it that you wish to learn?

Perhaps you would have me discourse on different breeds, explaining how the markings rendered on one cat's coat make it a medal winner of great value, whereas the markings on another leave it no better than a guttersnipe? Or perhaps it would please you to have me recollect well-known felines from cartoons and television shows? Or better still, what if I were to discuss the cats made famous by the internet, their faces printed onto T-shirts and their antics popular with millions of people?

These topics are of great interest to humans, but herein lies a conundrum: if these are the types of things that you wish to know about, then you *don't really wish to know about cats!* Discussing them would only serve to reveal your own petty machinations, because they are inventions of man, and of no interest to felines. What do we care about whether the sheen of a cat's coat corresponds to a breeder's manual? This is hardly how we judge amongst one another. As well, we have scant interest in cartoon characters who provide a vehicle to express loutish human behavior, made comical by being projected into a feline body. And the cats you have elevated to the status of celebrity? They ring the bells on your cash registers, but they offer not one whit of a clue about the gravitas of the feline condition. Empty stereotypes, they imply that the *raison d'être* of our species is to be cute, and thereby serve human amusement—hardly a discussion any dignified cat would deign to undertake.

If you really wish to learn about us, it is necessary that you put aside the topics with which you are familiar. In their stead, you must relive our tale. It is a saga that starts in days long past, when proud among nature's creations we prowled primordial forests in which humankind lived no differently than beasts. As it winds through the millennia, you will find as much love and honor as any species has known, and heroism to boot. Of great names there are plenty, cats of achievement and distinction whose paw prints stand large even after the passage of centuries. And don't think there isn't sadness too, because our story tells of far more than its fair share of suffering and loss.

Wait, Baba, feline history? You ask as if it is some peculiar topic. The ego of your kind is so vast that it lays claim to the past as if it is entirely the product of human endeavor. In your accountings, you credit history only to humanity, and offer scant mention of the contributions of other species, without whose assistance you would have in truth gotten next to nowhere. Shall I prove my point? When you speak of Alexander the Great, you recount the grandest of triumphs, with exploits that have ever since stirred hearts and filled books too numerous to count. But how many of you speak with equal reverence of Bucephalus?

If you remember the name at all, you consider him to be merely the steed that served a great man's bidding. But I ask you, did not this "mere" horse carry Alexander through every conquest, share equally in every feat of daring do, risk his life charging with the force of the winds into battle—and then with equal resolve sprint to safety when his human companion's life was in peril? Trusting in one another and sharing in every turn, the two were partners at the least. And should you be tempted to consign to the horse the role of junior partner, ask yourself where Alexander would have been without Bucephalus. Hmm, I'll tell you where: stuck in Macedonia, because I hardly think he could have walked all the way to India, and from there to Egypt!

So you see, all species have had a hand—or claw or hoof, as the case may be—in shaping history. Each has its own storied past, and all of them are incontrovertibly connected. This fact is at its most certain when it comes to cats and humans, because the historical connection between us is as intimate as any. We stood at your side at the very dawn of civilization. Raised by your hands to the thrones of the gods, we witnessed from on high your greatest glories. We marched with you through the passage of time and migrated to exotic lands. And we stand at your side still to this very day.

Despite this, our journey through history has been consistently overlooked by humans, and our greatest achievements dismissed as trivial. It is typical for you now to see us as your wards, as helpless creatures who would be lost without you, a proposition which is equally amusing and insulting. "Don't let the poor cat out!" you whisper, as we stare through the window or dart toward an open door. In your estimation we would scarcely survive even a minute out in the world. If only you knew what our kind has overcome! And truth be told, I suspect even the stoutest humans have nary the survival skills born into the average street cat.

Those of you who see us as meek little creatures shall find that notion dispelled in no uncertain terms within these pages. I will introduce you to cats who have not just traveled the globe, but traveled all the way into space (so much for not letting the cat out, eh?); others who have stood fast during the world's great conflicts, choosing sides among the armies of man, and earning for themselves medals of valor; and still other cats whose exploits garnered great adulation. Why, in honor of Trim, who sailed the Seven Seas in the eighteenth and nineteenth centuries and is remembered as the world's most famous maritime cat, there have been erected four statues. How many of even the most heroic humans can match that?

Yes, friends, if you really want to know about cats, our tale will turn many of your ideas on their heads. If you believe us to be selfish, you will find more than ample proof of our loyalty in the accounts of felines who willingly risked their lives for the humans they loved. Should you consider us lazy, you will be squarely rebuked by the stories of cats who undertook perilous journeys over thousands of miles. And any who doubt our influence will find that we have consorted with some of the finest names in art, literature, and politics, inspiring some of their greatest achievements—and oftentimes winding up enmeshed in their intrigues.

Likewise, those who think our lives are nothing but comfort will find that we have endured calumnies beyond which any species has known. I warn you right now that these pages contain not only joy. The hands which raised us high would later cast us back down to the pit of our greatest despair. I will not for the sake of good manners hide the truth of our sorrows and tribulations, and I don't imagine you yourself will be unscathed by the accounting. But my kind is resilient, and in the end I will show you how modern felines vanquished the slings and arrows of misfortune—a triumph that may force you to take further stock of the little cat that sits in your very living room as you read these words!

So now I must ask, is it still your desire to learn of my kind, knowing all that I have forewarned? Will you follow our path? If so, I extend my paw as your guide. Our tale will unfold before you as I pilot us through centuries long forgotten. We shall sail placid waters glowing golden under an ancient sun, past the rocky shores of volatile ages, and through the rough currents that lead to the modern world. A grand journey is in the offing. But the point of departure nears. The choice to sally forth is of course yours to make, but you have come this far, so I advise you hustle yourself to the dock! With but a mere turn of the page, we will alight in the deepest mists of time.

A CAT'S TALE

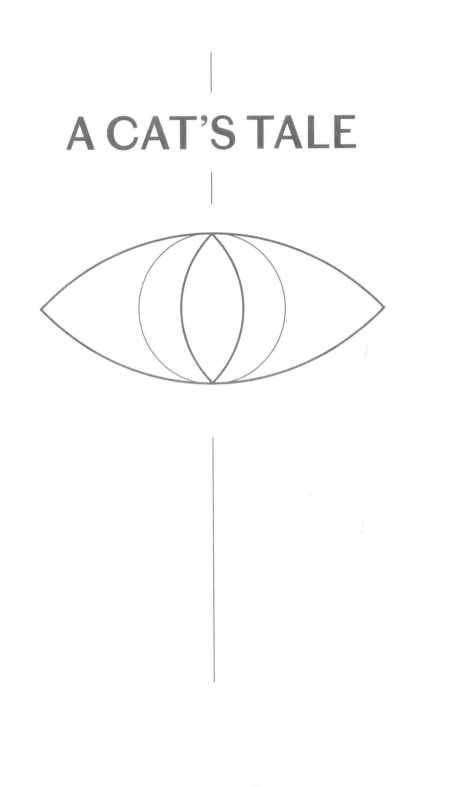

THE GOLDEN AGE: CATS IN PREHISTORY AND ANCIENT EGYPT

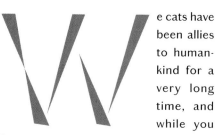

We cats have been allies to humankind for a very long time, and while you have reserved the sobriquet "man's best friend" for the dog, I may now provide you reasons to judge differently. In fact, archeological evidence offers hints that felines have been your companions for as long if not longer than canines—or to put it this way, the partnership between cats and humans is older than currency, older than man's use of metals, and older even than written language. It dates to the very foundation of civilization itself, and we might reasonably argue that without our assistance, your civilization may not have gotten very far. Human pride is such that you assume this is bluster on my part. But consider the view of your great ancestors in the matter, being so thankful for our presence that they believed us to be representatives of deities. We have arrived in the glory days, my friends, when humans and cats together marched from the most humble of beginnings to heights undreamt.

These early feline companions were descended from *Felis silvestris lybica*, a common wildcat found in the Near East and North Africa. Only slightly larger than a modern domestic cat and sporting a tawny coat with brindled markings, our great-grandfather many times removed would not be too terribly different in appearance from a tabby such as myself. But despite all the virtues we domestic cats possess, I am forced to acknowledge that comparing us to little *Felis* pays him a grave disservice. He was as cunning and quick as only a wildcat can be, and with a strength that greatly belied his size. You humans who are impressed by a modern cat's ability to bring in a lizard now and again would find *Felis* possessed of skills that would put ours to shame.

But why wouldn't *Felis* be a fierce and dangerous hunter? There's something about thirteen million years of evolution that tends to leave a cat pretty well adapted to its environment. And we house cats in turn claim a direct line of descent from him, which makes humans far our juniors. *Homo sapiens* is a mere three hundred thousand years old in comparison, so pardon us if we seem periodically snooty, but we're well aware that we have been tested and crafted by time. And to counter a common misconception on your part, I'll have you know that big cats evolved only three million years ago, so any of you who consider domestic cats to be a lion or tiger cut down to size need to think again. When it comes to felines, it was the small who begat the large.

Another issue you may need to rethink is the idea that humans domesticated us. Sorry, the truth is we domesticated ourselves. *Felis* did not need your help to survive, and as he was no dummy, you certainly would not have succeeded in tricking or coercing him into accepting your company. Rather, he willingly entered into your communities, and on recognizing that a mutually beneficial relationship could exist between felines and humans, he agreed to stay. In fact, rather than the term "domestication," I would prefer we use "partnership." As I've noted in our introduction, isn't it much closer to the truth, after all? But let me tell you the story and we'll see if you don't concur.

It was during the tail end of prehistory, the Neolithic, when humans in Mesopotamia began to practice agriculture, and this development would have many consequences. For one thing, it required that you cease your wandering ways and establish the first towns and villages. Oh, how your pride would sink if you could see those conclaves of huts constructed of mud and twigs—why, you were practically living in grandiose beaver lodges! But I do give credit where it is due: you tended your crops brilliantly, establishing such a surplus of grain that it would alter not just your own evolutionary path but those of all the species around you.

Among them were rats and mice, crafty types whose nefarious doings we will hear much of in our story. Scavenging from your excess was easy pickings, and they soon began gravitating around your dwellings. In typical human fashion you hadn't thought things through. You had considered with great astuteness the growing of crops, but

nary did you ponder if anyone else might want to eat them! And without any plan, you were caught off guard. Silent, nimble, and scarcely seen by your eyes, the greedy little vermin took what they wished and often spoilt the rest.

So you despaired. But not for long— because little *Felis* offered a solution. If you didn't want those rodents, he was glad to take them off your hands. They were an important food source for him, you see, and since there was an undeniable advantage in having his quarry massed in predictable locations, he began to congregate around your settlements as well. Of course, he was initially wary of your kind. And to be fair, you can't fault him. Consider yourselves through feline eyes. You are big—huge, even! You lumber about on two feet in a manner that seems to the more dexterous species to be nothing but clumsy, and, even more off-putting, you're *loud*. I won't go so far as to call you boorish, but you must admit you lack subtlety when it comes to dominating the world around you.

But little *Felis* had no lack of fortitude. He dared approach your homes in search of prey, and in the process found an additional advantage. For your own security you had been eliminating large and dangerous mammals from the outskirts of your villages, and this had the effect of creating a safe haven for smaller predators. This was a place where cats could prosper, *Felis* realized! In your orbit he became an apex hunter, blessed

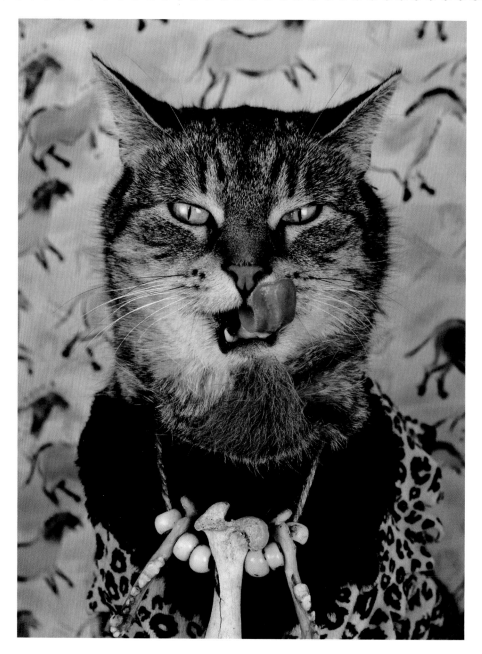

4

with an ample supply of game and a limited threat from larger animals. And as he decimated the rodents who had decimated your grain, the foundation for a symbiotic relationship between felines and humans was laid.

Of course, even if each provided benefit to the other, it didn't mean that the path leading to home and hearth would be trod quickly or easily. Just as *Felis* was reticent to trust the notoriously unpredictable humans, it's also a safe bet that prehistoric people were more than a little leery of him. Your great ancestors were well aware that while wildcats were small in stature, they were well equipped with claw and tooth. If *Felis* could eviscerate a rat with a single swipe, what he might do to a human hand?

But the relationship prospered in spite of such trepidations. After all, the last thing you wanted was for us to leave, lest you again become inundated with rodents. So if we hunted too well, you began to leave scraps of food from your tables for us, to ensure that we stayed nearby. Cuttings of prepared meat would have seemed a peculiar meal to a prehistoric cat, but then again they were tasty, and the fact that they miraculously appeared made life all the easier, so *Felis* accepted the offer. I doubt either could see it, the process occurring too slowly, but human and feline were becoming increasingly reliant upon each other. A cat's affections are of course won slowly, and in the case of little *Felis*, it would have

taken the passage of centuries. But as the relationship grew ever closer, the end result was inevitable.

If you will permit a bit of romantic vision, I imagine the historic breakthrough occurring on the outskirts of a ramshackle village in perhaps Iraq or Syria, some ten thousand years ago. Let us say sometime after midday, with the sun still high after warming the fields. I envision a man looking out toward the brush where the domain of humans officially stops. This is the border of his world, the place beyond which wildness lives, and as he squints into the shadows he sees bright eyes peering back. They are everywhere, hidden among the bushes and branches: dozens of eyes, sparkling green and almond-shaped. He knows of them, he and the other villagers having seen them countless times before. These eyes belong to the ones who prey on the rodents who prey on the crops.

Then a sudden flurry, and amid the scampering of paws the eyes disappear. Just as they always seem to when the man catches a glimpse of them. But this time there is something different. This time . . . one pair of eyes remains. These eyes are bold, they do not flinch and they do not waiver, instead staring back from the shadows as the man stares into the brush. The man bends low, squaring down on his haunches. Never has he seen the eyes so clearly as now. Slowly, as fear mixes with exhilaration, he reaches his hand forward with an open palm. And just

before him, at the very edge of his domain, stands little *Felis*. Ah, if the humans were curious about the eyes in the shadows, for how many generations had *Felis* and his kin been curious about the big, loud creatures standing among the fields? And he, equally filled with fear and exhilaration, steels his courage and steps forward, his body emerging from the brush.

The man's palm now descends. Slowly, slowly, oh so slowly — he knows what those claws can do, and he has no desire to be swatted by them. At the same time, *Felis* pushes his head upward, and the hand lands gently between the cat's ears. Just a touch, and then the fingers brush the neck and glide onto the back. Oh, a new sensation! The man's hand, cracked and callused from his labors, revels in the exultant feeling of the soft, plush fur. And . . . that will be enough of that! *Felis* vanishes back into the shadows, and the man's fingers grasp only emptiness, as the two nervous partners leave their encounter at nothing more than a simple stroke. It ends so quickly, a mere moment in time. Who could have guessed that with such a simple gesture two worlds were forever changed?

Such a scene would have been enacted again and again and again in villages across the Near East and North Africa. As little *Felis* continued to return to the edge of the brush and his skittishness dissipated, he would stand a little further out from the shadows. And as man returned to the edge of his fields and learned those claws were not meant for him, his own skittishness likewise dissipated and his hand lingered longer. He would then be joined by his kin, and a touch became a caress, which finally became an embrace. Eventually, man invited *Felis* to enter his domain and make residence. And *Felis*, grown accustomed to man's hand and the comfort it provided, overlooked his own independent nature.

What started with the chasing of mice had resulted in the unlikely union of two very different species, and one of the places that union would occur was along the Nile River in northern Africa. For millennia, rushing waters from the depths of the southern jungle had been picking up rich silt and carrying it northward. As the river ebbed and flowed along a four-thousand-mile path to the Mediterranean Sea, it wound through the Sahara Desert, and a land that was otherwise arid and inhospitable was not so on its banks. The silt deposited along this route had carved a lush corridor where plants and animals could thrive. Roving bands of hunters and cattle herders discovered this paradise and made a home of it, and by 4000 BC they began to plant crops and form permanent settlements like their brethren in the Near East.

I don't doubt that you know the second chapter of their story: the villages they founded prospered and, having been unified as Egypt, stood for three thousand years as the greatest civilization the world had yet seen. But that chapter was still another millennia in the future, and hardly could one have predicted such grandeur from beginnings which were not at all auspicious. Those poor farmers! Their land was good and their bounty plentiful, but their granaries were plagued by an especially troublesome breed of river rat from which they could find no relief. Ah, but who would come to their rescue? Our friend *Felis*, of course! The little wildcats began to appear on the outskirts of these towns too, hunting down the pernicious Nile vermin and endearing themselves to the hearts of the local farmers.

The bond that developed in this new land was particularly strong, and of all the ancient societies that took us to heart, it was in Egypt that the greatest gratitude for our service was felt. Our partnership with humanity called for you to serve us as much as we served you, but as time passed the people there allowed for the onus of servitude to fall more and more squarely onto mankind. Never forgetting their debt to the felines who had stood by their side at the dawn of their nation, the Egyptians allowed the fortunes of men and cats to become intertwined. And when they stepped forward to the vanguard of civilization, they asked us to walk alongside them, and we remained at their side, soaring to the zenith of feline culture as they soared to the pinnacles of human achievement.

Why was this so, Baba? What spell had cats wrought over the people along the Nile? That we had charmed them was beyond doubt. They were so delighted by our vocalizing skills that they took note and named us accordingly, using *miu* for male cats and *miit* for females, becoming the first humans to use words that you would later know as "meow." But truth being told, we have charmed any number of humans in any number of countries, and charming behavior alone can account for only so much. Clearly, there was something more at work in Egypt. The people who had taken us into their humble homes anticipated that we would control rodents, but found to their delight that our skills did not stop at rats and mice: we were deadly effective in hunting scorpions, cobras, and vipers as well.

Providing relief from these poisonous intruders not only heightened the sense of debt they felt toward us, it peaked their curiosity. The Egyptians began to pay more attention to our behavior and were shocked to find that felines appeared precognizant. Some cats seemed to know in advance about changes in the weather, others could sense impending earthquakes, and still others would warn their humans of seemingly invisible dangers. Our small size so belied our abilities that the Egyptians began to wonder whether our powers were something beyond natural. Perhaps we had indeed wrought a spell, and they began to conjecture about whether there might be an innate correspondence between felines and magic.

In the Ancient World, magic was no joke, nor was it malevolent. Accepted among all levels of human society, it was considered a transcendent force by which the travails of a chaotic and hostile world might be overcome. Be that as it may, perhaps you hold doubts and look upon the topic with condescension? After all, the abilities the Egyptians had mistaken for magic are easily explained as products of a sensory acuity which in felines is far superior to man's. Whereas humans will not receive foreboding of a storm until the clouds have gathered, we cats will sense it far in advance

due to changes in barometric pressure. Or a stealthy intruder will be seen and heard by us from far off in what to you is total darkness and silence.

And so on and so forth, and in this way we became conceived of as a bulwark against evil. That felines had apotropaic powers was unquestioned, and if a cat chose to favor a particular human, it would thereafter secure that person and his family from harm. But before you judge the Egyptians as simple people, realize that it was not only rational for them in such a time and place to put great stock in our abilities, it was wise to do so. In your modern hubris, you have turned a blind eye to messages from the species around you, but in observing cats closely and by understanding our behavior, the Egyptians did in truth receive some measure of the foresight they desired.

Magical? No, but the effect was nevertheless real, and they increasingly invoked us in rites of protection. They also placed our image on items designed to compel the supernatural, from the tiniest of amulets to the largest ever conceived: the Great Sphinx, history's most famous guardian figure, matched the head of the pharaoh, Egypt's divine king, to a gargantuan feline body. Among the potent items we were associated with was the mirror, which was used for something more than vanity back in the day. Polished pieces of flat copper, they could reflect evil and send it back to its source. Nice trick, but to ensure its effec-

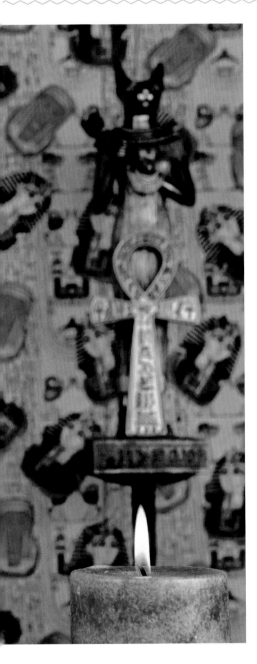

tiveness, a mirror needed *real* power, and thus the trusted image of a cat was often engraved upon the back or handle. We were also depicted on a bronze rattle which the Egyptians named the sistrum. It was considerably more than a musical instrument, however. Its rounded top was symbolic of the womb, and its pointed handle of the phallus. Potent indeed, as shaking it represented the agitation of the elements that governed birth, decay, and rebirth. And the feline standing at the top safeguarded this eternal process.

Think of how times have changed, as nowadays you watch over us, while back then it was we who watched over you. In fact, we so dominated the human psyche that each and every feline represented no less than a metaphor for Creation. This was in accordance with a popular legend that told of the time before time, when all was darkness and nary a living thing existed until the sun god Ra came forth, appearing in the form of the *Miu Oa*, or Great Tomcat. As the first paw prints trammeled upon the void, he wished for a world to be born into which man could be formed.

How wise Ra was to have chosen his feline form, because another soon appeared to stand in opposition. This rival was named Apophis, and his form was that of a serpent. He was the god of eternal darkness, and it was his wish that all remain as a void. But the Great Tomcat was determined that things should be, and he set upon the snake.

How long the primordial battle lasted, no one could say, because even time itself did not yet exist. That it was a fierce battle we can have no doubt, but the *Miu Oa* vanquished the serpent, and thus was the darkness loosened so that the world and all that would dwell in it were born. Ah, well, I told you the Egyptians valued our ability to hunt snakes! In so doing, we were not just protecting the home, but offering a metaphor for genesis itself.

Creation at the paws of a cat? Baba, this is news to me, you say. But maybe not, because you're well familiar with another part of the story, which has remained current to this very day. Ah, but you need a hint? The priests of Heliopolis recounted how afterward, Ra, in the form of a tomcat, begat other deities. First came the embodiments of air and water, respectively, who in turn issued forth earth and sky. And these responded with the great gods Osiris, Isis, Set, and Nephthys. Wait now . . . how many deities is this? We will allow Ra to count them for us: "I am one who becomes two, two who becomes four, four who becomes eight, and I am one more besides." In other words, the *Miu Oa*, the Great Tomcat, is eight and then another . . . He is one among nine! Yes, nine lives. The story outlasted Egypt itself to become the most long-standing of feline legends. And the American brand of cat food that bears the same name? It may be cheap, but it turns out it can rightfully claim its place as divine sustenance.

Felines were as irresistible to the gods as they were to the Egyptian people, and our legends evolved as we picked up associations with others among the pantheon. Chief among these in the early days of Egypt was the elegant and mysterious Isis, and she would prove a great force in shaping our history. As a mistress of magic, she had a natural connection to felines, and the Egyptians speculated on whether she played some role in our enigmatic abilities. She was also a goddess of the night, and despite our initial connection to the sun, by her hand, the moon rose above us. Black cats in particular,

their coats the color of nether night, were thought to have a special relationship with the goddess. Considered the most magical of our kind, it was speculated that they might even be epiphanies of Isis herself.

In the end, we became far more popular as lunar symbols than solar. It simply jibed better with our nocturnal nature, and later cultures also picked up on the same association. The Greeks and Romans went so far as to claim that the pupils of our eyes changed with the phases of the moon. The romantic—but crazy!—myth purported that our pupils became more round when the moon was full, and narrow when it waned. Oh, and be sure to monitor a cat's birthing patterns, ancient sages advised! If a female had seven litters, the first of one kitten, the second of two, and so on up to the seventh for a combined total of twenty-eight—well, that would be one kitten for every day of the lunar month. And you would have on your hands something more than a very busy mama cat . . . This was a moon goddess cat to be sure, a direct representative of a deity, and to be treated with all due respect and sanctimony.

Isis also governed over women as a patron of childbirth and motherhood. Perhaps we felines could again serve as her totem animal to represent femininity, domesticity, and the protection of children? We were already considered protectors of the household, and of course unchecked cats have a notably high fertility rate (yes, we've come to accept that spay and neuter isn't such a bad idea). And when it came to our own young, we had made a strong impression as the most fierce of defenders, with females of our kind famed for their willingness to risk their own lives to safeguard their kittens.

The pieces fit together quite nicely, the Egyptians decided, and every home's cat became a de facto household god. In particular, they asked us to guard over their young, placing around the necks of their infants amulets bearing a feline likeness in the hopes that we would protect them as we did our own. Once again it was all backed by legend, the Egyptians declaring that the infant Horus had been nursed by a cat. Bearing in mind that Horus represented the divine aspect of no less than the pharaoh, this meant that felines were worthy enough to be considered surrogate mothers for the king himself. And if you're unimpressed with that as a statement regarding our status, put it another way: modern-day humans hold their cats in outstanding regard, to be sure, but when was the last time you heard one of them claim that we suckled the president of the United States or the queen of England?

Over time, the association between cats and the feminine sphere grew even closer, until ideal femininity became codified in feline form. The consummate woman was catlike in her being and bearing, and so indelibly so that Egypt's most famous queen, Cleopatra, decided to style her own eye makeup after the distinctive facial markings of her beloved companion, Charmian. The queen clearly knew a good look when she saw it, and the cat's natural beauty inspired her to use thick black lines to exaggerate her eyes into an almond shape. The gesture would revolutionize fashion and has ever since stood the test of time as one of its most iconic statements. Of course, from an Egyptian perspective, there was nothing radical about it, being nothing more than the union of two harmonious principles.

It was only natural that our adherents would eventually seek a vessel into which those principles were perfectly fused, a deity in which the two archetypes could exist in an equally supreme state. Thus was born Bastet. Typically, she was represented as a beautiful woman with a cat's head, but she was not simply a goddess who was associated with cats. Bastet was something greater, a synthesis between the feline and human, and she was no less than the ultimate gift from your kind to ours. Later generations of humans turned on her, toppled her images and decried her name as unholy, but we have always held her dear. It was to her memory that we cats clung in our darkest hours, knowing that the union envisioned within her held the hope for a brighter future.

Fitting her feline nature, Bastet was not averse to a little bit of coy mystery. Her origins are not only considerably murky nowadays, they were even murky to the Egyptians. She was not known in their early history, and some among their scholars believed her to be the offspring of Isis from a union with Ra. Or perhaps, they theorized, a union with Osiris. Or perhaps—aha!—she was Isis herself, having attained a perfect feline incarnation? No one could ever get it straight, but one thing was clear: Bastet was a cat indeed, because like the ultimate stray, she showed up from parts unknown, and with her pedigree unspoken, but nevertheless stole a heart—and in her case, it was the heart of an entire nation.

It was during the second millennium BC that she began to gain popularity. And why wouldn't she have? Good kitty that she was, she guaranteed for her followers domestic tranquility and of course served in the traditional feline role of guardian. In her case, being conceived as an actual cat, all of our talents to protect humans were maximized, and a new one was even added, as she in addition became a warden of the dead. Traditionally, Egyptians had looked to Anubis, the jackal-headed god, to guide them into the afterlife. But you might as well teach that old dog some new tricks as far as the nation's cat worshippers were concerned, because it was Bastet who would now act as the soul's chaperone.

The cult of the cat proved an unstoppable force, and by the year 1000 had supplanted those of the other members of the Egyptian pantheon as the most popular in the country. By that time, we even had our own city, Bubastis, in the Nile Delta, the center of all things feline and the seat of Bastet herself. But all of this could not have been accomplished by her alone. The Egyptians understood us well. They saw in us a dichotomy that nowadays is overlooked. Yes, we are loving and sweet, and often desire nothing more than to cuddle in your arms, but the domestic companion sitting on your sofa is only one side of feline nature. We are also lethal predators. After all, was that not the ability that humans initially prized about cats, centuries before cuddling was even a thought?

To pay tribute to that aspect of our kind, the Egyptians had provided Bastet with a sister. Named Sekhmet, her head was that of a female lion, and she provided a ferocious counterpart to the loving domestic cat. Yet the two were complements rather than opposites, each incomplete without the other. "She rages like Sekhmet and is friendly like Bastet," went a saying from the era about the two poles of feline nature. Bastet ruled the heart and protected the household, representing the cat as adored by the common people. Sekhmet, meanwhile, was a symbol of feline strength and cunning, the fearsome patron of the army and protector of the nation.

Together the two sisters conquered. Egypt had been in political turmoil at the end of the second millennium BC, but the nation found in the cult of the cat common cause and was reunited by the start of the first. Eventually the crown fell to a royal dynasty from Bubastis, and it was there that power was consolidated. And when King Osorkon II offered to Bastet all his lands in obeisance, and unto her all the power of Ra, he declared the monarchy itself to be a servant of the divine feline. Think back now to those fields along the Nile tended by those humble humans and the wildcats who came to their defense. Who could have ever predicted such an outcome when the alliance was first made? But the seed that had been planted some three thousand years before now bore its fullest fruit: Egypt was but a toy in our paws.

What was life like for us back in that great, gilded era? Within the domicile, as you might guess, we were inviolable, nothing less than the very soul of a household. Caring for a cat was serious business. Our upkeep was the responsibility of the family's patriarch, and when he died it fell to the firstborn son. Heavy jeweled collars and golden ear cuffs provided us with marks of distinction, and have no doubts that families competed with one another when it came to feline couture since their own status rose and fell with their cat's. Since the question tends to arise, yes, it is true that felines are not typically fond of wearing such accoutrements that serve no purpose other than human vanity. But the dedication of these Egyptians was so far beyond reproach that their cats were willing to put up with a bit of foolishness and bear their jewelry in exchange for the genuine perks that came with being adored.

And nowhere was that adoration more greatly expressed than in the center of Bubastis itself. There stood the Temple of Bastet, the greatest monument ever erected in honor of feline power. It has been allowed to wither over time so that, to the horror of cats everywhere, only scant traces now remain—eh, well, considering how you humans have more often than not allowed even your own historic splendors to be destroyed, I suppose it would have been expecting far too much for you to be any more conscientious of ours. But even so, the cracked and scattered stones are for us magnificent relics. Our most treasured patrimony, each fragment holds within it the eternal memory of distant glory, a temple praised by no less than Herodotus—the most renowned of all ancient chroniclers—as the most beautiful sanctuary in all of Egypt.

Such a sight had not been seen before and has defied the imagination ever since! Surrounded by canals one hundred feet wide and planted all around with lush trees, the Temple of Bastet appeared as an island idyll upon which rose mighty walls of red granite, like a massive fortress 1,200 feet in length. But these walls were not Bastet's shrine. Rather, they concealed it from view, as if the temple itself was a treasure so sacred that it could not be openly exposed to the public. Entering within, what they hid was scarcely less impressive: a sanctuary measuring some five hundred feet long with

a sixty-foot-high vestibule, and massive pylon walls in front to give her home the imposing look one expected of monumental Egyptian architecture.

But that appearance was yet again a deception. Inside, one did not find a cold stone interior. The lady was a cat, after all, and that would hardly be to feline tastes. Instead the imposing walls gave way to a virtual feline paradise: an interior courtyard that was open to the sky and planted with an entire forest of beautiful trees to climb and play in. And the sanctum, where Bastet's sacred image was housed, was hidden within for visitors to seek and find . . . Nicely played, I'd say, since we all know cats love secret places! And therein, in that most sanctified of spaces, was her sacred statue, the goddess herself made manifest.

But Bastet was not alone. Surrounding her were maidens, unabashedly giving themselves over to the divine presence, and one can only imagine the commotion as they sang and danced and rattled their sistrums in wild ecstasy. It was a good thing the goddess was but a statue, because the ruckus would have been enough to scare a flesh-and-blood cat—and probably it did, because her own sacred felines were themselves housed within the sanctum. Living embodiments of divinity, they could be seen in the temple's grand hypostyle hall, bedecked in jewels, golden collars, and precious earrings, wandering at their leisure among offerings left by an adoring public.

These were piled high, stretching up toward the distant ceiling, and consisting of fruit, honey, and exotic oils.

Ah, the dear Egyptians. Generous to a fault, but we must acknowledge these were curious items to be bringing . . . Did they fail to see, even with all their wisdom, that such things were of no interest to felines? But the temple cats returned the generosity of their adherents with a generosity of their own: rather than turn their backs, they received these useless gifts with dignity, understanding them as the products of an enthusiasm which, even if misplaced, was absolutely sincere. And when the hubbub became too much, which no doubt it often did, the cats had their own living quarters to retreat to. Closed off by luxurious golden cloths were private areas restricted to only themselves and their priests, allowing relief from the adoring masses.

To speak of adoring masses, at no time were they more numerous than during the annual festival held in Bastet's honor. Lost in the throes of ecstasy, frenzied cat worshippers descended upon Bubastis, pilgrims to the most popular religious rite in the Ancient World. Oh, come now, Baba, was it really? I can sense the doubt among the skeptics, who find it unlikely that a sacred cat festival could indeed surpass all others. But we don't have to take my word for it. We can put our trust in your own kind, once again the renowned Herodotus, who just so happened to attend the festival himself and estimated its attendees to be seven hundred thousand strong. In awe, he watched as they arrived, a massive spectacle unfolding with flotillas of riverboats packed so tightly that they filled the breadth of the Nile from bank to bank. The faithful had come from every corner of Egypt, and, shouting praises as loudly as their mighty voices would allow, they created a cacophonous din that the faraway feline ears of Heaven could not help but hear.

And when this crazed crowd hit the docks? Herodotus had seen much in his life, but he had never seen anything like *this*! The statue of Bastet was brought forth, with the highest of honors, escorted by military commanders, and placed upon a barge. Moving slowly enough so that all could see, she began to sail the canals around her temple. This was the moment of climax that some among the pilgrims had waited a lifetime for, and all the cat shows in all the modern world can give you not even the slightest hint of the excitement. Any last vestiges of moderation among the cat-obsessed supplicants were now lost to hysteria. Shoulder to shoulder, they stood along the banks, crying and swooning as she passed, and calling out for a blessing from the mightiest of felines.

Herodotus continued his account by noting how much wine was imbibed during the festival—and remember, the Greeks were no teetotalers themselves, but this, he explained, was shocking. The celebrants drank more wine than during the entire rest of the year combined, resulting by the end

of the day in drunken orgies throughout the city. Shame, shame, shame, you wonder? Not in the least! Humans are the most prudish of all species, but this was a divine cat festival, and Bastet was also the patron of sexuality. And if the hysteria I describe sounds to you perhaps more feral than pious, well, friends, the festival in Bubastis was not intended to be a solemn ceremony. It was something akin to a Mardi Gras celebration, a raucous affair during which the congregants unburdened themselves of the oppressive mantel of humanity, and, in a mad catharsis, gave release to their own inner felines.

Of course, not *all* of the city could afford to be lost in reverie, because there was also work to be done. Many pilgrims had requests, for miraculous healings and other special favors, that could only be granted by the living incarnations of the goddess. These were people who had come in sober and somber entreaty to petition the priests of Bastet for an audience with her sacred felines. With all due gravitas and the most conscientious deliberation, it was decided which cases would be heard. Then it would begin, as the wardens would make a click-click-clicking sound with their tongues to call forth the cats.

Imagine the wonderment upon a poor, distressed human who has traveled a great distance hoping for miraculous redemption. Already he is awed to find himself in the far reaches of the holiest of holy places, and

as his eyes strain against a darkness, there is a flurry of motion from the other side of the hall. Suddenly, the cats come bounding forward! Too quick to count, as human eyes can scarcely keep up with their darting forms—there is one!—and there!—and there, as the candlelight flickers off the jeweled collars in the distance. In an instant, the cats of Bastet were everywhere, filling the sanctum with divine grace.

When it came down to it, there were among the Egyptians those who knew a good offering from bad, and there was to be no honey or fruit when the stakes were this high. Supplicating themselves to the presence of divinity, humans poured bowls of milk, and bits of fish were cut into bite-size slices and laid out in rows. And then they backed away to allow feline wisdom to run its course. Would the cats partake of these offerings? Were the petitioners sincere enough in their veneration to be worthy of assistance? The cats made their deliberations, and a priest would chant and stare into their deep emerald eyes. Miracles were in the balance, and in the wisdom and beneficence of those eyes the verdict was conveyed.

As humanity is now convinced that the source of all authority lies in itself only, the idea of such complete reverence being visited upon domestic cats no doubt seems entirely comical to you—and that very attitude, my friends, would have once gotten you into considerable trouble. The Egyptians had a saying: "Do not laugh at a cat." Those who transgressed decorum did so at the risk of grave consequences, with penalties including fines at least, if not flogging. Considering the internet memes and YouTube videos lampooning our kind which have become ubiquitous in the present day, you should count yourselves lucky the lashes have been stilled. In a more ethical world, a mighty price would have been due for this kind of juvenile humor, and judging by some of what I have seen, even flogging might be considered lenient.

And if mockery was prohibited, imagine the consequences for causing physical harm to a feline. Such was a matter most serious, and the retribution could be so severe as to make even PETA blanch. Not only was the malicious killing of a cat a capital offense (rightly so, I should say!), the punishment might be no less even if the death were caused by accident. Penalties were in theory at the discretion of priests, but in practice they might not have time to adjudicate since enraged mobs were often quick to enact their own justice. Such was the case in Alexandria, when an incident occurred which so shocked the Greek historian Diodorus Siculus that he made special note of it in his journal.

A Roman soldier had hit a cat with his chariot, dealing poor puss a fatal blow. That the incident was inadvertent, there could be no doubt, but nonetheless a throng of angry Egyptians descended upon the man's home, demanding that he receive his come-uppance. "No, no, no!" pleaded royal officials sent to the scene—after all, the man was Roman, and they were concerned that if the mob became violent it might spark an international incident. "Please stand down!" they begged. Can you guess the outcome? Their appeals were met by deaf ears! The Roman had inflicted fatal injury upon a feline and justice would be served: in defiance of the royal governors, the crowd dragged the man through the streets until he was dead.

And Diodorus explained that the story was no hyperbole, as he himself vouched for it as witness, leaving him with no doubts about the seriousness with which the Egyptians regarded their felines. There were other chroniclers who likewise mentioned the episode, and some went so far as to claim that in the aftermath, the Romans threatened reprisals, and when met with defiance, a quarrel resulted that was not settled until the death of Cleopatra and the conquest of Egypt by the Caesars. Well, the latter part is on flimsy grounds, and even I won't go so far as to argue that it was the death of a cat that sparked the war with Rome—but I can report at least one instance when the Egyptians' love for cats caused their army a crushing blow.

The chronicle of the military historian Polyaenus of Macedonia contains the account of a siege levied by the garrisons of the Persian king Cambyses II on the city of Pelusium in the year 525 BC. Located where the Nile Delta meets the Sinai Peninsula, the town was a gateway to the Egyptian mainland, and given its strategic importance, the troops of Pharaoh Psamtik III stood resolute in its defense. Or at least they did until the Egyptians suddenly saw the enemy leaving their lines en masse. Ah, could it be that they were backing down and giving up the fight? Was victory at hand?

Not so! The commanding Persian general, knowing the dedication of the Egyptians to their felines, had issued an order more perverse than any in military history. He had sent his soldiers to round up cats, as many as they could find, in order to tie them onto their shields. Oh, my poor brethren! Imagine the humiliation of those adored and pampered felines as they were callously lashed upon metal escutcheons that burnt hot against their fur. Cruelty and indignity in equal measure, and now the ruse was plain for all to see as the Persian soldiers reassembled in formation. What were the Egyptian archers and ground troops to do? Would they make battle against an enemy shielded by a wall of felines who were sure to suffer carnage? Or stand down and risk the invasion of their city?

The actions of the Persian general in this matter were unfair to the point of contemptible. How can we label grown men hiding in battle behind cats as anything other than cowards? But on the other side of the field stood true heroes, their status defined not by the blood they would spill, but that which they would save. Yes, the soldiers of Pelusium laid down their arms and refused the fight. The fall of their city was sounded not by the thunderous crashing of catapults and the clanking of steel, but rather the tender purr of love. A defeat? In human terms, the fall of Pelusium is counted as such, but we cats consider it the opposite—in ensuring that no cats were harmed, the defenders of the city earned a resounding victory for a bond between human and feline unlike any the world has since known.

And this was a bond that transcended even mortality. When the sad day came, as it inevitably did, that a beloved cat expired from this world, the relationship for the Egyptians was still not severed. This is a topic that I realize is difficult for you, my dear reader. Having witnessed my own brethren pass, I know the effect that the loss of a feline companion can have upon humans, even now in these less civilized times. There is a sadness upon your kind so palpable as to be debilitating, and I know full well that even by the mere mention of this topic the sadness is conjured again. But perhaps there is something to be learned from the rituals of passage enacted by those who understood us above all others.

The eternal happiness of beloved cats in Egyptian society received no less care and attention than that of human family members. Mummification and burial were typical, and while a family's means dictated the extent of the process, those cats whose companions were well endowed received rites that could mimic those of royalty. This included removal of the internal organs, which would be placed in canopic jars, and a beautifully carved coffin in a feline shape, inscribed with hieroglyphs offering prayers for the safe passage of the soul. There might even be gifts of gold and gems, and if the family owned a tomb the adored cat would be given its rest there after mourning rituals had been completed.

Such opulence could of course be afforded by very few. The bulk of us were laid to rest not in tombs, but in mass burials in feline necropoli—over three hundred thousand in the cemetery of Bubastis alone—to find final repose in the shadow of our patroness. But these cats, companions to those of limited resources, were considered no less precious to their humans than those who consorted with the wealthy. And if nothing more was possible, they would at least be treated with cedar oil and spices and then wrapped in linen. In the place of a golden funerary mask, feline facial features might be painted directly onto the bandages. Was such a treatment considered lesser, or a cause for shame, you wonder? Not in the least—or at least not by us! We felines are, after all, a classless society, and those humans who lavish luxury upon their companion animals in lieu of love should bear in mind that we are moved by the integrity of a gesture rather than by sheer expenditure.

Of course, in Egyptian cosmology death was simply a new beginning, so in the process of saying goodbye our companions had ensured that even as all else withers, within the immortal heart of the cosmos, we would remain connected to those who had cared for us. The feline soul would make the same journey as that of a human, traveling west to the land of the setting sun in order to reside with Osiris. You might wonder, would the journey be lonely and frightening for a cat who had never been on its own? Allay all fears, my friends, because the goddess Amenti, she who ruled over the western skies, would act as our guide—and being a wise deity, she knew that cats were naturally curious, and she kept diligent watch to ensure that we strayed not from the path.

And as for the path, it was lined with the offerings that had been lovingly left by the cat's human family. Think of it! Tributes from the hand of man—little bowls of milk, mummified mice, and bits of prepared food—would not only mark the route, they would multiply along the way. One became many, and many became more, as the gifts now stretched out further than even a cat's eyes could see. What a special feeling it must have been to know that love once shared had not dissipated, and in fact had been magnified countless times over by the passage to eternity.

Eventually, the path brought the intrepid feline to a ladder. It led upward to paradise, and the gods themselves held it firm as the soul climbed. This was unfamiliar territory to a worldly kitty, and the great gods Horus and Set stood by to take paw in hand and hoist the cat's spirit upward should it show any trepidation on the final rung. And it was during this ascent that the soul was reborn, entering into an ideal version of the world it had once known. A perfect feline utopia, complete with houses and ponds where in eternal youth a cat could hunt and play and run and jump to its heart's content, and roll in the sweet grass and lie under the warm rays of a sun that never set.

But this was not all, because there were more paradises beyond the first! In the second were tables filled with delights, free for the taking, on account of the terrestrial offerings that had been left by caring humans. The gods ensured that this generosity would be spread in perpetuity, and a cat could linger here as long as it wished—and no doubt some might linger for a very long time! But if and when the soul decided to move forward into the last paradise, it would find waiting for it a great ship. This was no earthly vessel that had been prepared for the final voyage, however, being rather the solar barque of the sun god Ra—he who himself brought light to the world as the Great Tomcat.

It was at the very end that we found the very beginning, as the feline soul would be invited to become one with the cosmos it had helped create. Heaven was merely a boat ride away! Ra ferried the cat's essence into the glittering night sky, allowing it to become a brilliant, eternal spirit of light. Back on earth, the humans who had loved this cat and made offerings in its honor could stare out into the night sky and think about their old friend. They might remember how, as a kitten, it had run recklessly through the house. Or all the years it had slept curled up at the foot of the bed. Or how, as an elder statesman, it sat nobly in the warm Egyptian sun. While the house might now seem empty, the humans who loved a cat could take solace in the knowledge that it lived on. And peering into those eternal depths they knew — they absolutely *knew* — that glittering bright against the pitch-black of night one of those innumerable stars was none other than their beloved companion.

As I know quite a bit about being a cat, I will promise you something in addition. We make a game of seeming coy and oft disinterested, but don't doubt that as human eyes scanned the heavens hoping to catch a glimpse of an old friend, feline eyes were scanning the world below for the same end. And fixing upon their beloved companions back down on earth, acknowledged their gaze with a blink of light, and surely no one in those days would doubt that the twinkle of a star is but the wink of a cat's eye.

Such was the journey completed by my Egyptian ancestors many centuries ago. And what a grand beginning for our own journey through feline history! While such a reminiscence is heartening, I shall not pine over what has been lost since those days, because we have only just begun, and we have stops ahead where I can show you grandeur nearly as great. We must leave the ship to the stars behind, but if you will travel by more mundane means, further ports of call await — once again, they are merely a flip of the page away.

Fig. 1.

Fig. 2.

Fig.

Fig. 4.

Fig. 5.

Fig. 6.

Icons of Bastet and Sekhmet were depicted in 1799 by Friedrich Bertuch in his *Bilderbuch für Kinder*. Their images were part of a series intended to teach children about the accomplishments of Ancients, although I reckon adults could also learn a thing or two by seeing how the Egyptians idolized us.

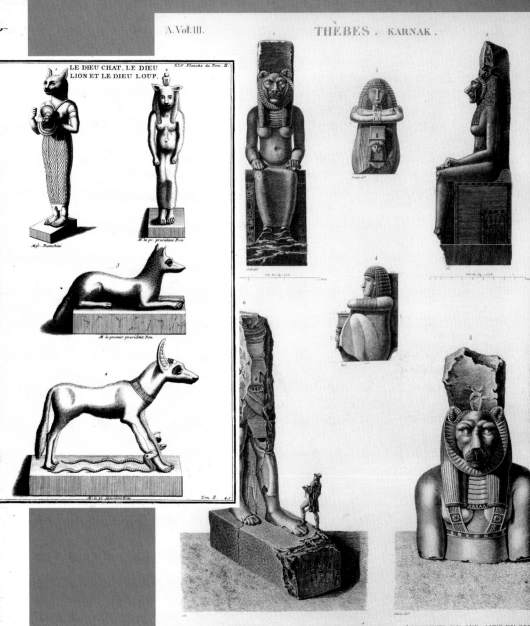

LE DIEU CHAT. LE DIEU
LION ET LE DIEU LOUP.
XLV.Planche du Tom.II.

1.2.3.4.5 STATUES DE GRANIT NOIR TROUVÉES DANS L'ENCEINTE DU SUD. 6 VUE DU COI

LEFT · *Le dieu chat* and *le dieu lion*: the cat and lion gods as engraved by Bernard de Montfaucon in 1719. A Benedictine monk who was one of the great scholars of antiquity, he was well aware of the important role we felines played in the spiritual lives of the Egyptians.

RIGHT · In 1802 Napoleon ordered the archeologist Edme-François Jomard to prepare a scholarly work titled *Description de l'Égypte*. The result was a book that provided the foundation for modern Egyptology—and included these images that left no doubt about the importance of Sekhmet in the royal cities of Luxor and Karnak!

Is it any wonder the Egyptians trusted in the sphinx? This one wasn't just impressive to behold; he demonstrated true feline loyalty by maintaining silent guard at Luxor when French scholars arrived in the early nineteenth century. Another engraving from Jomard's *Description de l'Égypte*.

How mighty we were! Royal power sublimating itself in the service of feline power in these reconstructions of the temple reliefs at Bubastis, with King Osorkon II making offerings to Bastet. From the excavation records of Swiss Egyptologist and biblical scholar Henri Édouard Naville in the 1880s.

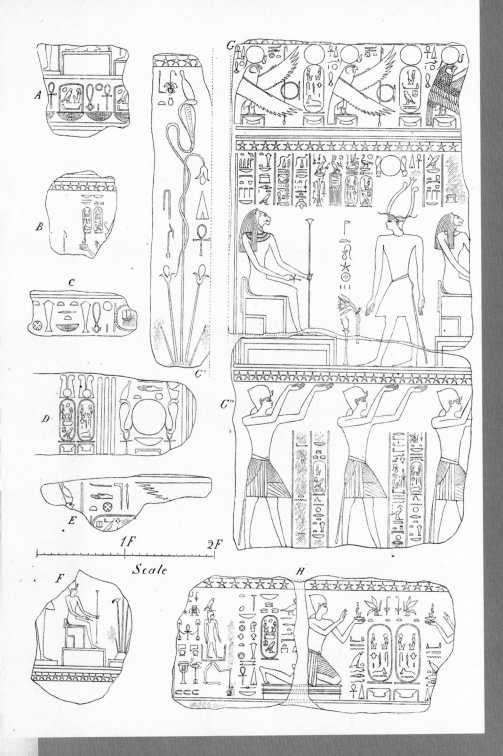

Scale

GLORY ROAD:

FELINE MIGRATION ACROSS PISA

The Egyptians carried us as far as the heavens. To be a cat adored by them was a privilege beyond any known to modern felines, even with all the creature comforts our humans may bestow upon us. But the people of the Nile were hardly alone in the gratitude and admiration they offered. Little *Felis* found just the same offered by many humans in many lands, for as a cat it was of his volition to wander near and far. Not all of them were people with the wealth and might to build temples in our honor, but even so, they let our esteem be known through legends and stories, thereby leaving no doubt about the gratitude they felt to us. The Ancient World was our Golden Age, and Egypt was not the only place where the days glittered.

Even the mighty Sahara could stop *Felis* from meandering, and he journeyed southward into Central Africa, from whence comes a folktale which serves as a metaphor for the alliance forged between cats and humans at the dawn of history. In the most ancient of times, the legend explains, when all things were new and man lived as the creatures of the wild, he one day had an idea. The rainy season was approaching and he conceived of building a dwelling—a fine thought to be sure—but he did not know how to manage it. So he went to a dog to beg assistance. "The rains will soon come.

Can I persuade you to aid me in building a house?" he asked. "No, I cannot help," came the dog's reply. He was far too busy, as there were important canine matters to attend to. Running, barking, chasing things, and sleeping must be done, and the dog simply had not the time to spare.

The man then went to a cat, asking of it the same. And the reply was similar. Important feline obligations such as licking one's coat, catching mice, and rubbing one's tail against things hardly left time for much else. "*However*," the cat paused in his reply, and after a moment of reflection continued, "it is *possible* that such duties might be put off for a day." He then rose from his perch and walked toward the man. "I shall help you!"

So it was that they built the house, man and feline working together. The rains did indeed come, and the drops fell in massive sheets, pregnant from the sticky African humidity. Suddenly, the dog appeared at the man's door and asked for shelter. "Hmmm, no," the man replied. "You will have to sleep outside." And as the dog searched for a dry patch on which to lie, the cat arrived. For him, the man opened the door of the house and extended an invitation to therein reside—after all, he deemed it a fair reward for an animal that had stood by his side at the founding of civilization.

Humans honored our contributions on Egypt's eastern flank as well. It was in the fertile triangle of Mesopotamia that we first made your company, and despite the pas-

sage of countless centuries, the partnership there established has always remained a prominent one. Did you know that no less than the great Muhammad, the very founder of Islam, favored us? The prophet described felines as pure animals, and himself owned a cat who was treated with such liberality that his relationship with it has become legendary among the examples of his charity. He even went so far as to grant the cat a place in paradise.

Muhammad called his companion Muezza, meaning "cherished," and his respect for it was so great that he was known to purify himself with water from which the cat drank. The story is still told about a quandary faced by the prophet when he discovered the cat napping on his sleeve just as it was time to leave for prayer. On the one hand, Allah was calling; on the other hand, there was a cat peacefully sleeping. Allah must be served and He cannot be asked to wait, but . . . was it possible to serve the One without disservice to the other? Faith reveals to the holy man paths that others do not see, and Muhammad cut the arm from his garment, thereby leaving for prayer without disturbing his sleeping friend.

Another legend recounts how Muhammad is responsible for the characteristic mark on a tabby's forehead. One day he was disturbed by a certain mouse while in the midst of his supplications. And he was not the only one disturbed by this sacrilege. The temerity of the intruder did not escape the attention of the vigilant Muezza, who immediately sprang into action and dispatched it. In thanks, the grateful prophet stroked the top of the cat's head to the ears, and it is said that on this occasion his fingers miraculously left four black lines in the shape of the initial M of his own name; they never faded, and were in fact passed on from generation to generation as a symbol of his blessing. A nice story, but you humans are a curiously gullible species. It is obvious even to a cat's ears that this is a tall tale: not that I doubt Muezza's sanctity, but in the Arabic alphabet, the letter M *does not exist*!

Even if it's not true, the fact that the legend of the phantom M has continued to be repeated serves as testimony to the enduring love Muhammad had for our kind. And this affection has been passed between generations in emulation, resulting in a legacy of extraordinary acts of kindness in the Islamic world. It was not uncommon, for example, for wealthy persons and even sultans to leave endowments sometimes lasting centuries in order to provide scraps of meat for local strays. Oh, and regarding tabbies, the Islamic world may not have provided us with our M, but it did provide us with our name. The English word is derived from *Attabiy*, the quarter in old Baghdad where the finest silk taffeta was made, and this cloth was at one time called *tabis*. Because it had a watered effect that produced stripes which bore a resemblance to a cat's coat, Europeans eventually began using the word for

felines showing a similar pattern.

But Baba, how did cats roam so far from the Middle East? Are they not known from ancient days even in the furthest corners of Asia? Indeed we are, and I will explain. Many centuries before Muhammad, we had signed on with merchants' caravans, tasked as mousers to protect their stock, and thereby plied the trade routes that crisscrossed Central Asia to arrive in places that had been unknown to little *Felis*. In lands where domestic cats had yet to be seen, we were greeted with such enthusiasm that we soon became commodities in our own right. Does not the vast number of breeds associated with differing regions of Asia stand as testimony to the warm embrace we received in each new area we were introduced? Almost everywhere along the breadth of the continent are cats proudly carrying a local pedigree, from the Persians in Iran all the way into Southeast Asia with the Siamese, Burmese, and Singapura.

But let me not jump too far ahead! I don't want to skip over the subcontinent. Why, did you know that Sanskrit texts indicate that domestic cats have been known in India for thousands of years? It is possible that *Felis* himself had once wandered so far east, and that we may have entered human households there not much later than we had in the Near East. Never in India did we attain the profile that we had in glittering Egypt, but since no one in those days could match the profile the Egyptians achieved in

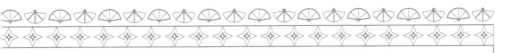
any regard, we shall not dismiss the love of a people for their cats as being lesser. Even though our role in India is far less celebrated than it was in Egypt, it was in fact quite similar. We were granted a place in the spiritual lives of humans, serving as totem animals of Shashti, a folk goddess who presided over domesticity, fertility, and the protection of children. Sounds familiar, doesn't it? These were the same feline values that were celebrated along the Nile, and Shashti has been likened by your scholars to none other than Bastet.

In one respect India outdid Egypt, as the people of the mighty Ganges passed down perhaps the greatest legend in all of feline folklore: the story of Patripatan, a cat for whom the love of the gods was so great that it caused time to stand still. He was the companion of a courtier who was competing with a Hindu priest of much esteem for the attention of a great king. This priest had vowed to prove his superiority by ascending to the Heaven of Devendiren and obtaining a flower from a sacred tree.

Such hubris! This heaven was home to twenty-four million deities who resided there with forty-eight million wives, and it was these gods themselves who tended the tree in question. But determined to demonstrate his virtue, the priest ascended higher and higher and higher until he was no longer visible to worldly eyes. All watched his ascent in wonderment—save for Patripatan's human, who waited in gleeful expectation of his rival's failure. But the priest did not return marred by the humiliation of divine rebuke, but rather in the glory of victory: he displayed in his hand the blessed flower, and the royal court proclaimed him to be the finest among them.

In the throes of jealousy, Patripatan's human made an unexpected declaration. If the people of the court thought this was a mighty deed, are they not aware that there is one among them who can do even better? "You yourself?" they inquired. "No," he replied. "Patripatan!" There was considerable snickering, as you might imagine. Patripatan was as fine a cat by any estimation, but all agreed he could not acquit himself of virtue greater than the greatest of humans. But the challenge had been lain and must be acquitted.

Humans are notorious for placing us cats in awkward situations, although the most typical form involves dragging us out from some comfy place and setting us in front of complete strangers with the expectation that we will act toward them as if they were the closest of friends. But the grand performance asked of Patripatan was a level of awkwardness unmatched before or since. Nevertheless, he was a devoutly loyal cat. Determined to fulfill the wishes of his human, it was now Patripatan who ascended to Heaven.

Imagine this if you can: Heaven, being very remote, even among all the splendors it contained, never before had a cat set paw

there. Well, you can guess how the gods delighted in Patripatan's presence. He was surrounded by divine hands, pushing forward by the hundreds and even thousands to reward him with caresses, as if he himself were a mighty idol. In fact, they delighted a bit *too* much, because while they were happy to grant him a flower from the sacred tree, they were unwilling to grant his departure. Far be it for a cat to contradict the gods, but he explained that he was expected back on earth. A challenge had been lain, after all, and the court awaited his return.

Heaven was smitten but sympathetic, and a compromise was offered. So that his sojourn not end too quickly, it was agreed that Patripatan should wait for three hundred years before returning. Centuries are of course mere moments in Heaven, but since the life spans of mortals are puny enough to have made this an excessive period for those who waited below, it was further arranged that for them time would stand still. So it was that weeks passed into years, which passed into decades and beyond, and none aged even a day.

All agreed this was peculiar indeed, although no one had the thought that it might be somehow connected to a cat who had gone missing so long ago. But the truth was known at the end of three centuries when the sky suddenly glowed like a burst of flame, and eyes turned upward in wonderment to see a cloud of a thousand colors, which then opened in the center to reveal a

throne, entirely composed of flowers from the sacred tree! And who was seated on this throne? None other than Patripatan, who descended back to earth to offer proof that feline virtue could match or even better that of the finest of humans!

I will concede that the story of Patripatan is but a myth, but shall we not esteem it nonetheless? Surely such a tale could only be conceived by a culture which held us in high regard. This was in no small measure due to the regional belief in reincarnation, which I might note is among the most appealing of your spiritual concepts from the perspective of animals. This is not so much because it gives all among us a chance to share the human soul (I'm fine with my own, thank you!), but because your kind often needs a bit of cajoling to do the right thing, and the idea that a former human might now inhabit a beast provides an added incentive to treat the rest of us with due respect.

And reincarnation into a feline form in particular has been considered in various regions within Asia as a final stage before which human souls might at last attain enlightenment, resulting in considerable esteem for cats in such areas. This idea proved long-standing enough to be still current when the British colonized India in the nineteenth century, allowing for one of feline history's more curious anecdotes. General Sir Thomas Edward Gordon, a British commander whose troops occupied the area around Bombay, recorded in his journals

what he considered a perplexing custom at the local Government House: the Indian guards would salute and present arms for any cat who happened to pass out the front door. "And good for them!" would be the feline reaction, although the British reaction was something a bit different. Presenting arms for cats was an egregious breach of military protocol, so the good general set out to investigate.

It turned out that Sir Robert Grant, the governor of Bombay, had died at the house as evening fell in 1838, and it just so happened that as he expired a cat was seen to walk out the front door and down the exact same path that the governor had walked each day at dusk. The British inclination was to chalk this up to coincidence, but the Hindu sentries believed that it might portend something more . . . After all, the cat had exactly mirrored the governor's routine. And would the soul of an esteemed man not be likely to wind up in the esteemed form of a feline? Consulting a member of a priestly caste confirmed the suspicion: Governor Grant's soul had transmigrated to one of the cats that lived on the property.

If such were the case, the guards felt it incumbent upon them to offer to this cat all ceremony that had previously been due the governor. But there was a certain quandary, as the feline in question had been seen only from a distance and in dim light, so no one was sure which of the many local cats it was. If any among them might potentially

be the incarnation of the governor, what were the sentries to do? Thenceforth they decided to offer the same formality to all felines, lest they fail to offer it to the correct one. Best to err on the side of caution, after all. And by the time the general arrived in Bombay, they had been presenting arms to cats for over a quarter of a century.

The British found this incident highly perplexing, but it would not have been so to many millions of people in Asia. For centuries, certain breeds of feline had been deemed blessed due to the belief that they could serve as vessels for departed human souls. In old Burma, the long-haired, silky-coated, blue-eyed Birman was one such cat, and legends held that the very first of its kind was created by the gods in order to house a great soul at a critical juncture in national history. Among the most famed of all cats, he was named Sinh and lived at a mountain temple which afterward became synonymous with the breed.

This temple was named Lao-Tsun and located near Lake Indawgyi in the very northern part of Burma. Its ancient history told of a time when it housed a group of Lamaist monks, their abbot being the venerable Mun Ha, whose life was devoted to the absolute adoration of Tsun Kyankze, a goddess with glowing sapphire eyes who presided over the passage of the soul. Mun Ha had taken Sinh as a companion, and all who encountered this cat considered him to be of great wisdom, with some commenting

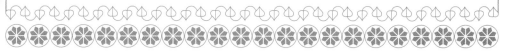

that he might be equal even to a sage. And he was handsome in addition, with golden eyes that shimmered like the temple's gilt statues, and his torso a hue of iridescent white.

Yet despite these virtues, he was not without defect. He was no proper Birman as we would recognize the breed today, and it was particularly notable that his ears, tail, nose, and paws all carried a dark tinge resembling the color of soil. Given the cat's sanctimonious bearing, there were those who felt that such discolorations should best be considered symbolic, perhaps Sinh's means of reminding those within the temple that the earth and all that tread upon it are tainted, and not even the most outstanding of its creatures could escape a truth so universal.

Together the wise priest and his wise cat spent many years, but time is relentless and it eventually made of Mun Ha an old and frail man. He was seated on his throne when the inevitable end came and his heart ceded to stillness. But his passing was not a moment of simple peace. Sinh had been by Mun Ha's side, having refused to leave his human during illness, and now jumped atop his lifeless master's head. "Hey there, what are you doing?" all the temple's priests no doubt wondered, but before any had a chance to raise a word in complaint, he arched his back and fixed an intense gaze straight ahead. His eyes locked on the very same statue of Tsun Kyankze that Mun Ha had so long venerated, and Sinh's meaning

was clear: there had been an immediate transmigration of the priest's soul into the cat's body.

Should any have their doubts, they were erased by what occurred next. The hairs on Sinh's fine white back bristled and took on a golden hue. And the gold of his eyes changed their color to a deep blue, being the very same shade as the eyes of the goddess herself. As for the extremities that were tinged with the color of base matter, they also transformed, becoming white. These are none other than the characteristics of a Birman cat, and Sinh not only absorbed the soul of the holy man, but in the process became the first of the breed. But as miraculous as this metamorphosis was, it was merely a prelude to the drama soon to come.

Burma was at this time at war with Siam, and a garrison of enemy soldiers was approaching. But within the temple, all were so absorbed with the extraordinary events that had already transpired as to be unaware . . . save for the cat, who finally broke his gaze from the statue and fixed it firmly on the southern portal. His eyes were ablaze like a sapphire flame, and their meaning was once again clear. Danger was near to hand, and the priests immediately moved to barricade the entrance. And just in time, as it turned out. The arriving invaders struck hard, but the doors held tight. The priests continued to reinforce them through the night until finally, with their blows coming

to naught, the Siamese troops passed on in search of an easier target. Lao-Tsun had been saved from profanation and pillage.

But even then, the episode was not complete. Sinh had not left the throne during this entire time, nor would he for seven days more. His gaze had re-fixed itself on the statue of Tsun Kyankze and did not waver, and even after the withdrawal of the enemy his eyes burned with no less fire. It was as if the cat was locked in communion with she who presided over passage of the soul. But once those seven days had passed, Sinh's stare finally faltered. His eyelids suddenly grew heavy and fell closed, and his earthly body wavered. It was now the cat who fell lifeless, and on the same spot that the old priest had. At Sinh's passing, the soul of Mun Ha was at last released into the loving arms of the goddess herself.

The surviving priests withdrew to their cells and allowed themselves to contemplate all that they had seen. But after another seven days, worldly matters beckoned. The first order of business was to appoint a successor to Mun Ha as abbot. They gathered again in front of the statue of Tsun Kyankze to deliberate, and at that time the final miracle occurred. All of the cats of the temple came running toward them—there had been many others besides Sinh who lived at Lao-Tsun.

But they no longer appeared as they had been. Each and every one had changed, transformed exactly as Sinh had been, all of them showing their coats golden and their paws white and their eyes a deep sapphire blue. All now appeared as Birman cats! They surrounded the youngest of the priests, and, by showing him their favor, made it clear that they wished him to assume the throne of Mun Ha. None would now doubt the wisdom of the temple's cats, and this priest was immediately appointed. And from then on, it was taken as fact by those who therein reside that whenever a Birman cat dies, it carries with it the soul of a holy man to Nirvana.

As for the Siamese, they had found themselves on the wrong side of the paw when it came to the story of Sinh, but I doubt they would have been surprised by the outcome since they likewise considered us to be receptacles for humans souls. Their belief was in fact so unwavering that a living feline was sometimes included in the tombs of important or royal personages. Wait, Baba, this sounds like the utmost cruelty! Ah, well, don't be alarmed, the cat was not buried alive, since entombing it would have defeated the purpose. Holes were provided through which it could crawl up and out, and when the kitty emerged, it marked the soul's return from the realm of the dead. Great celebrations ensued, and the born-again feline was escorted to a temple, where it was thereafter allowed to live in luxury—a well-earned reward from a feline perspective for having to suffer through the nuisance of being locked in a box with a corpse.

But when we speak of my brethren in Siam, one breed in particular comes to mind, being so associated with the country as to have become synonymous. The Siamese cats, as you humans refer to them, are among the oldest of purebred cats, and famed as the smartest of the world's felines. Well, that's a prideful boast indeed. Although keeping in mind that American street cats like myself did not yet exist, we can conjecture that perhaps it may have been true at one time. Regardless, the Siamese cats raised their own banner high. They carried proof of their virtue on the tips of their tails, in accordance with a legend which explained that a characteristic kink was not a defect, but rather a symbol of the breed's remarkable character.

The story was told of a prince in Old Siam who needed to travel far from his palace and was concerned about the safekeeping of a certain very precious ring. He would not dare leave it with any but the most trustworthy of parties! Thinking hard on the matter, he had no doubts that all of his courtiers were very fine men, but his inescapable conclusion was it was his cat who was the most loyal and true. Now, while I don't mean to disparage humankind, I suspect he judged correctly since greed is a vice common even among fine men, but unknown amongst felines. So the prince, in his wisdom, requested that the cat take the ring for safekeeping, and the cat agreed—but, the cat, in his own wisdom, proffered an unusual request, asking that the prince slip the ring over the tip of his tail. Fortunately, Thai royalty understood that we cats know best, so it was done. And when the prince returned, he found that the end of the tail had been twisted into a knot— his trusty palace feline had kinked his own tail in order to safeguard the precious cargo.

From then on, the cat's kin adopted the kink as a symbol of their honor, which should have proven a source of pride for all of Siam—except that sadly no one outside of the Royal Palace in Bangkok had a chance to actually *see* these meritorious felines. Humans can be highly protective of their cats, and this is a trait which we generally find charming even if it's unnecessary. But in the case of the Siamese cats, royalty was possessive to the point of tyranny, having claimed them all for themselves and restricting the breed to the palace grounds. How serious were they about this? Considering that the penalty for removing a cat was death, we should guess pretty serious indeed. And this left the Siamese cat as the great feline enigma, shrouded in mystery to the outside world even as people peered through the gates hoping to catch a mere glimpse of these mythic beasts.

I must state that depriving the citizenry of cats in order to serve the demands of status is nothing other than elitism, and very much against feline nature. Fortunately, the restriction was only on the Siamese as a breed, which meant the masses had plenty of other felines with which to happily

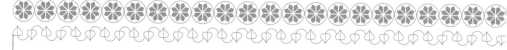

occupy themselves. And lest anyone think that the crown had siphoned off the best because they had chosen purebreds, listen up: we cats don't judge you humans by race or breed, so please do us the same courtesy! Certainly as far as the common people were concerned, their plebian cats deserved to be no less exalted than those behind the palace walls.

Consider the words of the *Tamra Maeo Thai*, or "Thai Treatise on Cats," an authoritative compendium of feline lore passed down over generations. The text listed seventeen other types of cats that would

ensure prosperity and well-being if kept as companions. No doubt you're curious about the nature of these auspicious felines. Surely they must have been nearly as rare as those guarded by the crown to bring such blessings? Oh, rare indeed, yes. Let's see . . . The list included cats with coats of white, black, or gray; those with various iterations of black-and-white patterns; also coats with various brownish or copper colorations; as well as . . . wait . . . in other words, pretty much *all* cats. Well then! The royal court could have theirs, because as far as the rest of Siam was concerned, simply keeping any type of cat at all brought blessings.

The impressive welcome we had received in Asia would get more impressive still as we continued onward to the easternmost shores, although there was a certain issue which first had to be cleared up. Would you believe there was at one time an interlude of animosity toward us in the Buddhist world? This unfortunate episode was the consequence of a misunderstanding that not surprisingly occurred entirely through the fault of mankind. I hate to even broach the topic since we no longer hold it against you, but I shall tell you about it nonetheless, just so you will understand that even in the best of times, being a cat among humans is not all bowls of sweet cream.

Have you ever wondered why domestic felines are not included among the animals of the Chinese zodiac? Does this not seem a glaring oversight, if not an outright insult?

Especially considering rabbits and snakes and other animals who are far less useful than cats are included, and a dragon— which *does not even exist*—and for Heaven's sake, there's even a rat! Well then, here is the story. It was around the time that we were entering into China that an entirely unjust accusation began to be spoken. Whether this was part of a conspiracy designed to stop the migration of felines, I do not know, but it certainly has the hallmarks of one.

The rumor being told was that at the Buddha's funeral, representatives of all types of living creatures presented themselves in order to pay homage, and that of all of them, of every species known to exist in the world, it was the cat and only the cat who was ill-behaved. At the moment of greatest sorrow, when all hung their heads in sadness, it was claimed that the cat jumped upon the rat and killed it. And since killing another creature would have transgressed the very laws that the Buddha had considered inviolable (he, knowing everything about civility and nothing whatsoever about living with rats), a prejudice was thus instilled against us, and for once, we were . . . not liked.

This prejudice, fortunately, did not carry over to the common people, who, especially in rural areas, had always been more impressed by our ability to control rodents than to behave ourselves at funerals. But we were not welcome in many temples, where humans not yet familiar with our character were led to believe we were a poor choice of companion. Of course, time heals all wounds, and as it turns out, the healing is especially quick when vermin are once again involved. Many of these same temples eventually found themselves faced with the threat of having important manuscripts nibbled at by rats and mice. Maybe, they finally wondered, there was something to this cat business after all, and they turned to us for assistance. What irony, eh? Felines were defamed by a false legend about killing a rat at the Buddha's funeral, but then Buddhists themselves asked us to *please kill real-life rats on their behalf*! And humans claim that it is we cats who are the capricious ones.

But there you have it. And in the end, the Buddhists came down on the side of adoring us, with many temples becoming veritable cat colonies. As our prestige sky-rocketed, it became traditional in China for cats to be owned by humans of renown, Confucius among them. And the Buddhists made up for their indiscretion by letting us hitch a ride to our final Asian destination: Japan, where we began to arrive in the company of Chinese monks during the sixth century of your common era. By that time, of course, Bubastis was rubble and the great pharaohs had been consigned to memory, but who could have imagined that our own eminence had diminished so little that it was as if we had alighted back to the glory days. Even as the ancient sun slipped into its dusk, those emerald isles raised it back up for the dawn of a new Golden Age.

The first cats to arrive in Japan were considered priceless and served as companions for aristocrats, who not only thought it appropriate to indulge us in conversation but even had the wisdom to inquire of our opinions on important matters. At the imperial court, felines were so adored that if one wished the emperor's favor, it became customary to present him with an outstanding cat as a gift. Our highest esteem came under the emperor Ichigo. Reigning from 986 to 1011, he was a man possessed of such righteous passion for us that when a dog attempted to chase a cat at the royal palace, he had the miscreant canine's owner imprisoned. Hurrah! An enlightened monarch indeed to dispense such justice, since let's face it, nine times out of ten, a human is somehow at the root of canine malfeasance.

Ichigo's favorite cat was as white as snow and had been brought from China. Named Myobu no Omoto (a courtly title meaning "Lady in Waiting"), she gave birth to a litter on the tenth day of the fifth moon of the year 999, and the emperor deemed the event to be an omen so propitious that it was decreed that her kittens be brought up with the same attention and care as young princes. But this was merely a prelude to his greatest act, an edict that *all* felines should be elevated to noble status! Henceforth we were to be accordingly pampered in high-ranking houses, where we would be treated as children of the elite class. Our es-

teem at this time was such that we were referred to by the word *tama*, meaning "jewel."

Unforeseen consequences would arise out of elevating us to nobility, however. Japanese custom meant that we were no longer permitted to perform anything that would be considered manual labor. Ah, is it ignoble to work with one's paws? Well, you can debate this issue among yourselves since you humans like to argue the virtues of social class far more than we felines do. I will offer only this much on the topic: when one lives with all four paws firmly pressed to the dirt, one does not shirk to use them, and to not do so in nature defies the primal need to labor for one's own survival. From a feline perspective, then, work is not only advisable, but necessary to the formation of character.

While the debate may seem moot to you, in the case at hand it would have far-reaching consequences. Because while Ichigo's edict was without a doubt magnanimous, it unfortunately meant that the menial task of catching mice was now considered below our station. Go figure. Not only did our ability to catch rodents create our bond with humans in the first place, it is something that we greatly enjoy—and now we were *too good* for it? A curious twist, Japan being the only country in the world where cats were ever discouraged from mousing.

And as it turned out, this spelled big trouble for Japan's cloth manufacturers. We had been combating the vermin which prayed on their silkworm cocoons, but in lieu of living cats, they now placed feline statues in their warehouses and workshops, something like scarecrows—or scarecats, to be precise. I can only laugh at the naïveté of humans who thought that mice, as wily as they are, might be taken in by such a ridiculous ruse, although I'm sure the situation was far less amusing to Japan's cats. Yes, they were sequestered in comfy suites, but at the expense of emboldening their old enemies, who fed as they wished on the cocoons and brought a near catastrophe to an entire industry.

For their stubborn dedication to the feline cause, however misplaced, the Japanese imperial house deserves kudos: even with Japan's cats chomping at the bit to get back into action, it still took them three centuries to finally acquiesce. In the end, of course, there was no choice but to put us back to work, and with that our noble status was of necessity withdrawn. One might in this case credit the mice with a rare triumph, seeing that they did manage to force us from our lofty pedestals, but any victory they might claim was offset by the cost. Do we not here witness the folly of mice? All they had to do was leave the cocoons alone and they could have prospered nearly as much as we did. Instead their smug satisfaction was answered by the return of our claws to the silk factories.

If you wonder whether being reduced to regular old working stiffs engendered any resentment, I can assure you it did not. Keep in mind that as a species immune to human insecurities, we cats are confident of our own nobility without any need of official titles. And while I will freely admit that we enjoy being pampered, we're equally fond of such pedestrian pastimes as rolling in the dirt and climbing trees, and it is irksome to be deprived of simple pleasures solely because humans consider them undignified. The hunting of mice gives us joy and a feeling of accomplishment that the nicety of sitting on silk cushions cannot match—as if there could have even been silk cushions to sit on

without us there to protect the cocoons, which, in the end, perhaps finally settles the argument about the nobility of labor.

In any event, our efforts on behalf of the nation had the effect of affirming our place as friends of the people, and the loss of title was more than made up for by the depth of affection which we have always received from the general public. Passed down in Japanese folklore are some of the world's most impressive feline tales, revealing esteem for us as wise, dedicated, and even heroic companions. Consider, for example, the story of a cat with wisdom enough to impart even onto a mighty lord.

A samurai of impressive standing was plagued by a monstrous rat, which ran roughshod through his home, doing as it pleased. It was of such great size that it chased away the samurai's own cat—and before we denigrate this feline, know that it was considered outstanding enough under all but this most exceptional of circumstances. And the same could be said for all the others among the local cats, various of whom were enlisted, and none, not even those thought to be the most brave, fared any better. In despair, the samurai attempted to hunt the beast himself. Indignity enough for a samurai to take his own blade to vermin, and to add insult to injury, even this was to no avail, as the rat proved too fast, too smart, and too bold for his blows.

Finally, the samurai was told of a certain cat reputed to be a hunter more accomplished than any in the region. He arranged for it to be brought to his home, but when this one arrived . . . well, let us say that his status was given the lie by his appearance and demeanor. His reputation must have been made in days gone by—or rather, I should say, years, and many of them at that, as he was old and worn, little more than a frail feline with no hint of his former glory. And to make matters worse, he seemed to have no interest whatsoever in *hunting*, preferring to sit like a bump on a log as the giant rat ran about and made him seem a fool.

Quite some time passed like this, and the samurai was unsure whether to laugh or to cry about the cat's fallen reputation. Until finally, and with a pronounced lethargy, the cat got up. Slowly, he walked over to the rat, who looked on with mocking eyes. And then it happened: with a sudden burst, quick as the wind and as nimble as a deer, the cat pounced and the monster was no more. It was over in a flash, and with a renewed lethargy, he seated himself back down as if he had performed the most mundane of tasks.

But the samurai looked on in awe. His own blade could not as much as nick the rat, yet this old cat, worn by the years, had dispatched it with ease. In reverence, he beseeched the cat to impart his secrets, as clearly this one knew a thing or two he had not let on. Finally, the cat acquiesced, disclosing to the lord the truth about combat: It is not based upon might, but upon self-control.

Don't rush into the fight. Take time to study the enemy and learn his movements and tendencies—and do not fall victim to pride. Worry not about your adversary's opinion of you, the cat explained, allow him even to see you as meek if he wishes, in order to lull him into a false sense of security. And when his guard is down, strike quickly and conquer. It was a wise old cat indeed that could teach a warrior how to fight.

But let us now turn from legends to the story of a real cat, for the greatest of all Japan's feline tales is no fable. While there are differing versions, to be sure, and none can be confirmed as definitive, know that the blame lies with the human faculty of memory, because all accounts hold to such certain similarities that there is every reason to believe that behind the legend is truth. It is set at the monastery of Gōtokuji in Tokyo, and with certainty, it can be said that a venerable temple was founded in the fifteenth century and had by the seventeenth become impoverished and dilapidated. This was a time when but a single monk therein resided, and as Gōtokuji was in its death throes there came to the rescue the most important piece of the story: a very special cat who would return the monastery to glory.

He was a stray, all white in color, and had been taken in by the monk, who, being a man of good heart, made a point to care for his companion as best he could. But intentions alone do not fill one's dinner bowl, and the pair were in dire straits. The monk's faith had always proved his bulwark, but worn down by poverty, even this began to waver, and looking at the shambles of his shrine, he confided his despair. "There is nothing more I can do, kitty," he lamented. "I know you would help if you could, but after all, you're just a cat. I don't know what hope there is left." With that, his spirit was broken. The string had finally been played out, and the monk himself was reeling it in to its sad end.

Ah, but that silly monk! Had he forgotten what happens when you pass a string in front of a cat? His companion would now grab destiny in his paws, and the monk would soon learn that there is no such thing as "just a cat." A violent storm broke out soon after, and a samurai named Ii Naotaka, who had been traveling with his retinue along the road near Gōtokuji, was caught in the downpour. Pelted by hard rain, he began looking about for shelter, and suddenly he saw a white cat in the distance. But what was it doing? It appeared to be motioning with its paw and . . . beckoning them?

An unexpected encounter, but the traveling party trusted feline wisdom, and when the cat turned and began to walk, they followed, and through the gale it led them down a short path to refuge at the temple. It was there that the samurai met the monk, and the wisdom and humble devotion of Gōtokuji's human resident made a deep impression on the mighty lord. Saddened by the state of the property, he vowed to become its benefactor, declaring it his family shrine.

From then on, Gōtokuji not only prospered, it became one of the wealthiest and most beautiful temples in all of Japan. And in gratitude to the cat who welcomed the property's savior, felines have ever since been honored there. Some among you humans even refer to it as the Cat Temple, as the grounds now stand crowded with cat statues, prayers are offered for sick or missing felines, and there is even a necropolis—the only one since the days of Egypt—where invocations are said to the Buddha in the hopes that the souls of departed cats will attain Nirvana.

Naturally, hundreds of living cats can be found roaming the grounds there too. But could you have ever imagined that the original cat from the story is himself still there? Well, in a *way* . . . because, you see, he's pretty much *everywhere*, as he became one of the world's most famous feline figures. Ah, I'm sorry, how mindless of me. Did I neglect to tell you this cat's name at the outset? Well, perhaps you have already guessed, since he happens to be the most recognizable of us all. He is none other than Maneki-Neko, the familiar good-luck cat with one paw raised in a gesture of beckoning, his pose a tribute to the moment he called to the samurai to lead him to the temple. So those skeptics who insist that we cats are self-centered might consider how an act of feline gratitude has been transformed into the most popular symbol of good fortune in your human world.

Well, friends, I can bluster on with enthusiasm about the Japanese love for cats, but we have traveled as far as the Pacific, and we should now direct our attention elsewhere. Another adventure had been long underway, and it rightly demands our regard: the conquest of Europe. Let us turn the clock back some 2,500 years, back even to the days when Bubastis still reigned supreme. The northern shores of the Mediterranean Sea had been of no interest to our old friend *Felis*, and this had put farmers there at a distinct disadvantage to those who had been prospering in the Middle East and Egypt.

But there was at this time a culture known as the Phoenicians, who made their homes upon the coasts of Lebanon. They were not builders of great monuments, nor had they a powerful army. But they were crafty, and therein lies their brilliance, as they had cast themselves as the great maritime merchants of the Ancient World, and sent their ships to ply the ocean and conquer by commerce rather than by the sword. In order to survive through trade, the Phoenicians had trained their eyes to know a good thing when they saw it, and in domesticated felines they saw a very good thing.

If we can just get these cats to the other side of the sea, they reasoned, we will certainly find a profitable market. This they knew with some certainty because—think about this and shudder—in lieu of felines, the early Greeks were forced to use weasels and stone martens to protect their grain from rodents. Need I tell you what a terrible proposition that is? Resolutely feral, such animals are difficult to deal with even in the best case, and if we are to be judgmental, they are uncouth in addition.

Cats in Greece would be an easy sale, and the Phoenicians determined to take us aboard their vessels. The finest of our kind were, naturally, to be found in Egypt. Strong and healthy felines, impressive to the eye and brought up well so as to be responsive to humans, these would bring the very best return. Alas, there was a problem. Egyptian esteem for us was such that cats were considered no mere commodity, and our removal from the country was forbidden.

But I have told you that these Phoenicians were crafty—meaning, when it comes to your kind, dishonest, ahem—and unbeknownst to Egyptian officials, they began to smuggle us out, hidden below the decks of their great galleys. Imagine the intrigue: daring pirates slipping out of port, their hulls laden with felines, and sailing off into the darkness of night. What must the reaction of the cats themselves have been? Some, no doubt, were offended at being handled by foreigners, and others perhaps frightened by such doings. Yet others rapt in anticipation, knowing that new adventures were afoot. And I intend that we shall join them, so come quick and slip aboard the ships with me as we head to the far shores!

毛川木美依多

Our love is eternal, and the Japanese were providing felines with funerals long before Westerners had even figured out canned cat food. Niches to hold a cat's ashes, like this one at Tokyo's largest cemetery for animals at Jindaiji Temple, provide humans a place to return and honor our spirits.

Dgi-Guerdgi Albanois
qui porte au Bezestein des Foyes de Mouton
pour nourrir les Chats.

ℬ

60.

G. Scotin maj. sculp.

Avec Privil Du Roi

ABOVE · Middle Eastern merchants made sure we didn't go hungry. This man offering sheep's liver to cats in a Cairo bazaar is moving a bit too slowly for the fellow at his waist, but we will admire his charity nonetheless. Dated 1714, designed by Jean-Baptiste Vanmour and engraved by Gérard Scotin.

OPPOSITE · The May 1891 edition of *The Animal World*, the journal of the Royal Society for the Prevention of Cruelty to Animals, reported the charity of a Cairo sultan. He had endowed a garden for local strays, and even many generations after his passing they were still being fed there.

Issued by the R.S.P.C.A.]

[The Editor's Address is 105, Jermyn Street, London.

THE ANIMAL WORLD

He prayeth best, who loveth best,
All things both great and small;

For the dear God who loveth us,
He made and loveth all.—COLERIDGE.

No. 260.—VOL. XXII. "BOTH MAN, AND BIRD, AND BEAST." MAY 1, 1891.

A CAT'S TALE

Twopence.]

THE CATS' HOME, CAIRO.

67

薄雲

仙且

けいて
くる玉の春
お

OPPOSITE · We don't know who this cat is but no doubt he's pampered, wearing a golden collar and carried in his mistress's robes. The Japanese weren't joking when they called us *tama*, or jewel. This c. 1820 woodblock print by Yashima Gakutei is a *surimono*, a private image for a special occasion.

ABOVE · Even in Japan there were a few concessions we had to make. This cat, for example, is seen gnawing on a dried fish in an 1814 woodblock print by Hokuba Arisaka. We cats greatly prefer the fresh stuff, but maybe his human was saving that for sushi.

TRIUMPH AND TRAGEDY IN EUROPE: THE RISE AND FALL OF THE FELINE EMPIRE

urope was a new land, and one ripe for conquest, and a warm reception on the northern shores of the Mediterranean further strengthened the bond between human and feline . . . or so we thought. Centuries of adoration had left us blind to what was to come. This new land would later bring us to our greatest despair, as it was there that we met with the treachery of man, and thereafter struggled to survive against cruelty of a kind no other species has ever suffered. But we will leave the dark days for later in our tale. For now, sail on through bright skies, being the brilliant blue that hung over the Greek docks—where the Phoenician sailors were unloading their marvelous cargo.

We were seen as a living miracle when the first ships carrying us arrived. This was some seven or eight centuries before the common era, and the Greeks were still a crude people who knew only of rough-and-tumble wildcats. The domestic variant appeared to them as wondrous. They were entranced by the softness of our fur and amazed by our gentle personalities. Why, we were amenable to the touch, and even—well, depending—allowed humans to *hold us in their arms*! "But they are so much more than novelties," the traders exulted, "for these cats are also useful!" They explained how we were far superior to the mousers the Greeks had previously relied upon. Oh, sure, weasels and martens could kill vermin, but they were wild creatures, indiscriminate hunters who might eat your chickens too.

But these were genuine Egyptian felines, domesticated animals who could be relied on (well, in theory) to kill only the desired rodents. The Phoenicians were nothing if not brilliant pitchmen, and it took little convincing before the Greeks were sold. They even agreed to pay added premiums for black cats—they were the most effective hunters of all, the merchants claimed, since their dark coloring made them invisible to their prey! *Is that so?* Ha, no! Mice have highly refined senses of smell and hearing, which they rely upon in the darkness instead of sight, thus making the color of the cat entirely irrelevant. Yes, a sucker is born every minute, but in the excitement, no one seemed to be bothered by such details.

The people of the northern Mediterranean were rank amateurs when it came to cats back then. But they had expertise in another field, and it was there that they offered their most important contribution to our history: words. Initially, the Greeks called us *galê*, being a catchall for small mammals and the same word they used for weasels, since at first we were all considered to be in the same category. Hmph! But by the fifth century BC, new words were evolving, and they are still with us today. *Feles* came into use first, eventually being replaced by *feline*, and this was followed by

catta, from which the modern English cat, as well as *chat*, *gato*, *katze*, and all the other similar-sounding variations in the many human tongues are derived.

A popular legend also gave birth to another—albeit less pleasant—word. The story involved a cat named Aielouros. The name was derived from the words *aiolos*, meaning "to move," and *ouros*, meaning "tail"—in effect, the "tail wagger." The loveliest of all felines, she was transformed into a human woman of such beauty that she rivaled no less than Aphrodite, so as punishment, the spiteful goddess transformed her back into her original form. The story itself was hokey and marked the predictable presumption of your kind (what makes any of you think we would prefer to be human than feline?), but from it the term "ailurophobe," being a person with an irrational fear or hatred of cats, was born.

This was still the golden age, however, and other than cranky Aphrodite, there were scarcely any ailurophobes to be found in what was rapidly becoming a country of *ailurophiles*—the word for cat lover. Eager to share their newfound wonders, the Greeks picked up where the Phoenicians had left off, carting us even further afield as their own power and prestige grew. Cats were again on the move, and oh how far we traveled! Greek colonists brought us to outposts in the Balkans and along the Black Sea, and to their settlement in Massalia—perhaps you know it better as Marseille, France? From there, it was an easy cruise with local traders up the Rhone River into Germany.

Italy was also introduced to cats through the Greeks, who brought us to their colonies in Sicily, from whence we made our way up the Italian peninsula. And by the time we got to Rome, well . . . what Caesar saw, Caesar conquered, and we followed in his wake. We had been entreated to join his armies in order to protect Roman stores from vermin, and, locked in step with the Imperial Legions, we marched all the way to Britannia.

"Hardly such a triumph!" the skeptics will scoff. "Were you not taken into servitude and carried about the continent as nothing more than forced labor?" I will not deny that we were introduced to Europe as humble mousers, but we knew the winning formula that had been passed down since the days of little *Felis*: through diligent work safeguarding the supplies of humans, we once again earned a place in even the most hardened of hearts. And if you trust not my word, consider the fondness of the Roman soldiers for us, as they were the first to adopt the domestic cat as a heraldic animal. Why, not even the Egyptians had gone so far, their army preferring the lion-headed Sekhmet. But the Roman *Ordines Augusti* marked their shields with the image of a green cat, and the *Felices Seniores* with one in red.

Of course, up north, many of Caesar's soldiers were mercenaries rather than being Roman by birth, and this provided a further boon to our conquest. The cats who had traveled with the legions were assigned to fortresses and would not typically have been seen outside of them. Had the soldiers been entirely Roman, we would have remained a secret, but locals serving among them had a chance to learn firsthand of our virtues. And so it was that even as the power of the empire ebbed, ours grew greater still. When the great battlements were abandoned, we returned not to the Eternal City,

but were claimed as prizes by men-at-arms hired from nearby villages, who took us with them to their homes.

And as we prospered in these new communities, our triumph in the end turned out to be even greater than the mighty Caesar's. It's true, my friends! I don't wish to embarrass the Imperial Throne too badly, but it was left to Rome's felines to complete the conquest of which Trajan had only dreamed; consider that his army was stopped by warring tribes and never succeeded in breaching Scotland . . . but we did. And by cuddles and purrs, rather than blood and steel. But we pressed on further still, forging boldly ahead on merchant ships toward Scandinavia, to those rugged northern climes from which the mighty Vikings would emerge.

To other humans, these fearsome Norsemen were nothing less than a terror. Ah, but to us they fell meekly. Their strong, callused hands, marked by the scars of battle and stained with blood, became for us soft palms as they put aside their axes in exchange for the simple joy of stroking warm feline fur on frostbitten nights. Why, they were so enamored that they specially bred us to serve on their ships, this heritage being preserved in the modern Norwegian Forest cats. So shall we end a debate right here and now? Should any among you think there is an effeminate stigma about being a "cat guy," well, feel free to take the matter up with a Viking.

As the pagan world was ever sympathetic to our kind, our newfound human friends continued the tradition of sharing their spiritual lives with us. The Greeks were quick to accept the sacred nature of cats and declared us to be companions of Artemis, and the Romans followed suit with Diana.

Both of these goddesses possessed the ability to take on feline form, and Artemis in particular was so closely associated with domestic cats that it became a staple of Greek lore that it was she who had created us.

And we had not arrived in Europe with empty paws, having brought the feline

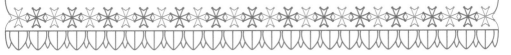

archetype constructed by the Egyptians to further augment the powers of our new patron deities. Artemis and Diana became protectors of the domestic realm, guarantors of well-being, and champions of fertility. And carrying on the Egyptian tradition of associating felines with lunar deities, both also became patrons of the moon. We even accompanied Artemis as she rode upon her chariot each evening to pull its great silver disk up into the night sky, a phalanx of cats following in her wake to gobble up the mice of twilight.

But as estimable as those goddesses were, they did not completely meet our needs. What of the feline's affinity for magic? The Greeks and Romans likewise sensed it, and for this reason gave us union with Hecate. Enduring goddess of mystery, she ruled over those arcane things which humans could sense but not see. Her powers were wielded over the underworld, liminal spaces, dreams, and magical practice, and it was she who was invoked by all of the famed enchantresses of the classical world, including Circe, Medea, and the Witches of Thessaly. I'm sure it will come as no surprise to learn that her shrines were often populated by cats, and once again black ones in particular, since a shared affinity for night gave them a natural connection to the goddess.

Hecate even took in a troubled stray as a companion—and giving credit where credit is due, history's first recorded rescue cat was thus a product of Greek mythology.

Her name was Galinthias, and she had formerly been a human maid of Alcmene, the woman whom Zeus had impregnated as the mother of Hercules. Hera was furious over this act of infidelity, and endeavored to stay the birth. But clever Galinthias distracted the goddess long enough that her grip was loosened. In retaliation, Hera changed Galinthias's form to that of a cat. Hecate in turn took her in, having recognized in Galinthias's sacrifice a perfect example of feline loyalty. A precedent was thereby set, and Hecate's priestesses were spurred to seek out their own feline confidants, thus giving birth to the tradition of sorceresses owning cats—and not as "witches' familiars," mind you, but as ideal spiritual companions!

Anywhere you looked in pagan Europe, it was the same. As far away as the northern realms, the Vikings also considered us as spiritual beings. They declared us consorts of the flaxen-haired Freya, yet another goddess associated with domestic bliss and fertility, and she and her cats were inseparable. Why, they even provided her locomotion by pulling her carriage through the sky as she traveled the land to bless the harvest. Ah, perhaps there is some confusion among my readers. But Baba, wasn't Freya the fierce warrior goddess who led the Valkyries to battle? Yes, one and the same!

With her armor gleaming, Freya would descend onto the field of honor and choose only the most heroic among the slain to be transported to paradise, and when the fight-

ing was done, she would return to preside over the hearth. And should the dichotomy between her two different personas seem jarring to you, know that it suits us cats just fine. Keep in mind that the Egyptians noted the two divergent aspects of our personality, the domestic and the fierce, and to differentiate between them, they had assigned one half each to Bastet and Sekhmet. But in Freya, both were united—making her perhaps the most truly feline of all ancient deities.

Similar deities to Freya were known in Germany and around the Baltic Sea, although they called them instead Hel or Holda. But while the names may change, the felines remained the same. Thankful farmers even held a tradition of leaving a dish of milk in their fields for the refreshment of the cats who pulled Hel's chariot, a sweet gesture to be sure, since carting a goddess across the heavens was no doubt hard work. Over time, the farmers even started to venerate the cats themselves, as they evolved into a popular feline figure they could appeal to when assistance with their crops was necessary.

And why not? We had, after all, been there to protect your crops from the very start, so what could be more appropriate than appointing a feline folk god to bless agriculture? All was as it should be, and as it had been for millennia, as a friendship born in the mists of prehistory had grown into a long-standing partnership defined by love and respect. We cats had been universally recognized as mankind's closest friend, and rested upon a perch that we had every reason to believe was unequivocal.

Oh, how wrong we were.

Our perch crumbled from under our paws, and when we fell, we plummeted to depths we could never have imagined. Perhaps domestication had come at the expense of our wiles. We had trusted too freely in mankind, and were wholly unprepared when humans turned on us with a wrath they had previously reserved for their most mortal enemies. And to this betrayal, we had no recourse. Having adapted over thousands of years to life among you, we could not simply return to the wild. Trapped in your cities, we looked in horror as the faces in which we had once seen love became contorted with rage. "But what of *Felis*?" we pleaded. "What of the partnership that had been formed, and has for so long served human and feline in equal measure?"

This was suddenly as nothing! For thousands of years we had seen humanity's very best side, and now the cheek was turned to confront with its very worst. Yes, friends, our downfall was quite real. The culprit was a new faith, although hardly would this have raised any alarm at first—we had, after all, lived in harmony with humans of any number of faiths in any number of lands. And certainly this faith seemed innocent enough. It had come from the Middle East, the very place where the alliance between cats and people had been formed, and based on the teachings of a prophet, Jesus Christ, who had never in all of the stories of his life shown one whit of animosity toward cats.

By the late fourth century of the common era, however, when their triumph was near at hand, the Christians decided they did not wish for their faith to coexist with those of the Ancients. The Old Ways did not sit well with them. Belief systems that had inspired some of humanity's finest accomplishments were now judged to be the work of the Devil, and anything associated with the pagan world was considered suspect. The goddesses with whom we had stood for centuries were suddenly reviled as demons, and we as their companions were as reviled as well. It was a topsy-turvy new world, and since the pagans had held us up in esteem, the Christians determined to cast us down low.

But even as they disparaged us, they didn't strip us of our powers, as they believed all too well in the magical abilities bestowed upon us by the pagans. Instead they turned them about so as to stigmatize us even further. Our power to protect became a power to curse, and what had once been foresight now became the eyes and ears of the Devil himself. Black cats became especially vilified. The pagans had considered them to be the most esteemed, so they must be the ones most favored by the Dark Lord. And didn't the color of their coats admit as much? Black as the deepest night to signify their connection to evil, they were creatures of the netherworld and bringers of bad luck.

Of course, it was one thing for theologians to turn against us, but quite another to convince the rest of Europe to do the same. During the early part of the Christian age, the hatred of cats was more theoretical than practical. We were no longer revered, that much was certain, but common people, accustomed to our company, held us fast in their hearts. In some areas, the chatter was disregarded entirely. The monastic communities on Mount Athos, for instance, may have been in service to God, but refused to give up their cats. They wanted to ensure that their stock of ratting felines was maintained, but more than that, they simply *liked* us. Ah, the Greeks had welcomed us into Europe and they continued to stand by us!

And in Wales, King Howell the Good lived up to his moniker by respecting the ancient pact between humans and felines. He had gathered the wisest minds in his realms to promulgate a legal code, and while others might carp upon cats, Howell and his advisers still acknowledged our immense value to society as mousers. Lest there be any questions on the matter, they answered them within their statutes. In order to qualify for status as a hamlet, a group of dwellings must have a minimum of nine buildings, a plow, various other implements . . . and a cat. Further, should anyone question our worth, an adult feline who had proven itself in the hunt was decreed equal to four pennies— at a time when a penny was a pretty thing indeed!—and anyone found culpable in the

death of a cat was fined this much in restitution, plus further penalties levied in grain. This wasn't Bubastis to be sure, but it was at least a cause for hope. The theologians left no doubt as to their contempt for us, but perhaps through the innate goodness of humanity we might weather the storm.

It was not to be. Such tokens of respect were little more than archaic holdovers, and the church would not be at peace until all such vestiges of the bygone era had been destroyed. In the eighth century, during the time of Charlemagne, sledgehammers reduced the great buildings of the forefathers to dust, and the death penalty was instituted for humans who still persisted in the Old Ways. The Ancient World was finally laid in its grave, and the cats of Europe no longer walked among humankind as friends but instead visible symbols of the diabolic age that had been overcome. We had trusted ourselves to humanity and were carried to a new land—only to now find ourselves abandoned there and judged as agents of evil.

But wait, what evil could cats possibly be guilty of? And no smarmy answers, please, because this is a serious topic. By the Middle Ages, the rumors had been spread. We were in service to the Devil, it was said. We acted as his little spies, stealthy, clever, and always on the lookout—as if every cobbler in the street and every peasant on every ramshackle farm somehow warranted His (and our!) attentions. And in the still of night,

we summoned Him, the cries of cats in heat being now mistaken for calls to beckon our Infernal Overlord to appear in our midst.

But these were piddling offenses compared to . . . stealing souls? Indeed. The old belief that we could act as soul houses had also been perverted into a wild notion that at the moment of passing, a cat might appear from the shadows to abscond with the deceased's soul in order to ferry it to Hell and condemn a good Christian to eternal torment. And so the accusations went, paranoid ramblings that might seem laughable in any rational age. But this was an age of a different type, and the paranoid superstitions were codified as doctrine by the thirteenth century, when the highest authority in Christendom, Pope Gregory IX, officially condemned us as vessels of the Devil and enemies of God.

But we were not alone as adversaries of the Faith. The various heretical groups accused of opposing Christian society were considered our comrades in arms—in effect, the domestic goddesses of the past had been traded for godless heathens as our natural allies. Did you know that heretics in Germany were at one time referred to as *Ketzer*, meaning cats? Makes the connection pretty clear, I'd say. But we were more than simply their accomplices, serving instead as the Devil's own proxy to receive their obeisance. The Luciferans, for instance, were accused of worshipping a tomcat the color of nether night and sacrificing children in his honor. Meanwhile both the Waldensians and Cathars were said to demonstrate their diabolic allegiances by ritually kissing the posterior of cats as part of their assemblies. And as these delirious condemnations were spread to a public already wary due to sermons, lectures, and the rulings of Inquisition tribunals, our stigmatization became all the greater. But it was with the Knights Templar that our infamy received its most public proclamation. A crusading order that had gained fame fighting in the Holy Land, the Templars possessed wealth and prestige beyond all other brotherhoods. This

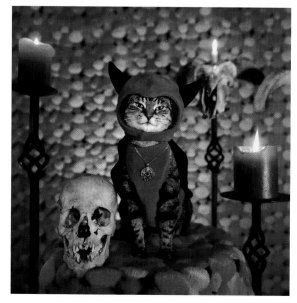

only force vile enough to besmirch a noble order, we received a starring role in the ensuing drama as a whole kit and kaboodle of improprieties was brought forth against the Templars. They had been worshipping the Devil in the form of a black cat! They had been kissing its posterior! This felonious feline would lead them in acts of sacrilege such as trampling the cross and spitting upon it! They had sacrificed infants in the cat's honor! Outlandish charges, each and every one. Yet the enmity toward our kind had grown so vast that no argument could clear from the air the stench of feline, and when the per-

spurred the jealousy of King Philip IV of France, who contrived an insidious plot: disparage the Order so severely that he could justify arresting them and confiscating their holdings. But how? What power could be brought to bear so as to irreparably damage the reputation of such an esteemed fraternity?

Cats could, he reckoned. As the

verse charade was finally concluded, the most famed of Christian knights, with a string of fortresses once a thousand strong, were outcasts of the Faith, and their leaders were sent to the stake.

And as tragic as it is to consider innocent men killed, think now of this: If the mere imputation of consorting with cats demanded a price so high in human terms, what cost would come due from the feline side? By the time the Templars burned in 1314, we were already burning, mercilessly tossed onto bonfires all across Europe. And with consciences hardened by propaganda that had convinced millions of people that we were in league with the Devil, who could object?

This is what we cats know as the Great Reckoning, the darkest age of feline history. As if by eradicating the memory of love one can, through hatred, achieve orthodoxy, the Christians tossed us into the flames to purify themselves of their own pagan past. Starting in the late twelfth century and continuing in some areas unabated for more than half a millennia, we were the targets of a persecution, the magnitude of which had never before been seen. All we could do was hide, scavenge, and endure, as countless generations of felines passed knowing humankind as nothing other than a tormenter. And torment alone was not enough, as it was even turned into spectacle. Our murder was

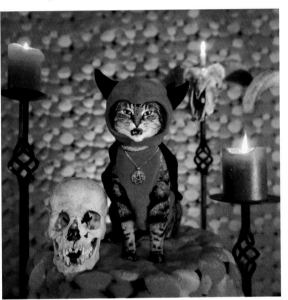

treated as a sacred act and incorporated into religious holidays, as if God had asked humanity to do Him the service of eradicating one of His own Creations.

His worldly Son's resurrection on Easter Sunday was celebrated by burning cats in large numbers—in the Alsace, we were thrown into the fires by the hundreds. Lent was also a popular time for butchery, and not a day went by when some village, somewhere, wasn't killing cats. In Picardy, we were attached to poles and lowered into the flames as slowly as possible in order to increase the drama, as if merit were measured through cruelty. And as the howls of agony rang out loud and true, spectators were told to pay no heed since our cries were nothing more than the language of devils.

One could at least find a few towns that had voted against burning. Ah, a few humans who still believed in mercy? Not exactly, they just didn't care to waste the firewood. In Ypres, Belgium, they tossed us to our deaths from the highest tower in the city, while in Albrighton, England, they whipped us to death, a rite considered such good fun that a rhymed couplet became popular: "The finest pastime that is under the sun, is whipping the cat at Albrighton."

And let us give special mention to the celebrations for the feast of Corpus Christi. The presence of Christ in the Eucharist was popularly commemorated with untold savagery against felines, including a uniquely barbaric ritual in Aix-en-Provence. A fine tomcat, the best that could be found in the region, was swaddled in fine cloth and placed upon an altar. Surrounded by flowers and incense, people came before him to bow in prayer. But they were not supplicating themselves to feline power as in days of yore. Rather, this innocent cat was conceived as a communal receptacle onto which the townsfolk could project their vile thoughts and deeds—and then expunge themselves of sin by destroying him.

Confused and at the mercy of man, what must this cat's thoughts have been? Surrounded by smiling faces of joyous humans, did he fancy that he was at last among friends? After all, these folks treated him gently, tending and even feeding him. At sundown he was placed in a wicker basket and they carried him through the town. Where they were taking him was a mystery, but perhaps he trusted them still as they walked in procession, merrily chanting the words of some human wisdom. Maybe he thought

they were going to provide him with a home among man, where he could be safe and well cared for.

But now, the curious day became curiouser. Rather than taking him to a home they placed him . . . upon a pile of wood? And then they all began to back away. Surely they didn't intend to abandon him there, inside of a basket? His answers came soon enough. The facade of kindness was dropped at the end, and in the final moments, he glimpsed evil in the faces of those who had tended him. It was then that the torch was thrown. The flames began slowly, at first known only by the smell of kindling, but you know the rest, so there is no need to narrate further. Another victim burned, and all the while the cavalcade of sinners rejoiced, believing that through their act of abject cruelty they had gained a clean slate with God.

I wish I could comfort you with the knowledge that these "celebrations" were borne of a sudden madness and passed just as suddenly. Alas, that was not the case. Consider, for example Metz, France, where the burnings began in the year 1344, when a black cat was blamed for an outbreak of St. Vitus's Dance. Ah, that odd medieval affliction that caused humans to show outward signs of joy—an intolerable display to the medieval mind! Henceforth on the eve of St. John's Day, thirteen cats would be suspended in a cage and dropped into a bonfire, lest the dancing perchance return.

Shall I tell you when this mindless cruelty finally ceased? In 1773. Yes, for 429 years—as generations passed from one to the next, and a child burned cats as had his father, and his father before, all the way back to relations whose names were no longer even remembered—our wails were heard in Metz. So if you have read thus far with dry eyes, perhaps you will now loosen a tear when we total the victims for one city alone, amounting to 5,577 innocent felines, many perhaps no different than the one you have taken as your own companion. All burned with neither conscience nor compunction, save that the people of Metz believed that through our suffering they might be free from dancing.

History is as bitter as it is sweet. I have told you these stories because I must, even though I know they are as painful for you to hear as they are for me to recount. For our end, yes, we know forgiveness, and humans have proven themselves once again to be our friends. But memories hold long on to the consciousness, and it is something you should keep in mind when you see a cat unknown to you and bend down to offer it a hand in kindness only to see it dart off: history has taught us all too well that it is not always love that is borne in the hands of a stranger.

But hear now of a further tragic twist to this sordid story, as the price due for the misguided cruelty of humans was not paid by cats alone. Those who sang out in joy at our demise did not realize that the penalty they levied upon us would be levied upon themselves also, as within a century of the first great massacres, the stigmatization of felines would result in nothing less than the devastation of Europe. Wait, Baba, how can this be so?

In betraying their pact with *Felis*, humans had invited vermin back into their lives. Holding the line against rats in the premodern world was precarious even with a full complement of feline defenders, and with our numbers decimated and the remaining cats ostracized, oh, how they prospered! You understand so little about them. Did you know that left unchecked, a single pair of rats can produce a *million* offspring in a three-year period? And now, without us to stop them, they took up residence in your towns and villages at a level that can hardly be imagined. They averaged ten per household, meaning they vastly outnumbered humans even in their own homes.

They devastated your goods and food supplies, and that was just their opening gambit. Even worse was the contamination they brought, as they spread disease and pestilence in all corners. Mind you, these were brown rats, and they were trouble enough. But they had cousins in Africa who soon arrived on the scene, black rats who came hidden within the holds of ships bringing crusaders back from the Holy Land. And these stowaways themselves carried stowaways: parasites that bore a plague

unlike any Europe had ever known, a deadly cargo which the rats dutifully delivered from field to field and town to town. Humans began to contract it in 1347, and the consequences soon became catastrophic as your ancestors cowered in advance of the fearful disease that they called by the name Black Death.

As a comeuppance for Europe's war against cats, some twenty-five million lives were lost within five years, a third of its population gone. But still no lesson was learned. Imagine the obstinacy of humankind being such that even as the plague ravaged city after city, and the bodies were piled in the streets, the hatred of us abated not a whit. Your best hope for deliverance was reduced to cinders as we continued to be thrown into the fires. And as unimaginable as it might seem, our dark age would soon turn even darker. Europe would discover a new enemy, one that was likewise descended from the Old Ways. She was the great-granddaughter of Isis, Hecate, and the other patrons of magic from the Ancient World, but while we once stood by these goddesses in an expression of benevolence, we now stood damned alongside the one they called the witch.

She arrived on the scene even as the plague still swept its deadly path, and for the next three centuries provided as much fuel as the bonfires could burn. By adding magic and overt sexuality to the basic package of sacrilege heretics had already been accused of, the witch became a sensation, something considerably more than the sum of her parts. And cats?—oh my, yes, we were the ideal complement. Both witch and cat were creatures of the night, and considering our long-standing connection to magic it was a sure bet that we were somehow linked to her powers. Some accounts even claimed that the Devil appeared at her sabbaths not in the form of a goat or ram or as any other modern conception, but as a large tomcat. A perfect pair, cat and witch. Like two forces of evil operating in tandem, one incomplete without the other, but together magnifying the threat each posed to the Christian world.

Given such a buildup, many of the accusations involving felines and witches seem a bit prosaic, being no more than recycled charges from the war against heresy. We're talking about simple matters that all cat owners must attend to; you're familiar with the daily tasks, no doubt, things like sacrificing infants in our honor, participating in unholy congregations, and kissing under our tail. But the witches were also brewing up something new on those dank and sinister nights under the bloodred moon. Cats were becoming intimately bonded to them in a way we had never been with heretics. When it came to witchcraft, we were cast as familiars, extensions of the body and power of the witch herself.

This was according to the Devil's own plan, he having devised the role of familiar so that we could give special assistance to

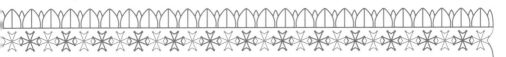

his army of hags. There were advantages to our small size and stealth, as we could go unnoticed in places where a woman could not, and thereby provide a discreet set of eyes and ears. But that was the least we had to offer since we were believed to have our own magical talents. By communing with our matron, we could augment her powers, and snippets of our fur or claws could be used to make potions which provided the witch with abilities as varied as clairvoyance, invisibility, and weather control.

And did you know that a witch could even adopt her familiar's form? Imagine the havoc she could wreak, as with her identity thus disguised she could roam freely and cause whatever mischief her little black heart desired. As if a cat's life wasn't difficult enough in those days, this new delusion led to a particularly loathsome belief that witches could be unmasked by inflicting injuries on suspicious felines. The idea was that one might attack the cat, and if a local woman was found the next day to have a wound on her body in a corresponding place, her status as a witch was thereby confirmed. Ah, yes, yet another danger to look out for, and yet another impetus to avoid humans entirely.

But we cannot call the accounting complete until we give audience to Europe's demonologists. Their hysterical meanderings in those days had credence, and they declared that affairs were even worse than anyone had guessed since cats were, in addition, at great risk of being possessed by demons. Well! How was that left out of *The Exorcist*? As ridiculous as the charge now sounds, back in the day it was understood that demons could possess all manner of creatures, and of the entire animal kingdom it was we who were most amenable. In the demented logic of the time it made sense. We served the Devil, after all, so why wouldn't we be delighted to offer our bodies to his minions?

We were simultaneously at the height of our powers and the depths of our despair, helpless to protect ourselves despite the potent abilities your kind believed we possessed, and in fact punished all the more for them. Our crimes might include no less than murder, and numerous were the witches who admitted to having set cats to that very task. Of course, these were women who had been tortured to a breaking point and were ready to acquiesce to any confession that might bring even a moment's respite from the rack. But credible or not, their testimony confirmed the zeal to believe, heightening further still the vitriol directed against us.

If you think it can get no worse, guess again. A banner year in the history of feline deviltry came in 1484, when the Vatican proclaimed us to be as culpable for the evils of sorcery as the witches themselves, and decreed that we should be burned alongside them. From then on, any cats sharing the home of a suspected witch would share the ignominy of her fate. And if the accused perchance had no cat? She had better come up

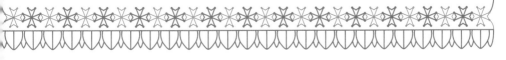

with one and quick, lest the inquisitors disbelieve her confession. Any cat she could think of might be implicated and brought to their demise, even local felines roaming the streets and scarcely of her acquaintance. But I will place no blame upon these tormented souls for testimony that caused untold further deaths of my kind. They were victims of the same perversion of faith as we, driven to madness as their whole reality was reduced to excruciating pain. Relief would come, but only in the form of death, as the witch and whatever unsuspecting cats she named in accomplice were together bound and condemned to the flames.

Think now of the irony that was perhaps

the cruelest turn of all. It was older, unmarried women looking for companionship who were the most likely to show us compassion. Ah, you know the kind! You joke about them now as crazy cat ladies—but back then it was no joke. As a group, they were forced to the margins of society, where their gender and lack of status rendered them defenseless against charges of witchcraft. And once accused, the very goodness of their hearts as evidenced by their charity toward local felines was turned against them. A suffering animal and a lonely human, a pair of outcasts each offering the other a modest measure of comfort in a wicked world, saw an offer of love turned into a death sentence

for both. Can an age be darker than to ex-change kindness for murder?

But this was also an era populated by some of mankind's most brilliant minds. Your major cities were transforming into vi-brant centers of intellectual discourse and sweeping cultural change. Surely the vision-ary thinkers born of the Renaissance would give a stern rebuke to the horrors perpe-trated upon defenseless felines. What, for instance, would a man like William Shake-speare make of us? He did indeed include cats in his work . . . but creativity for once escaped him and he cast us in the most pre-dictable of all roles, the companions of the witches in Macbeth. At least back in gentile London, his queen offered us a place in her coronation. It's true—we were honored participants to Elizabeth's ascension to the throne, front and center . . . packed into a wicker dummy which was set ablaze to demonstrate the forthright power of Prot-estant English faith.

But what of Paris, being no less than the intellectual capital of the continent? It was there that Pierre de Ronsard, famed in his day as the "prince of poets" and so esteemed as to be provided a suite of rooms in the royal palace, penned these words: "There does not live a man in the world who so greatly hates cats as I . . . I hate their eyes, their brow, their gaze." And not many people at court would have objected to such a senti-ment, since in the midsummer celebration in the Place de Grève, baskets of felines

were placed atop tall poles and burned before cheering crowds. Are you curious about who would attend such a sadistic spectacle? Rabble, no doubt? Yes—if that is how you consider the very kings of France. It's true. Henry IV in particular was said to take great pleasure in listening to our anguished howls. And as for the Sun King, Louis XIV, the monarch who defined a nation and an epoch like no other, he didn't just watch—crowned in a wreath of roses, he personally lit the fire in 1648.

All right then, what of philosophers? Could minds that study the broader questions of existence countenance such cruelty to a living creature? Let us check in with the greatest of the age, René Descartes. He paved the way for the Enlightenment, but he was hardly so enlightened himself. In his case at least we had company, since it wasn't just felines he denigrated. He declared that all animals lack souls, and without them they further lacked the ability to reason or even feel. We amounted to a vast army of exceptionally wrought mechanisms whose behavior was a form of complex parody. And to prove his point, this titan of the age threw a living cat out a window. Helpless, it cried in fear and fell hard against the street below, and as it writhed in pain, an amazed Descartes exulted about how it so perfectly mimicked authentic sensation.

Perhaps we should try our luck with men of science? Trained in clinical thought, would they see through the delusions?

Actually, they managed to make things worse. The physicians of the day advised that it was more than just a feline's sorcery that one must be leery of because we possessed certain physical properties that were no less dangerous. Pietro Andrea Mattioli, the personal doctor of the Holy Roman Emperor Maximilian II, warned that cats carried leprosy. Meanwhile the leading surgeon of the Renaissance, Ambrose Paré, explained that our breath, hair, and brains are all poisonous. They generate fumes that escape through our mouths, like little chimneys expelling toxic vapors. If inhaled, they have a consumptive effect, and those of you who allow us to share your beds have no doubt noticed the onset of tuberculosis. No? Odd, considering that Paré ensured his readers that would be the consequence if they slept close to a cat.

In a modern world where cats and humans live together so contentedly, this history is infuriating to recount, and I don't doubt that the reader wishes for me to bring this sordid history to a close. Baba, can you offer us no positive stories which portend the love we share with our own felines? Yes, I can. There were some beautiful legends passed down, heartwarming stories that stood squarely in defiance of the myths spread by the cat haters.

Have you heard the tale of a very brave cat and his companion, an impoverished fellow named Dick Whittington? This tale involved exotic lands and a faraway king, and it was said that this cat by his wiles secured such a fortune in gold that his human became wealthy and was elected mayor of London. As this story was told and told again, it became so popular that a statue was dedicated in London in honor of this very same cat, and it still stands to this day. And the story inspired others from among those humans who dared see us as virtuous.

These included Giovanni Straparola, who in the sixteenth century wrote a caprice in Italian based on the same theme, with a poor boy inheriting as his bequest nothing more than a little feline. Eh, a petty endowment? Not so! This cat was as clever as could be and orchestrated a series of schemes that eventually saw the boy crowned a prince. And this story was likewise told time and again, and people began to call it by a certain name, *Il gatto con gli stivali*. Or, in English . . . "the cat with boots." Well, I suppose you can guess the rest. A century later, Charles Perrault would write his own version in French, and *Puss in Boots* would become forever a classic of feline literature.

These are charming tales to be sure but again I sense objections. They are mere fables, after all, and you want to know about cats of flesh and blood, fur and claw. You wish finally for stories of real felines that might redeem the malfeasance of man. Ah, it was hard to love a cat in that era, my friends—and I should point out at least as hard for a cat to love a human, making such stories sadly scarce. But if one searches

hard enough they can be found, and nothing will please me more than to now regale you with some of the outstanding personages who defied public scrutiny to openly declare their affection for us.

They include no less than Petrarch! The great scribe of the Early Renaissance dared offer his love to a cat even while his contemporaries were burning us, and this love was so true that upon his companion's passing, the poet went into a period of deep mourning. To mollify his sadness, he insisted on preserving the little body in a glass shrine in his home, which no doubt raised a few eyebrows. But I will venture that they were raised even higher by an inscription he placed upon the case which compared his favorite cat to the muse who inspired his poetry. And Petrarch was not the only Renaissance poet to love a cat. In France, Joachim du Bellay took as a companion a tabby named Belaud, and on her death composed a two-hundred-verse-long epitaph which called her "nature's most beautiful work," and deserving of no less than the immortality promised to us by the Ancients.

Among our supporters I can offer you an even greater personage. Michel de Montaigne is esteemed by your kind as a philosopher whose 107-volume *Essays* contain some of the most influential thought of his day, but we felines remember him as one of history's great advocates for our cause. Possessing gentility and discernment which elevated him well above his contemporaries, he

had no doubts whatsoever about our keen intellect. In fact, he had been personally instructed in the topic by his own prodigious companion cat, Madame Vanité. And while it may have been veritable heresy at the time, Montaigne considered our two species to be equals. He was the first of your kind to pierce the facade of the human/feline relationship, laying the issue bare for all to see when he broached the question of who was actually in charge. "When I play with my cat," he asked, "is it not she who is amusing herself with me more than I with her?"

And here is another surprise for you: despite the antagonism directed at felines by Christianity, we nonetheless found champions among men of the cloth. Among these true men of God was Cardinal Wolsey, the Archbishop of York and Primate of England from 1514–1530. His cats were so dear to him that he brazenly allowed them to cavort in his lap during important audiences. Scandalous, to be sure—a perversion of such magnitude has not been seen since the days of Caligula, remarked the Venetian envoy. But Wolsey cared not a whit. Sadly, he fell from grace and died an outcast, although his propensity for felines was not to blame. Henry VIII decided he preferred the charms of Anne Boleyn to those of his wife and instructed the cardinal to secure for him a divorce. When Wolsey failed to convince the Vatican to comply, he was accused of treason and stripped of his titles. So there you see, the culprit in his downfall was human lechery, which has historically proven itself a far greater enemy to your kind than we cats could ever be.

But of this much I will assure you: if there had been any way in which Wolsey's cats could have saved him from turmoil, they would have, and in fact they probably tried their best, because back in those dark days we *never* forgot a friend. Some of the greatest examples of loyalty in feline history involve certain special cats who transcended the hatred and oppression of a bleak age to act heroically on behalf of the special humans who took them to heart.

Take the case of the English courtier Sir Henry Wyatt. In 1483 he was arrested on charges of treason for publicly supporting Henry Tudor, Henry VIII's father, as the rival to the throne of King Richard III. He was shut away in the Tower of London, a place where people were sent to die. And indeed, he had been left to starve. But not so fast! In his hour of despair, Wyatt met a stray female cat lost among the cells. He took this wandering feline to heart and offered the single gift he had left, his friendship. As if any of us have ever asked for more from a human. Wyatt hoped only that his furry visitor might provide him with a bit of solace in his final, lonely days—never did he dream that she would provide his salvation.

The cat began to return daily, bringing pigeons caught on the grounds as food. And on cold nights she would climb onto Wyatt's chest, keeping him warm in his freezing cell.

Through the cat's dedication, he survived his incarceration, eventually seeing the light of day two years later when Henry Tudor was crowned king. For his part, Wyatt honored the debt, taking with him the feline who had tended him so loyally, and commissioning a stone memorial in Kent to the intrepid companion whom he credited with saving his life.

And this was hardly the only cat who came to the rescue of a prisoner in the Tower of London. That nasty Queen Elizabeth got a measure of comeuppance for the felines that were burned at her coronation, courtesy of Trixie, the companion of Sir Henry Wriothesley, 3rd Earl of Southampton. After he backed a rebellion against the throne in 1601, he was locked in the Tower, far out of sight of those who might offer him aid . . . save for one. Intrepid Trixie managed to find her human sequestered in his cell, and embarked on a surreptitious campaign to smuggle in morsels of food. For two years her efforts sustained poor Henry. Her loyalty left no doubts about her nobility, and after the earl's release in 1603, she was given an honor unique for cats of the day: she was depicted in a portrait, sitting proudly by his side.

A mighty huzzah for such stalwart kitties! Can we assume that by demonstrating such virtue these cats helped vanquish the negative feline stereotype and finally garnered us a clean slate? Not entirely. Humans change their attitudes *verrrry* slowly, and many of you stubbornly clung to the idea that we were evil well into the 1800s,

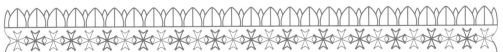

and in some areas even longer. Only a century ago people in remote parts of Europe still circulated stories about witches transformed into cats. Or tales of an evil cat king who ruled over the rest of us, appearing as a run-of-the-mill feline by day, but at night . . . ah, well, that was when he exerted the Devil's powers, and people best be wary if they venture out after dark since no one could say where he might be hiding.

By the late nineteenth century, the belief in demonically possessed cats even managed to cross the Atlantic. One was accused of plaguing Richfield Center, Ohio, in 1897, and while that town managed to slip from the Devil's paws, soon enough it was the turn of Schuylkill Haven, Pennsylvania, to face the evil (cat's) eye. It started innocently enough on the face of things, when a local mama cat gave birth to a litter. But the residents were no bumpkins and they knew something was amiss. They noted the date—being the sixth day of the sixth month of the year 1906—and what's more, there were exactly six kittens born and the sixth one happened to be black. That's an awful lot of sixes, and if you add them all up you get no less than the Number of the Beast.

The prophecy appeared to be fulfilled when a large black cat suspected of being either a disguised witch or the Devil himself began appearing at night, prowling around local farms. Word spread of sinister doings: it was said that the hens started to crow like roosters and the pigs barked like dogs when it was near. The climax came when the owner of the property on which the kittens had been born died suddenly. The coroner could not determine the cause, but the locals had no doubts that the "Hex Cat," as they now called it, had lain the man low.

Posses were formed and went to the forest in search of this unholy foe. Their rifles were loaded with bullets cast of melted gold—an expensive indulgence but apparently effective, because even though none of their shots hit the mark, the cat ran off and was not seen again. The townsfolk explained that the diabolic feline had been scared off by the power of their faith. Or, alternately, might we conjecture that an otherwise normal stray cat hit the road in search of a town where it wouldn't be shot at by hillbillies?

But these goings on were scarcely a ruckus compared to the wickedness afoot in Washington, DC. It was there, more than a thousand years after we were first cast as the Devil's minions, that the most feared of all demonic cats was finally summoned forth from the pit—meaning in this case the basement of the US Capitol Building. With its dome under construction in the 1850s, the Capitol was left open to an influx of vermin. Before you quibble about whether the term might refer to the elected officials, let me state categorically that I refer to an invasion of rats. Feral cats were collected and released into the basement to combat them, but within a decade, a very different sort of cat was claimed to be prowling the halls.

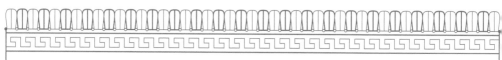

The apparition was black as pitch, but generally appeared at first sight no different than an ordinary domestic feline, and would not have caused undue alarm, save for the matter of its glowing red eyes. These proved a portent of further devilment, and the cat grew larger and more menacing as it returned over a series of nights until, with fangs gleaming and claws glistening, it took on the form of a ferocious panther. As terrified maintenance staff spread word that a monster had come, the terrible specter just as mysteriously disappeared. It then reappeared some months later, only to dis-

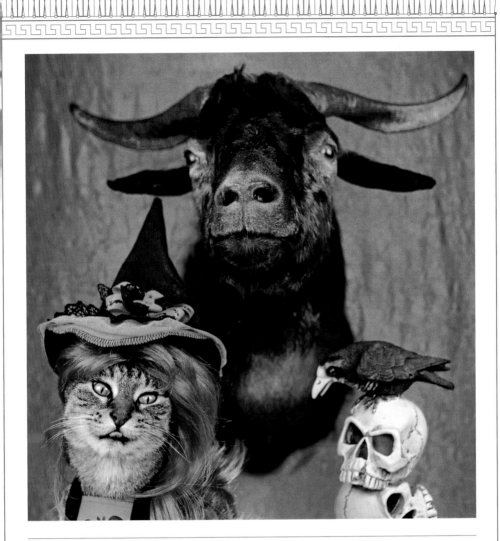

appear and reappear again and again in a terrifying game of hide-and-seek.

Rumors began to circulate, and they did not tell of the quantities of moonshine whiskey or whatever other swill might be quaffed by bored night staff in order to induce such visions. Rather, they told of the horror of horrors, as it became common knowledge that one of the cats released into the Capitol Building to combat mice had carried within it . . . a demon! Oh, come now, would anyone believe such a thing? As the United States was preparing to take a starring role on the world stage, could the people in its very seat of power be gullible enough to believe that their capitol was afflicted with a feline phantasm?

Should that question occur to you, I am afraid you have not learned your lesson still. Yes, they believed! And continued to for decades. Newspapermen spread the word, and even if they themselves had never seen it and the evidence was dubious, they concocted sketches showing a giant, razor-toothed cat chasing laborers through the halls to provide all the confirmation that was needed for a credulous public. With a disappointing lack of inspiration, the apparition was named "D.C.," referring to both Demonic Cat and the District of Columbia, and it became a staple of Capitol lore and nearly as well known a presence as the senators themselves.

And lest in your innocence you take this all as a joke, know that to the pundits it was a matter most serious. They whispered of certain tidings associated with the beast, as it seemed to appear immediately before natural disasters. They noted with alarm how sightings had occurred before a terrible flood hit Pennsylvania, and a hurricane came ashore in Texas, and an earthquake rocked San Francisco, and many other tragedies of the Devil's doing. "Was the cat a harbinger?" they asked. "Or had its presence caused these disasters?" Or—was it instead a tale based in old slanders that refused to die, and to which modern man should pay no heed? This question they did not ask, as too many people continued to accept as the most natural thing possible that a cat should be connected to evil.

Beliefs die hard with your kind, and the centuries of oppression had by this time extended over millennia. But we cats are nothing if not determined, and among us were those who refused to submit to tyranny. They dreamed of a place where the somber clouds of a dark age would finally part, and a cat could once again bask in the warm glow of love and acceptance. And it was not a dream! Such a place did exist, a respite where humans put aside their prejudices and accepted us for our own merits.

Ah, a secret feline paradise, perhaps?

Eh, well, not exactly, for it was fraught with its own dangers and challenges. And the path itself was perilous enough that only the hardiest of Europe's felines had the fortitude to follow it. That place was the sea. We had come to Europe aboard ships, and during the dark ages the greatest adventurers kitten-kind has ever known began to board them again. They were not headed back to the world that had once embraced us, for that was long gone. Rather, they risked voyage into the great unknown in search of freedom. So let us scupper these sad days and weigh anchor! Join me as we follow the journey of the pugnacious pussies who dared dream of escape not to greener pastures, but rather over great expanses of the ocean blue.

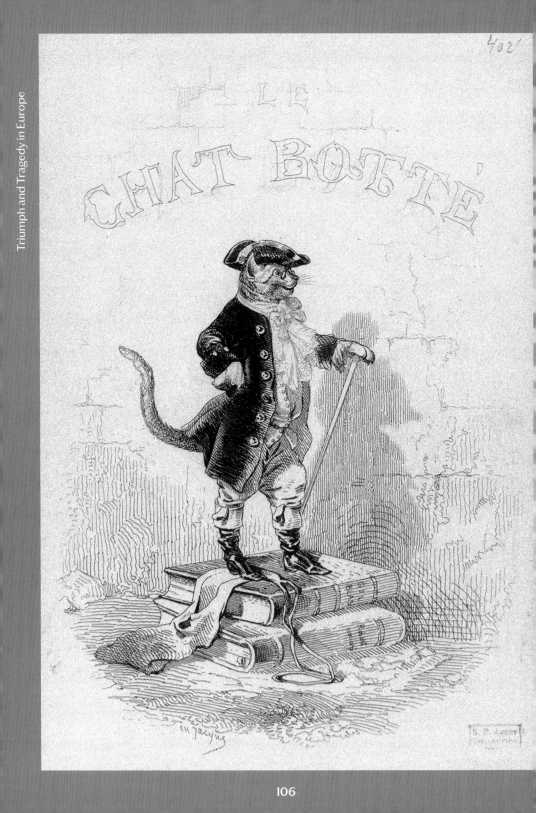

"HEX" CAT FAILS TO TURN UP TO BE SHOT WITH A GOLD BULLET

POTTSVILLE, Pa., Oct. 6.—Failure of the celebrated "hex," or witch cat, to turn up at the home of Miss Mary Isabella Thomas delayed his execution by means of shooting with a golden bullet, the only simon-pure method, according to the credulous, of effectively dispatching a feline capable of expanding to a height of four feet and contracting to the normal at will.

In the seriously expressed belief of the members of the Thomas family and of many of the superstitious dwellers in Tumbling Run valley, this "hex" cat caused the death of Howell Thomas, whose funeral occurred here today, and the fear engendered by the influence of the beast, which has probably become disgusted with the childishness of the Thomases and sought a home among more sensible people, has induced Miss Mary Thomas to move from the "haunted" house in which her father died.

A curious development today was the reconciliation of Miss Thomas with her sister, Mrs. Sarah Potts, of Orwigsburg, whom she at first charged with being the director of the operations of the "hex" cat. This return to the sisterly relations was ratified by an invitation from Mrs. Potts for Miss Thomas to become a member of her family circle. Miss Thomas declined, however, and is now at the home of a neighbor.

Gives Aid to Strkers.

Sometimes liver, kidneys and bowels seem to go on a strike and refuse to work right. Then you need those pleasant little strike-breakers —Dr. King's New Life Pills—to give them natural aid and gently compel proper action. Excellent health soon follows. Try them. 25c at all druggists.

—Herald Want Ads Bring Quick Results.

OPPOSITE · Standing proud, as his status in feline literature merits: Puss in Boots depicted in an 1841 French engraving by Charles Emile Jacques. The story is most famous in the telling of Charles Perrault, but has been published in almost every language and even made into feature films. A true legend!

ABOVE · We cats have never been known for our punctuality, so they should have expected no better from the so-called "Hex Cat," the demonic feline believed to be terrorizing a Pennsylvania town. Especially when the appointment was for him to be shot. From the *New Castle Herald* (PA), October 6, 1911.

lice would not let her.

DEMON CAT

Causing All the Sickness and Trouble at Richfield Center, Ohio.

SPECIAL DISPATCH TO THE ENQUIRER.

TOLEDO, OHIO, January 21.—The inclement weather here to-day has prevented any investigator from driving to the bewitched community of Richfield Center, 22 miles west of Toledo. A farmer named Henry Niemen came to this city, however, and fully corroborated the strange story told last night by Farmer Miller when he came to this city to ask for aid. Everything about the case sounds like a story from the days of Salem witchcraft, the sick now numbering the majority of individuals in 20 families. All claim to have been visited by a demon cat, after which they are simply wasted away by a disease that makes them indifferent to life itself. This cat, by the way, has been hunted with the belief that its death would kill the witch who is making the trouble. All other "witch signs" are said to be present. Many cattle have died, and some that are living give bloody milk, feather wreaths in pillows and beds, and one woman has burned 10 pounds of them which she claims has formed a wreath as hard as stone. The sick claim to be unable to stay in their beds, and sleep in the kitchen and living rooms. One man took his entire family to his barn, but were chased back by the demon cat. Miller's relatives, who went back with him to nurse the sick, first visited a priest, who is said to have given them directions for laying the evil spirit.

THAT DEMON CAT.

Mysterious Thing That Continues to Haunt the People of Richfield Center, O.

A special to the Cleveland Plain Dealer from Toledo, O., says: Additional details from the bewitched community of Richfield Center were brought to this city today by Henry Niemen, which fully corroborate the strange story told by A. M. Miller yesterday. Whatever the cause, the whole town, or at least the larger German element in the village, is as thoroughly stampeded as a drove of wild cattle.

Miller, although in what seemed nearly a dying condition himself, came to Toledo last night to take some relatives to nurse his stricken family, which consists of his wife and four sons. They, together with 20 other families, feel that they have been bewitched and unless help can be given them in some manner there will be many human deaths, just as cattle have already wasted away and died.

Before Miller's relatives accompanied him last night they visited a priest, who in all seriousness gave them rules for exorcising and "laying" the evil spirit, just as would have been done 200 years ago.

None of the elements is missing from the story, according to the accounts given by Miller and Niemen. The community is haunted by a demon cat and the sick aver, in all honesty, that the visits of the cat precede the demoniacal possession. This cat has been hunted in every manner, for it is believed that its death would result in the death of the witch.

Peculiarity of the Disease.

A peculiarity of the disease is the fact that many of the sick cannot remain in their rooms. They have made their beds in the kitchen and living rooms, while one man, named Woolson, moved his entire family to the barn in the hope of escaping this symptom. This was to no avail, as the dreaded cat still followed them, and the Woolson family returned in despair to the house, where they are all extremely ill. Cattle affected give bloody milk, which has long been recognized as an infallible "witch sign."

Another sign that is not wanting is the "wreathing" of feathers. Miller says that his wife has burned over 10 pounds, in the hope of breaking the spell. The feathers wreathed themselves in hard shapes, and one man reported the same phenomenon in the case of a bundle of shavings that he had brought to the house from the barn.

It is thought that the water in the locality is bad, which would account for the fact that both people and cattle are affected. The sick, however, do not show typhoid symptoms, but simply waste away, and after once affected the sick show an utter indifference whether they get well or die.

The strange part of the case is the fact that this trouble has been going on for over a month without attracting outside attention. Richfield Center is 22 miles from Toledo and not on any railroad. The inclement weather here has prevented any investigators from undertaking the long ride to the town today.

ABOVE · Richfield Center, Ohio, was wasting away in 1897. Pestilence and evil! People suffering illnesses that defied diagnosis and cows giving milk mixed with blood. Newspaper reporters came to town and told the rest of the state how it was all the fault of . . . a stray cat?

OPPOSITE · Oh, how you humans like to play when you're the big ones, but see how you run when the tables are turned. This syndicated news story from 1898 was accompanied by an artist's rendition of D.C. the Demonic Cat, the most legendary of the specters haunting the United States Capital.

According to the Washington correspondent of the Chicago Inter Ocean, the demon cat has reappeared at the capitol, spreading terror among the employes. The capitol is most prolific in such apparitions, no less than 15 ghosts claiming it as their heritage. But of them all the demon cat is the most horrible. It possesses much more remarkable features than any of the others, inasmuch as it has the appearance of an ordinary pussy when first seen, and presently swells up to the size of an elephant before the eyes of the terrified observer.

The demon cat, in whose regard testimony of the utmost seeming authenticity was put on record 35 years ago, has been missing since 1892. One of the watchman on duty in the building shot at it then, and it disappeared. Since then, until now, nothing more had been heard of it, though one or two of the older policemen of the capitol force still speak of the spectral animal in awed whispers.

THE DEMON CAT.

109

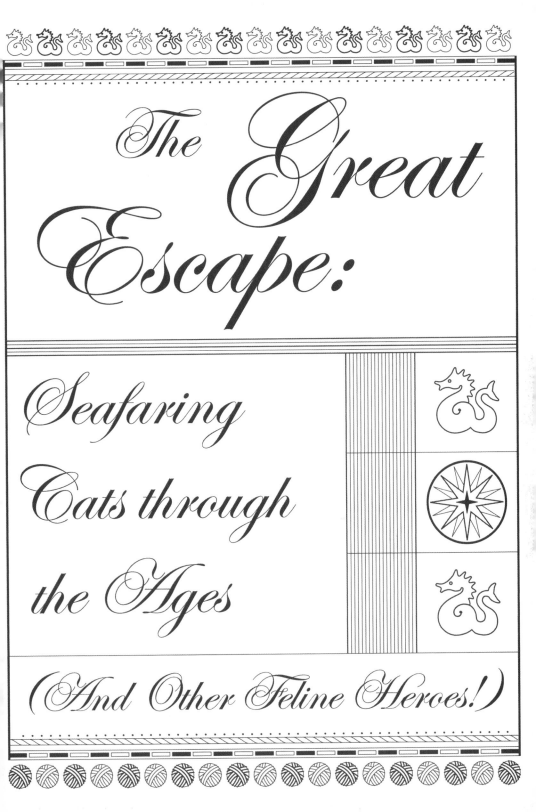

The Great Escape:

Seafaring Cats through the Ages

(And Other Feline Heroes!)

The great oppression that surrounded us for so many centuries of Western history allowed but a single escape, and an unlikely one at that. But those cats who boarded ships headed out to sea ventured forth to a place where they might find respect and even love. The pounding waves had the power to wash clean the accusations of witchcraft and deviltry, and the fetters of old world prejudice fell by the wayside as the cities of humankind flickered in the distance and then disappeared over the horizon. Adapting to a mariner's life was by no means easy, but those cats who made the transition were afforded an equality not only with other animals—but dare I say even with humans.

You may be surprised to learn of cats living aboard ships, but in truth, we had been sailing since the Ancient World. The Phoenicians had of course brought us across the Mediterranean aboard their galleys, but long before then Egyptians of noble rank were known to travel with us aboard their barques. Those were different times, and we were esteemed guests on the flotillas that traversed the Nile. But in the dark days, nothing was easy, and we worked hard to earn our keep on the vessels that carried us from European ports.

Not surprisingly, we were assigned to control rodents. Ships were wooden and creaky, providing easy entry for rats, who were capable of wreaking havoc upon provisions and leaving entire crews in jeopardy of starvation. This was serious business, and sailors understood the extent to which they were reliant upon us. No crew would risk leaving port without a cat, and in some cases more than one. So it was that your Age of Exploration likewise became an age of feline expansion. As you colonized the world, we colonized it at your side, and in many cases cat colonies were established in far-off ports so that needy ships might avail themselves of our services.

But to sailing men, we were more than just a vermin-control system. Living with us in close quarters, they learned the truth about cats, and while we might still be considered consorts of witches back home, out on the high seas we were friends. And with the sea being a harsh mistress, a friend was often needed, resulting over generations in the fondness of sailors for their cats being reflected in nautical lingo. The passageway above decks became a "catwalk," and "the ship's cat kittened," was a common phrase used by sailors as they logged off duty. Among a multitude of other examples, crew members who misbehaved might face the "cat-o'-nine-tails"—the term used in the British navy to describe a whip with multiple strands, and similar parlance was found in Holland and Spain, where the sailors also needed a bit of feline discipline.

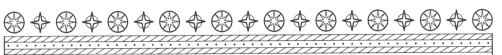

Mariners became even more indebted to us as they discovered the many unexpected skills we possessed. We became a trusted tool for predicting changes in weather, for instance. Pishposh, Baba, isn't this simply some shipboard superstition? Before you render judgment, remember the great acuity we cats have to natural phenomena, being far superior to human faculties. In the days before modern meteorological devices, our sensitivity to changes in barometric pressure might be as accurate if not more so than any other technology of the time. According to one common theory, if the ship's cat held its tail straight up, the weather would be fair for the next forty-eight hours, whereas if its tail sagged, squalls were coming. Naturally each feline might use its own unique set of mannerisms and postures to communicate its forecast, but a good sailor knew the gist of it: if he could read his cat, he could read the weather!

We were also esteemed for our natural ability as navigators. If you're tempted to doubt that a professional sailor would seek feline guidance, remember that we are well known for our outstanding homing instincts. After all, when we disappear from the yard, it's you who panic—we're not worried since we have absolute confidence in our ability to find our way back. And in cases of zero visibility on the high seas, a savvy captain might seek the wisdom of his ship's cat, in the hope that its finely honed sense of direction could point the ship along the proper course.

Unconvinced? I offer as a cautionary tale the fate of the crew of the American cargo steamer *Lake Eliko*. While moored off Grangemouth, Scotland, in February 1920, eleven sailors took a rowboat for shore leave, bringing with them their cat, Tabby. But as they made back for the ship that night, they were hit by an unexpected storm. Waves rose in a violent crescendo! Their small boat flicked about like a toy! All hands and paws tossed into the choppy waters! The men floundered hopelessly as the fearsome rain pounded their faces, and with the black of night concealing both ship and shore, they knew not where to turn.

But then came a sound from the darkness. Rising against the maelstrom was a familiar mewing sound. The men strained their eyes to see Tabby swimming off and calling for them to follow. Trust in the cat? Do you doubt still? With their lives in the balance, nine of the eleven men made haste after Tabby, and in his wake they arrived safely back at the ship. As for the other two? If you still question a cat's ability to navigate the open ocean, I will let you inquire of them directly. They can be found at the bottom of Davy Jones's locker.

Of course, not every cat would adapt to the nautical life, but those with enough dedication and fortitude came to love it, and there are even recorded cases of some who refused to ever set foot on dry land again. How far might such cats travel, you ask?

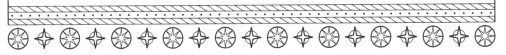

Why, as far as the seven seas would take them. While the cats themselves rarely (well, never) kept adequate logs of their journeys, we can take as a tantalizing hint Princess Truban Tao-Tai, the modern leader for miles sailed. A mixed-breed Siamese who joined the crew of the ore carrier SS *Sagamore* in 1959 and spent over two decades at sea, she was credited with logging . . . would you care to register a guess?

An amazing *one and a half million miles*! Shall we put that in perspective? It's the equivalent of over four hundred trips between New York and London, or three round trips between the earth and the moon. Of course, a lifetime spent at sea naturally made for a different kind of cat. A journalist fascinated by the topic explained to her readers that "ships' cats are an independent, self-sufficient breed, as different from the usual feline as their human counterpart, the seafaring man, is different from his landlubber brothers and sisters." Meanwhile a captain in Marseille told another inquisitive writer that some among us developed such a passion for sailing that if the vessel we had arrived on lingered too long in port, well, time waits for no cat, and we would simply hop onto the next ship headed out. These types of cats were called by nautical men pier jumpers or sea rovers due to their habit of switching boats on a whim.

But there were also plenty who stayed loyal to a single craft and crew, exhibiting an oft uncanny ability to remain with their ship even in the face of great adversity. "They are an amazing species," the same captain continued. "They seem to know instinctively when a vessel is leaving port. I have seen them disappear down the gangway a few minutes after we had docked, and never show themselves again until just before sailing time. And I have heard of them quitting a ship in one port and rejoining it at the other side of the globe." Certainly, anyone who knows cats will believe we might show up in the exact nick of time to catch our boat, but I'm sure you scoff at the latter claim as romantic hyperbole. After all, a cat separated from its ship at one harbor certainly can't catch up with it in another. Or can it?

Again, suspend your disbelief, because many are the stories of nautical cats who did exactly that, and there are plenty of documented modern accounts. Consider, for example, Minnie, a tuxedo cat who served as the mascot of the *Fort St. George*, a liner operating out of New York in the 1920s. On fifteen occasions, the captain attempted to evict Minnie from the ship, and each and every time she made it back on deck. Wait, now, fifteen times? That sounds like terribly rude behavior on the captain's part!

I will in this case show him a little sympathy, however. Minnie was prone to, eh, "screw around" in port, if you know what I mean, resulting in litters of kittens suddenly appearing on deck some weeks after shipping out. Don't judge! Hers was a traditional mariner's vice, after all, and being that ship

cats were sailors, they were no more or less loose with their morals than their human crewmates. Of course, a working vessel is no place for children, and Minnie's repeated litters firmed the captain's resolve to remove her.

His final attempt cemented her status as a legend among sea cats. While in New York, she was given over to a crew member with instructions that she be put ashore in a place from which she could not possibly return. The sailor did as he was told and bid poor Minnie fair wind at Broadway and Seventy-Second Street. This was a long way from the port, to be sure, and considerably further over open ocean from Bermuda, where the *Fort St. George* was next headed. Yet when the ship docked in Hamilton Harbor, lo and behold, she walked straight up the gangway to present herself for inspection, having found her own transportation across seven hundred miles of the Atlantic. The captain at this point had no choice but to admit defeat. Kittens and all, the indomitable Minnie could stay: a just outcome, I should say, considering she had proven herself a more adept mariner than he!

As amazing as Minnie's story is, I can offer one even greater. The Norwegian cargo ship *Hjalmar Wessel* sailed during World War II with a cat named Puss, much beloved by those with whom she served. But in 1943 she was lost in the port of Algiers. The sailors searched, searched, and searched again—but to no avail. Puss was not to be

found, and the ship, well, it had waited as long as it could. Brokenhearted, the crew was forced to sail on. But it was through no fault of her own that Puss was not aboard. She was lying injured, having been mauled by a dog. And now finding herself alone in some remote corner of the port, this ailing cat gathered her strength for the journey ahead.

From the northern coast of Africa, she scanned the vast horizon. She knew that somewhere beyond where blue sea met blue sky was her crew, and she determined to find them. How she traveled no one knew but Puss herself. A stowaway, most likely, a wounded cat hiding belowdecks of a ship headed out of port, toward the far shore of the Mediterranean. Meanwhile her own crew was steaming up the heel of the Italian peninsula, their destination being Bari. And Puss was headed toward Italy also—could it be? But wait . . . Her ship was headed not to Bari but to Barletta. Had brave Puss guessed wrong? Had she come so very, very close but overshot her target by forty miles?

Ah, but wait again. And trust in that sixth sense we cats have—and in the case of nautical cats, maybe we should assume a seventh, because Puss knew more than even the crew. The day before the *Hjalmar Wessel* was to dock in Bari, the port there was bombed by the Allies. And it was rerouted to . . . yes, Barletta. Puss had guessed correctly, and as the ship sat at dock, the sailors suddenly saw a familiar friend crawling

116

meekly up the gangway. They rushed her aboard and took her belowdecks to treat her wounds. Alas, she had expended all she had left in the effort to find them, and by the next day she was dead. But before you shed tears for her passing, realize that there is beauty here even more than there is sadness. Puss had a final wish, and the strength enough to fulfill it: a true sailor, she spent her last hours in the embrace of the crew she loved.

While you are no doubt impressed at having already met some very fine nautical felines, in the following pages we shall tread onto hallowed ground as I impart to you the most revered tales (and tails!) of all. I am talking about our greatest heroes and most stalwart adventurers. These are the cats whose incredible triumphs—and sometimes tragedies—resonate far beyond the crews with whom they served, as they charted the course of even human history.

The most legendary of these was known by the name of Trim, being a large black tom with a white patch on his chest, and I can safely speak for all cats when I say that he is regarded by us as being the greatest of all feline mariners. Sailing with Captain Matthew Flinders at the start of the nineteenth century, Trim was the first cat to circumnavigate Australia. And when he continued onward to traverse the Indian, Pacific, and Atlantic Oceans he became in addition the earliest cat recorded as circumnavigating the entire globe. A ship's cat through and through, he took in the salty air with his first breath, having been born aboard the South Seas exploration vessel HMS *Reliance* in 1799.

A telling event occurred when he was but a kitten, and left no doubt that he was by nature a sea cat. Playing on deck and gamboling about, he rolled up along the ship's rails and fell into the ocean. "Cat overboard!" the crew yelled, and quickly scrambled all hands to the rescue. But Trim was not as helpless as they had thought, and considerably more resourceful. Swimming back through the brine, he clawed his way up the hull and climbed up onto a rope as the astonished crew looked on—the kitten had rescued himself!

Trim's intelligence and playful manner made him a favorite among the *Reliance*'s young officers, all of whom competed for his paw with the hope that they might have him as their own when they received a command. It was Flinders, at the time a lieutenant, who would gain custody of the prodigious feline. Together they sailed until 1803, and while it may be only four years as the calendar tells it, measured in adventure it was enough for many lifetimes. Flinders called Trim "the finest animal I have ever seen," and was so impressed that he even wrote a book detailing his cat's exploits. It was the first feline biography ever penned, and it is high praise indeed when a captain deigns to write the memoirs of a crewman.

Flinders freely admitted that his cat was not immune to trouble—and given that he

was both a cat and a sailor, we should expect nothing less. He was prideful and disposed toward vanity, and could at times be destructive. On a whim he might steal the food right off of other sailors' forks, and if there happened to be any dogs onboard, well, he took it as his bound duty to torment them without mercy. But these were footnotes to the real story: Trim was the finest cat to prowl the bounding main, a dedicated voyager who could be counted on to help navigate, control rodents, boost sailors' morale, and keep a keen eye on things, all done with a diligence worthy of the best sailing man.

Together, captain and cat successfully mapped the coast of Australia, and afterward sailed all the way back to England. Flinders had the notion to settle down and convert him to a landlubber, but Trim was even more born to the sea than his captain and the city did not sit well with him. He had been left in the custody of a woman in London while Flinders got his affairs in order and her appeals were soon heard. A bored and angry Trim was destroying her home, and she urged Flinders to get him back out on the blue.

So it was that they continued to sail, until Flinders again attempted to return to England from Australia in 1803, only to be detained by the French in Mauritius on suspicion of piracy and sentenced to seven years in the brig. Trim was taken in as well, being in all likelihood as much a pirate as his captain, if not more so, and his sentence

was no less severe: he was given over to a young girl and it was decreed that he should become a housecat. No thank you, mate! He promptly disappeared, much to the dismay of Flinders, who never saw him again. Brokenhearted, he feared that Trim might have fallen victim to the most dastardly form of foul play. Might the natives have eaten him, he wondered? The fate was so cruel that the captain was incapable of discussing the topic further.

But I laugh at that part of the story. I know full well where Trim disappeared to, and I think you, the reader, do also. The French Navy had as much a chance of holding him as they did the water itself. Trim was born to the waves and destined to die among them, not in the belly of some islander. Yes, Trim loved Flinders, but seven years is a long time to wait. What Flinders did not want to acknowledge is that there is an authority above captains, above even admirals, and it was to this one that his cat had in truth offered his lifelong devotion. We should have no doubt that Trim stowed away onto another ship and continued in the service of his true master: the sea.

Trim's story reminds us that great voyagers also faced great perils, and indeed many of these cats paid for their bravery with their lives. The most harrowing journey ever undertaken by a nautical feline was that of Mrs. Chippy, a fine-looking tabby who had the misfortune of sailing aboard the HMS *Endurance* with Ernest Shackleton's 1914

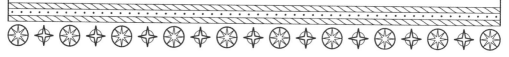

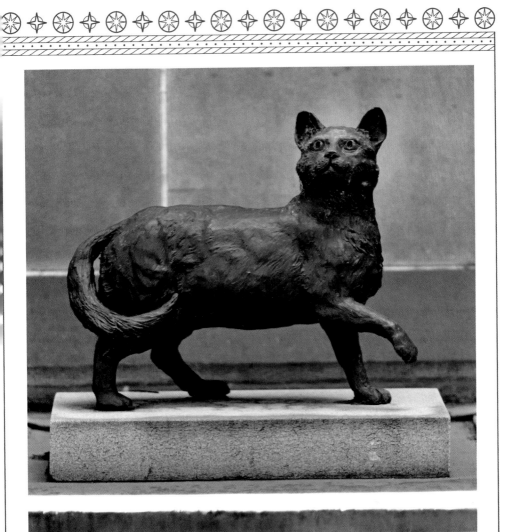

Antarctic expedition. Other daring cats had already sailed to the icy southern pole, a pair named Blackwall and Poplar having accompanied Robert Scott in 1901. But their journey was scarcely more than a Sunday cruise compared to Mrs. Chippy's star-crossed voyage, which started even with *his* name.

Yes, that's right, despite being referred to in the feminine, Mrs. Chippy was in fact male, being a Scottish tomcat who had been brought aboard by the ship's carpenter, Harry McNeish. This fellow was also nicknamed Chippy, and his close relationship to the cat, combined with the fact that sailors

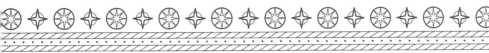

tend to be considerably more cognizant of female anatomy in humans than in cats, had caused a Mr. to be misidentified as a Mrs.

If the name weren't already a forewarning, feline intuition had provided him with such cause for alarm that, in a highly uncharacteristic gesture for a nautical cat, he broke ranks as the ship left port and jumped overboard in an attempt to swim back to England. The crew, not to be faulted since they were convinced they were doing the right thing, fished him out of the water. To Chippy's great credit, he did not sulk, instead settling into life on the *Endurance* and by all accounts serving winningly as a mouser and general morale booster. And it turned out the crew would desperately need him in both roles, because tragedy struck after their arrival in Antarctica.

But before continuing his story, I must pause for an aside. Your history books record Ernest Shackleton as a great man, but in light of what is to come, I think it is fair to consider from a feline perspective his qualifications for leading such a journey. He was neither a captain by trade nor did he come from a nautical background, having been the son of a well-to-do physician. And while he had apprenticed and risen through the ranks of the merchant navy, by the time the *Endeavor* sailed, he had not actively served for over a decade, a period during which he had already been involved in attempts to reach the South Pole that not only failed, but were nearly catastrophic.

His principal qualification therefore rested on an insatiable desire to plant a Union Jack at the southernmost point of the globe before the flag of another nation might arrive. To the English of the day, this made him fit for the task, although such a résumé would not suit any cat. Ah, but then we don't understand the human ego. The willingness to take great risks to plant the flag of a geographic region defined by fictive lines drawn on maps is to us nothing more than folly, and when it causes woe to other living creatures, it becomes something even worse. And it did indeed cause woe.

Experienced hands had warned Shackleton not to steer his vessel too far into the ice, but every inch forward he could drive the *Endeavor* placed his flag that much nearer. The ship drew closer and closer still, until lo and behold, crowds of mammoth icebergs, gawkers to the unexpected sight of visitors in their remote and frigid land, packed in behind, leaving no path to escape. Trapped at the bottom of the world, the goal of planting flags suddenly fell by the wayside, to be replaced by one that is eminently understandable to the feline psyche: survival. Rations were counted and found to be scant. And all on board braced themselves for the inevitable. Because there, in the loneliest place one can ever imagine, cat and crew could only watch as one by one the days of the calendar fell away, each bringing them closer to the fierce polar winter.

When it came, it showed no mercy. Winds faster than a motor car arrived to pummel the crew's spirit, followed in short order by temperatures in excess of fifty degrees below zero. As for the sun, it was stolen out from the sky and replaced by the black expanse of an endless night, broken only by the twinkle of distant and unfamiliar stars. This was no place for a cat! But huddled up on the freezing ship, Chippy and his crewmates endured as best they could. A cat's contributions were now seen to be all the more valuable, because every rat he had killed en route had saved a few

precious morsels in the commissary. Beyond the meager rations, they were left with only dried seal and penguin meat, whatever they had been able to catch and preserve, and there was not much even of that.

Little could they have imagined that worse was on the way. It was hoped that by October of 1915—the beginning of spring at the southern pole—the ice would break apart and provide a passage back to open waters. And the ice did break, but the huge, heavy bergs had not yet given up the game. Instead of moving aside to offer the ship freedom, their jagged edges pinched in its timbers. The *Endurance* had thus far lived up to its name, but as noble and strong as it might be, it was by then pushed to its limits, and the hull finally gave way. From its splinters, the crew salvaged what they could and moved out into makeshift camps and tents. Chippy had already gained one unwanted distinction, being the first cat to live through an Antarctic winter, and would now gain another as first to encamp out on the ice itself.

With the situation beyond critical, Shackleton determined that the only hope was to take the remaining lifeboats and make a daring attempt at escape, headed first for Elephant Island over three hundred miles away, and then the nearest populated land over seven hundred miles further at South Georgia Island. In that much there was nothing to quibble about. But he also ordered that everything which he deemed nonessential to the rescue attempt must

be disposed of, and that decision from the point of view of feline history was the greatest betrayal ever visited on a cat who had served diligently and with good conscience. Because on the list of items deemed expendable in the esteemed opinion of one Ernest Shackleton was . . . Chippy.

All must be willing to sacrifice, Shackleton explained in the face of the crew's protestations that he spare their cat's life. For his own part, he stressed the point by throwing some gold coins onto the ice, and then tore apart his Bible and threw parts of that away as well. Well, sir, there are plenty of gold coins in the world, and Shackleton was not a poor man. As for that Bible, mind you, he didn't even throw the whole thing away, having kept the flyleaf, although the text itself was rightly discarded since it explained how animals and humans were all creatures of the same God. Shackleton's sacrifice was hardly equitable with Chippy's very life, but his decision was firm. Only the "crew" was to be saved, he decreed.

"*Wait!*" you no doubt protest in sudden panic. Was Chippy not a member of the crew? A sailor just the same as any of the men? Is that not what you have taught us about ship cats, Baba? Indeed you are correct. And not only was Chippy a loyal member of the crew, to judge by the accounts of his fellows, he was the most popular among them. He and the men of the *Endurance* had bonded through long months of shared hardship, and the creed of the sea as passed

down by generations of proud sailors dictated that he be accorded respect no less than any human on board.

But I have already offered you an opinion on Ernest Shackleton. A dilettante who had set himself upon the ocean for the sake of flags and honors, he did not truly understand the bond between sailors and cats, nor how a crew member with four paws risks its life and serves as nobly as one with two feet. And since ignorance in humans is impervious to reason, he proved implacable to any entreaty. And so it was done. At Shackleton's command, Chippy was killed on the cold and barren Antarctic ice.

As for the escape, a lifeboat did indeed complete the trek to South Georgia Island. The human crew was saved, and while I won't claim that the rescue wasn't heroic, you will nevertheless pardon me if I find something empty in the outcome. Harry McNeish felt similarly since after all he was the one who had brought Chippy aboard. He never forgave Ernest Shackleton and refused afterward to speak of him other than to tell those who inquired that his former commander had killed his cat. A distraught McNeish abandoned even Britain, settling instead in New Zealand, where he died in 1930. There was one bit of humanity to come, however. Nearly three-quarters of a century after his death, the New Zealand Antarctic Society paid for a bronze statue of Chippy to be cast and placed atop his grave, symbolically return-

ing to a grieving man what he had lost on that tragic journey.

The British government heaped adulation upon Shackleton, selling the debacle to the public as a triumph. He was knighted, and gloried in the claim that "not a single member of the crew was lost." But I am not taken in by his words, and neither should you be. Because they are false. To this day, somewhere in the Antarctic ice lies the body of a crew member of the *Endurance*. Chippy is still there, his diligent and loyal service repaid by his commander with an unmarked grave in the desolate, unknowable expanse of a frozen continent.

For those who think I am being unfair to Shackleton, and that I denigrate a hero, the injustice of Chippy's death will be all the more evident when I contrast his fate to that of Nigeraukak, a tuxedo cat who served on the Canadian Arctic exploration vessel HMCS *Karluk*. Their stories are separated by only a year, and there are striking parallels between them. In 1913 the *Karluk* became icebound during an expedition to the North Pole. It was similarly crushed, and sank in January, in the middle of a harsh Arctic winter. Stranded at the top of the world in a life-or-death situation, the crew would face the same challenges—exposure, fierce cold, illness, and dwindling supplies—and even something that the men of the *Endurance* were spared: predations of polar bears.

Likewise confronted with the daunting prospect of a long and perilous journey

toward the nearest settlement, they did not, however, abandon their cat! To the contrary, they instead made a fur-lined pouch in which to carry Nigeraukak, and each among them provided bits from his rations for her sustenance. They acknowledged the cat as a member of their crew and for that reason alone they were loath to abandon her. But they also looked upon her as something more. For the men of the *Karluk*, she was a symbol of their ability to maintain their humanity in the harshest of conditions. Abandoning their cat would have meant abandoning faith in themselves, and they were convinced that as long as she survived, they would also.

It took nine brutal months before rescue came, with the tally at that time being fifteen survivors: fourteen human and one feline! Afterward Nigeraukak settled with a crew member in Philadelphia, and every time she had a litter of kittens, one was sent off to a member of the expedition. The kitten provided a reminder of what they had shared, suffered, and conquered—together, including their cat. This was, I think, a beautiful gesture (even if at some point they should have considered having her spayed, to be frank), and one that leaves me with a final thought in the matter: while it may not be easy or convenient, you humans should realize that there is always a compassionate solution to problems that confront both man and beast, if you are willing to look beyond selfishness to find it.

For centuries, our seafaring ancestors had labored in anonymity to all save the sailors with whom they served. But it was during this same decade, the 1910s, that the triumphs and tragedies of sea cats began to receive their due outside of nautical circles. And I'll have you know that some among these heroic felines gained no small degree of fame among the general public. By this time, as we shall see in the next chapters, the stigma against us had passed, and there was much hoopla as journalists reported on our service aboard the dreadnoughts of World War I.

Among the first to reap the benefits was Sideboy, a black cat who sailed off to war with HMS *Neptune*. The crew adored him so much that they had postcards featuring his image printed up, to send back home to show off to friends and relations. Did they send pictures of their captain? Eh, no way! Who wants to see a grizzled old navy officer? But a handsome sailing cat, now there was something to be proud of. Sideboy was equally popular with newspaper editors, who couldn't resist photos of him reclining in a mini-hammock his mates had constructed for him.

A long-haired tortie named Jimmy meanwhile sailed aboard the HMS *King George V* at the head of the British fleet at the Battle of Jutland in 1916, and also found himself a celebrity. It was dangerous out there, folks, and he nearly took the big swim when a cannon blast sent a piece of shrapnel toward

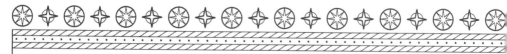

his face. Thanks to his cat-quick reflexes, Jimmy was saved from a head-on collision with the flying wreckage, but he still lost the tip of one of his ears. His injury earned him not only newspaper clippings touting his bravery, but an official commendation from the admiralty, making him history's first decorated naval cat. And the public didn't forget him after the war. As a decorated veteran, Jimmy was in much demand, making appearances to raise funds for the Chelsea pet home where he was living.

Humans were finally realizing just how valiant cats can be. And in fact had been for quite some time, since the adulation accorded these brave felines was recognition long overdue for a growing list of heroic cats—and not just on the high seas. One of the most famous to serve with land forces was a tabby named Tom, who saved the British and French armies during the Crimean War. Critically low on supplies while defending the port of Sebastopol in the Ukraine in 1854, they were in dire straits—that is, until Tom came along. A partisan Ukrainian cat, he refused to stand by and see his country fall to the Russians. Entering into the fray, he showed the British and French where the czar's troops had hidden caches of food, saving them from starvation in the defense of his city. And the thankful troops acknowledged their debt, adopting him as mascot and taking him back to Britain after the war.

The Russians lost that round, but they nevertheless have their own impressive his-

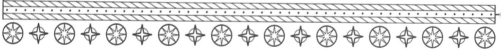

tory of feline heroes. A pair of their finest helped to turn the tide of the German advance during the Second World War, both serving in the fiercest battle of all, Stalingrad. Mourka, a brown tabby with a white bib, was stationed with a group of advanced scouts, and would sneak across the German lines with information about artillery positions hidden in his collar. Humans being the doubting type that they are, historians have cast aspersions on the motives behind Mourka's service. They have wondered if he was less interested in serving the Great Soviet than he was in the dinner he would receive upon arriving back at headquarters. Really now? I ask you, dear reader, if you doubt his heroism: would you sneak through battalions of Nazi soldiers solely for a few table scraps? No, I didn't think so. And neither would any cat who was less than a true comrade.

The other Stalingrad cat served with the 124th Rifle Brigade, defending the villages of Spartanovka and Rynok. He showed up as a hungry stray, on whom the Russian troops took pity and offered what food they could spare. Daily visits followed, and the soldiers noticed that when he left he always headed in the direction of the enemy lines, so they one day placed a collar on him and attached to it propaganda leaflets urging a German surrender. Sure enough, when he returned the leaflets were gone . . . the cat had delivered them to the Nazi soldiers! From this point on, the stray became the

Soviet propaganda cat, and was sent on daily missions to deliver messages undermining German morale. In thanks for his efforts, the troops of the 124th adopted him as their mascot. Oh, and if he was going to be part of the squad, he needed a name. So they called him *Geroy*, Russian for "hero."

We have also taken bravely to the sky, having served aboard planes during wartime—and one of us going higher up still. While the Soviet space dog program of the 1960s fascinates people to this day, history has sadly forgotten that France during the same era had a space *cat* program.

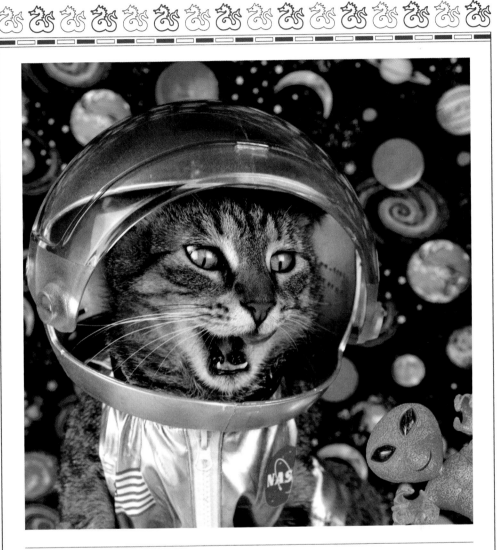

A crack team of fourteen of the finest strays from the alleys of Paris was assembled as potential test pilots. And from these, a tuxedo cat named Felicette was chosen as the feline Mercury, climbing higher than any cat had ever dreamed on a historic journey through the stratosphere. It was in a rocket named *Véronique* that she made her bid for the heavens, on October 18, 1963.

Launching from the Algerian town of Hammaguir, Felicette hurtled one hundred miles high over the Sahara Desert on a fifteen-minute flight—and by the way, if that doesn't sound like much, I might point

out that it was the same amount of time that the first American in space, Alan Shepard, spent aloft. All the while, electrodes relayed to scientists on the ground important data about her reactions. You've been told that we hate to travel? Well, this was one cool cat, remaining calm and collected throughout. In fact, it was the ground crew rather than the pilot whose nerves were racked, because as the rocket descended, the heat and the turbulence built to critical levels. Would they lose brave Felicette? Would she perish like Laika, the first space dog? Suddenly . . . poof! The capsule ejected and its parachute deployed! A recovery team raced through the desert, and when they pulled open the door of the capsule they heard a happy *miaou!* Felicette had survived and was returned to France as a hero.

But if it is heroes you wish, I have saved the greatest for last. I will now return you to the ships, because it is back at sea where we will find the finest of them all: Simon the Able Sea Cat. If any human wishes to know the history of ships' cats in a microcosm, they need only hear his story, because it is as if all the adventures, bonds, and hazards of all the centuries of sailing cats are in Simon combined. And as for the heroics, listen to his saga and tell me if you don't find all you could ever need.

Simon was born in the port of Hong Kong, and it was on a dock there that a group of British sailors discovered him in 1948. A scrawny young cat marked by the scars of

hard living, his coat was mostly black but accented by a wide white bib from his chest to his chin, and a further white streak running along the left side of his face almost to his eye. This little one was not afraid of the sailors, and not standoffish; instead, he was curious about them, and courted their friendship. Smart and bold, he carried in his manner something special, and the sailors decided they would sneak him onto their ship, the HMS *Amethyst*, a gunboat serving in the China Sea.

When their captain found out about the stowaway, he asked that the cat be brought before him. As a commanding officer he possessed a keen eye for all things nautical. The *Amethyst* was without a ship's cat, and the captain saw potential in what to landlubbers would be simply another mangy stray. The cat from the docks had passed muster! But with what will prove to be an uncanny foresight, a condition was laid down: the new crew member would have duties. He must prove that he can catch rats if he is to remain on board.

That was fine by the little cat, who enthusiastically embraced his new life. Imagine the excitement: he had scraped by on the docks as best he could, but now he was living with the sailors on their big boat. They played with him on the deck, and he chased after their fast-moving boots. New sounds and smells were everywhere, as winds blew in from the ocean and splashes of water flew over the bow. They even gave him a name,

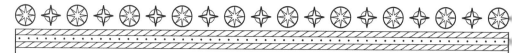
calling him Simon. He had been a lonely dock cat, but he was a part of something now, and it was something big.

And it was about to get bigger. In April of 1949 the Communist armies led by Mao Tse-Tung were sweeping across China, and orders came: Simon and his crewmates were going into action. Sail the *Amethyst* up the Yangtze River and relieve the British Embassy in Nanking, they were told. They had prepared themselves as best they could for whatever might come, but they were not prepared for the cannons that opened fire from the cover of the jungle along the river's long, winding banks. It was an ambush! Explosions rocked the vessel and caused enough damage to prevent the crew from returning fire. It was all the ship could do to limp up river, far enough to be out of range of the enemy artillery, but in bad shape.

The list of casualties included no less than the captain himself, killed when a shell hit his quarters. And what of little Simon? He had been asleep in the captain's own cabin when it was struck. In the chaos following the attack, and despite shrapnel wounds to his body and singed fur, he fought and scraped against the rubble, pulling himself free and limping to the deck. The wounded cat was rushed by his mates to sick bay, but there wasn't much that could be done. There were men of war to be tended, and the *Amethyst* hardly sailed with a medical staff for felines. Simon could be comforted and that was about all. Besides, the crew had bigger

problems. They were sixty men stuck on a lonely stretch of river, and the Communists were claiming them as hostages and threatening reprisals should any aid be sent. Deep in enemy territory and with limited supplies, they would have to find a way to survive.

There would be no quarter for the *Amethyst*, as a new and unexpected adversary now arrived to bring the already weakened sailors to their knees. Not a human adversary, but rather vermin: rats invading the ship in large numbers, swarming in from the surrounding brush. The leader, the king rat, was the toughest, meanest, smartest, and most determined the crew had ever seen. They nicknamed him Mao Tse-Tung, and not solely in jest, because the army of this new Mao was as much a threat as the old. The rats were stealing from the ship's provisions whatever they pleased, crawling through holes, hiding out in crevices, and coming and going in the darkness of the hull where the big, strong men were powerless to combat them. The situation with the ship's supplies had been grim to start with, and if these rats could not be stopped, the consequences would be disastrous.

If ever a hero was needed, it was now, and the bedraggled sailors were about to learn that providence had already sent them one, back on the docks in Hong Kong. Little Simon may have been injured, but he was a cat, and may I remind you that he was no longer just any cat—he was a *ship's* cat, a representative of millennia of tradition and

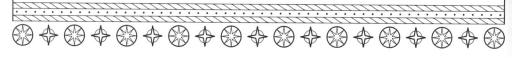

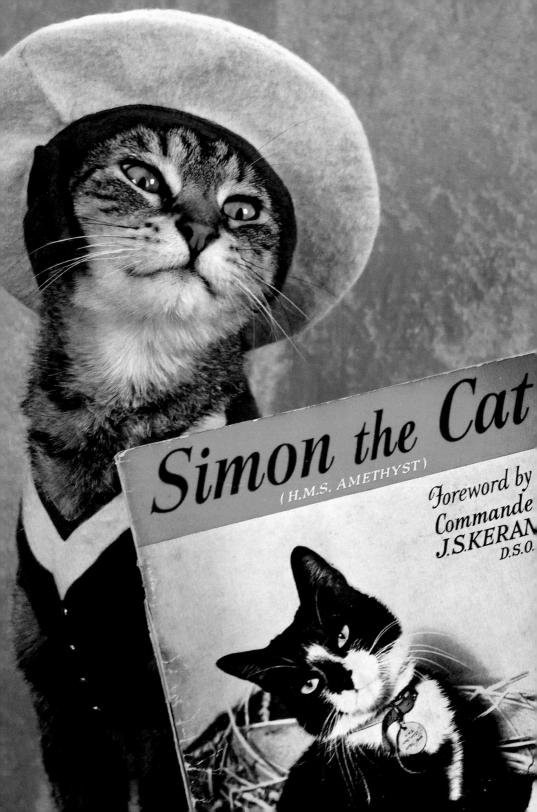

service. Wasn't this predicament the very reason cats had been taken aboard ships in the first place? And hadn't the captain made a deal with Simon when he accepted him among the crew? He could stay on board, but he had to prove he could catch rats.

Ah, but let me pause here for a moment to explain to you a little something about my kind. While we're often criticized as insouciant or inattentive, in truth we're highly sympathetic and caring. We may not feel a need to bother ourselves with mundane affairs, but trust me when I say that we know when there's trouble afoot, and Simon understood full well the dire straits his crewmates were in. And don't be fooled by our

diminutive size. The fact of the matter is, as every cat lover knows, we're as big as our heart will allow, and within Simon beat the heart of a lion. The men of the *Amethyst* had taken him in and given him a chance, and his own injuries be damned, he was prepared to give his all for them.

But was Simon prepared for the challenge, you may wonder, since he was still a relative neophyte when it came to being a ship's cat. Here I caution you to not underestimate his youth spent on the rough docks of Hong Kong. His very survival as a stray had depended upon instincts that were keen and reactions that were quick. He was a far tougher customer than he might at first glance appear, and he would now descend into the cramped cargo hold that would become his field of honor. Imagine the drama: silence in the darkness, as Simon crawled like a phantom among the nooks and the crannies. Still not a sound as he stopped suddenly and pushed himself up on his haunches. A sudden pounce! The sounds of clattering and hissing, scampering and things being knocked about! Then the return of silence, broken only by the soft pattering of paws, as from the darkness Simon emerged. And in his jaws? The limp and lifeless body of the king rat.

He had caught the leader the first time out! If only the captain had lived to see. Could little Simon catch rats? Like no other cat ever had, and he henceforth became an impassable barrier, a vigilant guardian who hunted down every rat that dared enter the *Amethyst*. And in the process he was doing something even greater. The crew was comprised of proud professional warriors who had been rendered helpless, their ability to fight stripped away. But Simon found a way to fight on their behalf. And not only fight, but win. Every rat that Simon caught was a victory for the debilitated sailors, and they kept a running tally as cheers rang out in celebration of each one that he brought forth.

Providing a stark rebuke in the face of cruel destiny, Simon was restoring the morale of the sailors. He knew it too. Soon enough he began making rounds in sick bay, checking on each man, giving a nuzzle here and a paw there. And he then extended his watch to the entire crew, his affection offering the promise of hope against despair. The men of the *Amethyst* had granted Simon their friendship, and he now returned the favor on a magnitude they could have never imagined. Under his watchful eye the rations held out, and the now resilient crew patched and repaired the ship. From the brink of tragedy, the *Amethyst* made a daring run for freedom under the cover of night, maneuvering past enemy cannons and back down the river to safety. They had survived!

Perhaps some among you think this is all some kind of joke, that a cat's heroism is a mere gimmick of feline fancy. Then let me reveal how long the *Amethyst* was stranded: one hundred and ten days. For a period of nearly four months Simon remained

diligently on duty to safeguard every last scrap in the commissary—and serve as a bulwark lest the hopes of his crewmates falter. Perhaps you see a way they would have survived without him, but I do not.

When the ship hit open water and word began to spread of the selfless actions of the ship's cat, little Simon suddenly became a very big deal. It started with the newspapers, which picked up the story of this unlikely hero. And as people heard the tale they were touched by Simon's loyalty and bravery, and began to send letters and gifts from all over the world. At every port the ship docked, there were bags of mail waiting, filled with thank-you notes, toys, and cat treats, all addressed to Simon of the HMS *Amethyst*. Awards and commendations began to arrive as well. He became the first cat to ever win the Dickin Medal, the animals' version of the Victoria Cross, and the Royal Navy bestowed upon him his own rank: Able Sea Cat. The stray cat from the dock had become such a cause for celebration, and while it probably all seemed a little much to one of such humble origins, will we not agree that the adulation was well deserved?

Most accounts of Simon's life conveniently make their exit here, allowing the audience to indulge the fantasy of a brave cat living happily ever after. But I will not do the same. Simon's story did not end with medals and mailbags, and I will not shirk my responsibility as narrator to tell it in full. My kind has learned to never take anything for granted

living among yours, and have we not already met the treachery of humans? The ensuing paragraphs may not contain the ending you expect, because as the ship sailed back to England—our hero was betrayed.

As the *Amethyst* was preparing to dock in Plymouth, word came that Simon would not be allowed to disembark with the crew. Why so ever not, you demand to know? Ah, well, you no doubt recall that he was born in Hong Kong. We have already made note of the human folly of drawing fictive lines and thereby separating one people from another under the guise of nations. And the folly is magnified by applying it to cats. Medals be damned, how dare Simon not be born in a place within the lines that contained the word Britain? For such an indiscretion it was necessary that purgation be imposed, since according to regulations this made him—horror of horrors—*an immigrant cat*. Simon must be confined upon the ship itself, the rules demanding a lengthy period of quarantine.

The crew of course protested. Simon was one of them. Not only was he one of them, he was perhaps the best of all of them! But the order had come from on high, not from fellow sailors but from men in offices, landlubbers who held authority despite having never in their lives wiped salty foam from their brow as they crested a wave. The type of men for whom hundreds of years of proud nautical heritage meant nothing. Men for whom a ship's cat was . . . *just a cat* . . . and

who could never understand that Simon was as much a member of the *Amethyst*'s crew as any human. The kind of men for whom rules are rules, and devoid of empathy they simply must be obeyed.

So it was that when the *Amethyst* docked, there was a public celebration awaiting the members of the crew, with cheering and good tidings and the waving of flags, all except for one. For that one crew member, the smallest on board, yet with the biggest heart, there was a cage. An appalling injustice! The journalists who had sung Simon's praises, responded with wan humor. Simon is in quarantine? He can play with his medals while he waits, they joked. But I can't blame them: in disbelief at this turn of events, they saw no choice but to cover the outrage by making light of it as a trivial thing. But it was no joking matter. It was on November 28, 1949, while in British quarantine, that Simon died.

The men in the offices offered feeble excuses. Simon died of his war wounds, they claimed. Is that so? Aren't these the same wounds that he overcame during months of active service without any adequate medical attention? The same wounds he traveled around the world with in order to arrive in England? And now, when he is in the hands of the British government and should have been receiving the best veterinary care available, he suddenly succumbs to them? I don't buy it, and neither would any other cat you ask. And while I can't tell you

with certainty of what Simon died, there are a few guesses that we might venture. Perhaps an infection brought on by his confinement? Or a British feline disease to which he lacked immunity?

Or so human logic would surmise, but feline logic suggests that it was perhaps something else, and pardon me if I now wax a bit too sentimental. In gratitude to the adoring men who had taken in an outcast cat, Simon had offered every ounce of his spirit. It had been enough to see tragedy turned to triumph, but his heroism was then pushed aside in the name of regulations. We cats do not respond to rules; most assuredly you know that about us. We respond only to bonds forged through love, and if you understand that perhaps you will find the real wound that felled Simon. Having given over his heart, how could he have now not found it broken?

But even in death his story is not yet concluded. The deed had been done, but we will now return to the sailors. They had not yet had their say in the matter of Simon, and were determined that the last word would come from his comrades in arms. He should not depart this earth without a statement of the respect which they felt for him, and from the deck of the *Amethyst* they proposed to pull strips of wood for his grave marker—after all, they reasoned, Simon was the soul of that very ship, so it was only right that he be buried under a piece of it. And on the appointed day, his crewmates

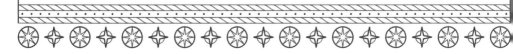

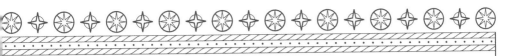

made the trek to a small pet cemetery on the eastern outskirts of London and laid their devoted friend to rest with military honors and under a Union Jack. It was against regulations, no doubt, but they had determined that the regulations should not now hide the truth: this grave held more than just a feline companion, for in it lay as fine a sailor of the Royal Navy as had ever served.

In the wake of Simon's passing, the crew did one thing more. They knew, of course, that they could never replace him, but their debt was so great that it was decided that to honor his memory, the *Amethyst* must continue to sail with a cat. So they found one, of the right kind—a cat with a zest for adventure, tough and smart, curious and loyal. But they needed to name him, and here came a quandary. A name is an important matter. They had to find one that stood for the best qualities of a nautical cat, a name that expressed honor, determination, and courage. It had to be a name that symbolized greatness, and most of all one that paid homage to tradition. Well, if a name must meet all of those criteria, I suppose there is but one choice . . . so they called him Simon II.

No, my friends, the original wouldn't have minded. Nautical cats know full well that the law of the sea demands that ships sail on, come what may, and it was the highest flattery for the crew to ensure that his memory was preserved as they headed back to the high seas. But the legacy would be short-lived, for Simon's heroic service was a climax to an age that was drawing nigh a close. By the 1970s, cats were being evicted wholesale from ships around the world. Vessels crossing the oceans were by then made of steel rather than creaky wood, and there were modern methods of pest control to deal with rodents. Why, in the modern age, would anyone need a cat on board a ship? Well, I suspect that generations of seafaring men would have had quite a lot to offer in reply, but their voices would not be heard as the final sands fell through the hourglass.

By then the wooden planks over Simon's grave had also fallen victim to time. But he was not forgotten by his crew, and the original marker was replaced with one carved in stone to stand in perpetuity. And while it bears the name of but a single cat, to us it is also a memorial to all who had preceded him, to the feline adventurers and sailors and scallywags and rogues who had turned their tails to oppression and served heroically among mankind—some of whose stories I have told you, and many, many more whose stories have been forgotten to all save the waves which now carry us back to port.

Yes, friends, we have been away from land for quite some time, and we must now disembark from the great schooners and galleons in order to resume our journey. Much had changed by the time of Simon's death. We felines were once again the

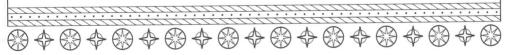

IN
MEMORY OF
"SIMON"
SERVED IN
H·M·S AMETHYST
MAY 1948 — NOVEMBER 1949
AWARDED DICKIN MEDAL
AUGUST 1949
DIED 28TH NOVEMBER 1949.
THROUGHOUT THE YANGTSE INCIDENT
HIS BEHAVIOUR WAS OF THE HIGHEST ORDER

darlings of humankind, so clearly we have a lot of catching up to do. But that change did not come easily, so batten down the hatches as we turn back into the winds of history, for they howl still as we land hard and fast in the seventeenth century. And keep your heads low as you come ashore, because scuttlebutt has it that shots are being fired. There is a battle underway — being no less than the Battle for Feline Redemption!

●

CATS THAT FOLLOW THE SEA AND ROAM THE WORLD

They Change Ships at Will and Are Known in Every Port From New York to Far-Off Hongkong and Nagasaki

"Hors d'Oeuvres"

By WARREN IRVIN

CAPTAIN RIDLEY TAYLOR of the Fabre Line freighter Bankdale first called the pier-jumpers to my attention in Marseilles. We were walking along the docks near a weather-beaten British tramp, which had been loading general cargo for Bombay and was preparing to shove off. The monotonous clanking of anchor chain forward stopped, and from the bridge came the command: "Rig in your gangway and let go the head lines."

At that instant a grimy black-and-white cat emerged from a pile of crates beside me, darted across my feet, ran up the gangway and disappeared. The animal displayed such amazing agility that I stopped to watch it, and Captain Taylor, noting my interest, explained: "That was a pier-jumper, a sea-rover cat. These are the drifters of the cat family and they roam about the world, changing ships at will."

"They are an amazing species. They seem to know instinctively when a vessel is leaving port. I have seen them disappear down the gangway a few minutes after we had docked, and never show themselves again until just before sailing time. And I have heard of them quitting a ship in one port and rejoining it at the other side of the globe.

"Sometimes in port you'll see a dozen of them congregated at the end of a dock, like sailors just home from a long voyage who have got together to swap yarns or compare the relative merits of their ships. I know of no other animal that hates constraint so much as a cat. In many respects they are remarkably like human beings."

Captain Taylor was right—cats are remarkably like humanity. There is the feline "four hundred," with its blue-blood ribbon-winners listed in special registers; there is the bourgeoisie, the pampered pets of shopkeepers or lonely spinsters; there is the prowling tom of the underworld that lurks in deserted alleyways at night, and then there is the adventurous, roving sailor cat that follows the call of the sea.

When the great ports of the world are sleeping these feline sea-rovers are gathering in the shadows of deserted warehouses to celebrate shore leave. There are tabbies from Antwerp and Cardiff, toms from Fiasco and Montreal, sly-eyed felines from Rio, Nagasaki and Hongkong, from Bangkok, Bombay and Aden. Grizzled and war-scarred veterans who have lost eyes or ears or tails rub noses with half-grown kittens spending their first nights ashore. Old cats, young cats, cats of all colors and breeds; cats who have stood in the cross-trees of barkentines and basked in the tropical sun; cats who have fled from the arctic blasts to the welcome shelter of engine rooms.

Almost from time immemorial cats have been going to sea. The ancient Romans were so well acquainted with their roaming habits that in Rome the cat became a symbol of liberty. The Goddess of Liberty was represented holding a cup in one hand, a broken sceptre in the other, and with a cat lying at her feet.

AT best cats are but indifferently submissive to human will. Aboard ship some become great pets, while others behave as though they owned the vessel and "high-hat" everybody—that is, everybody but the cooks. Cats have been known to stick to one ship for many years and then suddenly, for no apparent reason, desert it for another. Sometimes they will bring companion cats aboard as temporary guests while in port, or as passengers for a voyage. Females sometimes take unto themselves a tom; and, falling after one or two voyages to rid either the ship or themselves of him, leave that vessel flat. Roy Urban, wireless operator of the President Polk, tells a story of a ship's cat that deserted the San José while that ship was in Puerto Castella, and rejoined it later at New Orleans. But stories of ship's cats are as plentiful as rats in a

ship's holds. Most ships want them and are glad to have them aboard, for they kill rats and mice which do vast damage to a ship's cargo.

Usually, however, sailors dislike black cats, the popular superstition being that they bring bad luck. There are exceptions. The United Fruit Company's San Pablo carries four of the blackest cats that ever graced a steamer's deck. They were aboard when the San Pablo rode the hurricanes which did vast damage in Miami and Havana a few years ago and came through unscathed. And on other occasions, with these four mascots aboard, the San Pablo has encountered

took her to Broadway and Seventy-second Street and bade her a fond farewell, but when the liner entered Hamilton Harbor, Bermuda, a few days later Minnie appeared on deck.

Ben Fidd, the veteran watchman at the Cunard Line piers, used to say that London cats were always homesick in foggy weather, and he would point to Cuthbert, at that time a leader in feline society on the Chelsea piers, as proof of this assertion.

"It's a funny thing," Fidd would say, "how London cats get homesick in foggy weather. Cuthbert hasn't been the same cat since the fog started here two weeks ago. He's so homesick I can't even tempt him to eat a nice breakfast of fried fish. We had a fine cat just like him when I was bo'sun of the Saucy Sarah, trading from London to Rangoon in 1882. He was called Tinker, and was what you might call a haughty cat. He lived aft with the officers. Tinker tolerated the cook because 'Slushy' used to feed him bits from the cabin table, and he was fairly friendly with me because I had been shipmates with his father on the old Whampoa in the China trade. But he despised the crew for'ard. And that was his downfall.

"Tinker was so homesick when the ship ran into a fog, no matter what latitude we were in, that the Old Man and the mates could do

nothing with him. He would run up on deck and dash up the fore rigging as far as the futtock shrouds, through the lubber hole to the foretop and mew so long and so loud that the officer on watch on the poop couldn't hear the lookout man, and would cuss Tinker like a good 'un.

"One Christmas Eve we were homeward bound for London and off Dover we ran into a thick fog in the Channel. The Old Man finally decided to heave to and wait for a tugboat to tow the packet to London. When the hands went on the upper fore topsail yard to take a turn with a gasket to prevent the sail from flapping, Tinker was out on the yardarm and somehow he got knocked off, whether by accident or on purpose I never found out. The Old Man, who was on the poop, heard the frantic mewing as the cat dropped through the fog into the sea and was quite upset about it. But that was the last of Tinker. There was quite a procession of pals down the ship to meet him and we had a lot of trouble explaining why he wasn't there, and Cuthbert, I'm afraid, will disappear off the pier one of these foggy days if he's not a bit more careful in the way he behaves to longshoremen."

Benn Fidd's prophecy came true. Cuthbert did disappear after that, but whether he met the fate of Tinker or whether he just paid a flying visit to England was never found out.

THERE have been many "pier jumpers" who have made for themselves a world-wide reputation. There was a Minnie who selected Montreal as her home port, and who shipped from there to many ports, but always came back. Large families was her great drawback, also, and she seldom was permitted to make more than one voyage in a ship. No one ever knew what Minnie's exact mileage was, but she had been accounted for not once but many times in a score of ports in various sections of the world. However, in 1922 Minnie ap-

(Continued on page 16)

Cats Are Well Taken Care of by the Crew

waterspouts off Florida and escaped without damage.

Not long ago the crew of the fishing schooner Clifton of Wildwood, N. J., rebelled when they found Captain Hilding Peterson had taken aboard a black cat. They demanded the captain throw the cat overboard, but he refused and put it in his cabin for safe keeping. The cat escaped and ran up into the rigging. Captain Peterson dared not ask any of the crew to bring his pet down, so he climbed up after it himself. And lo! from the crow's nest, where the cat had lodged, the captain sighted a great shoal of baby mackerel trying to escape the attack of a school of bluefish. Dories were quickly lowered, encircling the entire school with seines, and three hours later the boats returned with their catch. They filled 400 barrels, which brought $7,000. Not only did that black cat stay aboard the Clifton, but the crew took up a collection to buy it a silk cushion and a case of condensed milk.

The case of Minnie, the black-and-white pet of the Furness-Bermuda liner Fort St. George, illustrates the stick-to-it-iveness of ships' cats. Fifteen times Minnie has been ejected from the Fort St. George, principally because of her numerous offsprings, but each time she has come back. Once a sailor

They Sleep in a Coil of Rope.

SAY BLACK CATS SAVED SHIP

Sailors on Fruit Steamer Declare Four Carry It Through Storms.

BOSTON, Dec. 1 (AP).—Four of the blackest cats that ever graced the heaving decks of a steamer went to sea today with the United Fruit steamer San Pablo, for the superstition associating black cats and bad luck means nothing to the crew.

The cats are mascots, and the crew points to the vessel's escape from the Miami hurricane as significant. When it seemed that the vessel was doomed to be dashed ashore in the hurricane the cats were aboard and the vessel escaped.

The cats were aboard when water spouts were encountered off Florida. Again the ship rode safely through. The cats were aboard when the ship passed through the Havana hurricane unscathed.

LEFT · So much for centuries of persecution. This clipping hit the newswires in December 1926, and American papers told the world how despite centuries of superstition the crew of a steamer out of Boston found black cats to be *good* luck—they refused to sail without them on board!

BELOW · I told you that no sailor worth his salt would sail without a cat. In a pinch and preparing to leave from New York for a yearlong voyage in the Pacific, the captain of the freighter *Woodfield* managed to get this notice posted in the *New York Times*.

SUNDAY, OCTOBER 1, 1922.

Captain Seeks a Sea-Going Ship's Cat To Sign On for a Trip Around the World

Captain Edwin Dyason, master of the freighter Woodfield, will welcome any ablebodied seafaring cat wishing to join the crew of his vessel, sailing today for Manila and China.

"We missed the ship's cat shortly after we put into port here," said the captain as he entertained a few friends aboard ship on the eve of a voyage which will take him almost around the world. "Her name was Cleopatra. She joined on at Fremantle, Australia, and did one voyage with us. Now she has left us "flat."

One of the party offered to give the captain a fine Angora kitten, but he refused the gift with thanks, saying: "It would be useless to try to keep it on board. Only seagoing cats are any use on a vessel.

"Joking aside, sea cats are a race in themselves. Why, a land-lubber cat wouldn't know how to take care of itself in a rough sea. But a sailor cat knows just what pile of ropes to hide under. It stays there and waits for fair weather before it reappears to demand rations.

"No, the seafaring cat is no joke. What is more, plenty of them have never been on shore at all. They are born at sea, live on ships and when they die they go down to Davy Jones's locker. Almost every time we start on a voyage we find one or more strange cats on board. They often change ships, but seldom give up the sea for the land. In-deed, I never heard of a sailor cat doing so.

"I know where the term 'jealous cat' originated. I once had a cat—my favorite of all—named Margaret. She became so attached to me that she wouldn't allow the other cats aboard to go into my cabin. She was even jealous of her own kittens.

"Sometimes when several cats are aboard they assign parts of the ship to themselves, and will not allow others within their particular precincts. One old boy we had kept every cat aft but himself, and proud he was of his power to do so. No, sir, ships' cats and the ordinary domestic variety appear to be two distinct species.

"I'll lay a wager we have a cat to replace the capricious Cleopatra before we leave the dock. What is more, the newcomer will undoubtedly bob up serenely of her own free will, having decided in her clever feline brain that she would like to join on for the voyage."

For twenty-seven years Captain Dyason has been a ship's master. His only other hobby is music, which he indulges by means of a specially seaworthy phonograph and cabinet containing a thousand records. During the war he was master of the Welsbach Hall, which was torpedoed in the Mediterranean, sinking within five minutes, with the loss of four men. The Woodfield's voyage will last almost a year.

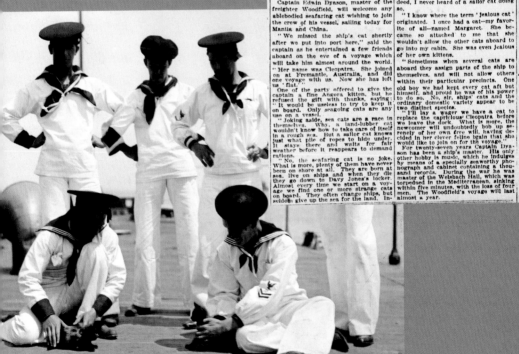

All paws on deck: the USS *Nahant* was a two-hundred-foot-long ironclad gunboat equipped with cannons firing fifteen-inch and eleven-inch shells, and a crew of seventy-five men . . . and two cats! . . . when this photo was taken during the Spanish-American War.

BIGGEST FELINE newsmaker was Trixie, born an alley cat but bred to the sea. When the steamship Stuart Star docked at London the other day the crew was mourning the loss of Trixie, their mascot. Somehow Trixie had missed the ship when it sailed from Cukatoo Island, near Sydney, Australia—more than 11,000 miles from London.

But they didn't mourn long. crew just started ashore when T showed up! Finding the Stuart had sailed without her, she "stowed away" on another Lor bound vessel. The matter of se ing the London waterfront fo own ship was then simple.

FOLLOWED SHIP'S CAT: SAVED THEIR LIVES.

GRANGEMOUTH, Firth of Forth, Scotland.—Nine men of the crew of the American cargo steamer Lake Eliko, were saved from drowning recently by the instincts of the ship's cat to swim toward the steamer in a storm and darkness when their small boat floundered. John Shrotne, 33, a sailor, of Marlboro, Mass., and Gilmer Stroud, 17, mess-room boy, of North Carolina, were drowned. The members of the crew had been ashore on leave. They had with them the ship's cat. A storm began and before reaching the steamer, their boat capsized. In the darkness no one could make out the lights of the ship. Tabby, however, with her instictive desire to get out of the water as quickly as possible, swam directly toward the steamer. The men swam after her and nine of them reached the ship. The other two went down.

LEFT · The June 27, 1937, edition of *Parade of Youth*, a popular Sunday supplement for American newspapers, carried this clipping documenting the longest recorded journey a ship's cat ever took to find its crew: Trixie missed the ship near Sydney, but caught up with it in London, nearly 11,000 miles away.

RIGHT · In 1920 Tabby wound up a hero by saving his crewmates on the cargo steamer *Lake Eliko* from drowning. Their vessel sank in Scotland but the story was told around the world—this press clipping is from the March 17 *Morning Republican*, a newspaper 5,000 miles away in Fresno, California.

Space Cat

Vive la Felicette!

THE United States used monkeys; Russia used dogs in space vehicle test flights. But with Gallic independence the French use cats. Felicette, shown here, was chosen from 14 feline candidates because her weight was right the morning of the flight; the others had eaten too much. Centered in her skull, an electrode recorded readings of her brain processes as she roared over the Sahara desert and 100 miles into space.

A technician prepares to insert the "harnessed" cat into the type of cylinder which will be her space capsule during the actual space flight.

I won't credit the *Centre National d'Études Spatiales* for designing a comfy cat carrier, but that contraption kept Felicette safe on her journey to the stars. The Parisian alley cat was a celebrity in 1963. This clipping is from the *Philadelphia Inquirer*, the photo from the *Pittsburgh Press*.

A MEDAL FOR SIMON

LONDON, Aug. 4 (A.A.P.).—Simon, the cat aboard H.M.S. Amethyst, who received shrapnel wounds during the ship's exploits on the Yangtse River, will be awarded the "animal's V.C." — the Dickin Medal.

Fifty-three dogs, horses, and pigeons have the medal, but Simon will be the first cat to receive it.

Simon—the Cat—Not Forgotten

IN A LONDON ANIMAL CEMETERY, two youngsters read inscription on a new tombstone erected o the grave of Simon, cat, mascot of H.M.S. Amethyst. British vessel involved in Yangtze River incident last year. As a result of his behavior dur the shelling of the ship, Simon was awarded the Dickin Medal the Victoria Cross for animals. The youngsters are Donald an S phanie Jones, 5-year-old children of an employe of the cemeter

Letter to a Hero

Following is a letter from Lottie the cat to Simon, hero cat of HMS Amethyst, wounded by shell splinters and awarded the Dickin Medal for catching rats under fire:

Dear Simon:—

I hope you won't think it too terrible of me to write to a perfect stranger, but I was so thrilled by your exploit that I felt I must.

Of course, we don't have rats in our house, so I have never seen one and feel sure I would be terrified if I did.

The cats I know often boast about the rats they have caught.

Some of the older ones talk of practically nothing else, the rats getting bigger every time they tell the story.

But although we live by the sea I don't know one who has ever been inside a boat, so you can imagine I was pop-eyed when I heard about you in that warship, wounded and carrying on as if nothing had happened.

Are you wearing a bandage round your head? I would like to think of you wearing a bandage, as I think they're so becoming.

Before going any further perhaps I ought to tell you something about myself.

I am a tabby, 2½ years old, with white chest and paws, large eyes, and have heard myself described by passing cats as a smasher.

My American boy friend, Manhattan Mouser, has described my figure as a "swell chassis," and calls me his "Sugar Puss."

He says I am the only she-cat he knows who sways her hips when she walks, and that I could knock all the cats on Broadway for a row of sardine cans.

Although we are friends, he is not my steady, as he is rather old for me, though full of life and always ready to "go places."

But even if an older cat has poise and knows his way around, and is inclined to spoil a girl, I always think of him as a sugar daddy rather than a boy friend, and one always has to consider the future when they get quite old and you are still attractive.

I expect you'll think I'm awful telling you all this, but I've always wanted to meet a sailor cat, especially navy types.

They must be so interesting and refreshing after all the dull cats you meet who never go anywhere but on the same old tiles and up and down the same old alley.

never go anywhere but on the same old tiles and up and down the same old alley.

I think of you as young, gay, and, of course, gallant, and would love to have a photograph of you.

When you get leave in England do pop in and see us. My people are awfully reasonable about callers and the butcher's awfully generous about lights. Don't forget now.

Your sincere admirer,

LOTTIE GUBBINS.

Simon, the Cat Is British...

Receives Dic... For Shipboar...

LONDON, ENG... quette, when refer... cat, to call him S...

The initials stan... al, which is the ... ish honor any cat... has won. Simon is...

Simon, about 2... guished himself... sloop Amethyst w... Yangtse river by... nist shell fire. ... by shrapnel and s... official dispatches... right on with his... the ship of rats.

Simon's attachment to the ship and its crew was hailed as an example of devotion which did much to bolster the morale of British sailors when the vessel ultimately made its sensational dash to the sea and freedom.

So Simon gets the Dickin medal, and when the Amethyst steams into Plymouth the bands will play, there will be a lot of gold braid about, and an admiral will make a formal presentation of the medal.

It is about as big as a mouse, and about the same color and what Simon will think of the fuss there will be no knowing. But he does join a distinguished company of birds and beasts who have received what the British call the "animals' Victoria cross." Fifty-three have received it.

It takes its name from a 79-year-old lady... in O.B.E... pire) fri... of the p... animals.

The n... name of... club, a ... associat...

No civ... club, or... strictly... or bird ... mascot ... be prop... comman...

So it'... the fact that some of the members are mongrels and broken down horses who wouldn't win any beauty prizes.

RAT CATCHING UNDER FIRE NETS FIRST MEDAL FOR CAT

London, Aug. 4.—(AP)—For catching rats in time of extreme danger, Simon, the sloop Amethyst's cat, is to get a medal.

It's the Dickin Medal which, to animals, ranks with the Victoria Cross, Britain's highest award. The Allied Forces' Mascot Club will present it.

Among the 53 mascots already holding the medal, Simon will stand out. He's the first cat. The others are dogs, horses and pigeons.

Simon was aboard the British sloop when it ran the Chinese Communist gauntlet down the Yangtze last week end after three months of virtual captivity. He had been wounded by Communist shrapnel when the ship was first attacked in April, but kept right on catching the rats that threatened the ship's meager supplies.

The Allied Forces Mascot Club will present the medal.

A CAT'S TALE

AMETHYST'S CAT DEAD

Simon, the Amethyst's cat, has died in quarantine at Hackbridge, Surrey. His death is thought to have been caused by the cold weather and by the wounds he received in the Yangtze action. He had been awarded the Dickin Medal and was also to receive a decoration from the Blue Cross Society. London. He will be buried in the cemetery of the People's Dispensary for Sick Animals at Ilford, Essex.

Twenty-One Guns for Simon, D.M.

"All hands on deck and stand muster!" the command rang out.

The sailors quickly formed ranks for roll call. Last of all came Simon, yawning and stretching from his sleep.

He was the only member of the crew of the H.M.S. Amethyst who didn't have a gun. But he had other weapons.

He had sharp teeth and claws. He used them with deadly effect on his enemies, the rats who came aboard. Simon was a cat.

The Amethyst was in the Yangtze River in 1949, trying to carry supplies to the people of the British Embassy. Each time the ship stopped at a port the rats would come aboard, carrying disease germs and fighting savagely to get at the food and supplies.

There was only Simon to fight back at them.

It was bad enough in any port but the worst came when the ship ran aground at Rose Island and damaged the gear. Within minutes the enemy shells were coming thick and fast. The Captain was killed and Lt. Commander Kearns took charge.

After the volunteers had left, there were only 115 men on board to defend the ship against the Chinese Reds. There was only Simon to defend the ship against the rats.

Of the entire crew, not one put up a more determined and courageous battle. He risked death every day from their poison-laden teeth and from the gunfire that whistled about him.

For three months the fighting went on. One day Commander Kearns said to Simon, "Our supplies are getting low. A lot depends upon you. Unless you can keep on fighting, the rats will carry off what little food we have left and we'll have to surrender."

Simon arched his back. He would fight to the bitter end.

Finally the gear was repaired and the ship made a run for safety. When Commander Kearns arrived in London he carried a dispatch recommending Simon "For gallantry in performing a vital service in behalf of H.M.S. Amethyst."

Simon had to obey the rules and stay in quarantine for six months but when the word went out that he was to receive the Dickin Medal he was visited by scores of reporters and photographers.

Simon was the first cat ever to be recommended for the medal, which is awarded to animals that perform deeds of heroism.

Unfortunately he was so weakened by his months of fighting that he died before the medal could be awarded. And so it was received by members of the crew for whom he had given his life.

...AY CLUB

...rthday Club, I will be ...... 195...

A collection of press clippings covering Simon's heroic service . . . and his tragic death. But my favorite is the fan letter from a fellow cat, Lottie. The plaudits of humans are much appreciated, but what higher praise can there be than having your own feline groupie?

149

REDEMPTION:

THE

ENLIGHTENMENT
AND THE RISE

OF THE

MODERN

FELINE

ack on *terra firma*, centuries of persecution had knocked us down, but not out. Europe's felines had suffered casualties that were incalculable, but know this much: a cat never gives up hope. We are survivors, and with gritty determination, we were clawing our way back into the hearts of humankind by the start of the seventeenth century. Make no mistake, our rise would not be quick nor would it be easy, but we had taken the worst blow humanity had to offer and were steeled for the fight to come. Battlements were being prepared by our allies and adversaries alike, with the front lines being in France and the trenches dug in the very salons of Paris, which subsequently set the taste for all of Europe. The fur would fly, but during the age you call the Enlightenment men of vision would take a stand against old superstitions—and in favor of felines. The tide that had been so long against us would turn, and when that tide came in, it carried back the love that had been stolen.

We had found a key ally by the 1620s, a public figure whose devotion to us was total, and for which he offered no apologies. Of course, felines had all along been taken in by certain mavericks. Some among them were great names, but even so it had been easy enough to write off their affections as eccentricity and thereby limit the influence of our champions. But this was a different case. We had gained a convert who could not be disregarded, one who stood at the pinnacle of power and from there cast his shadow over the entire continent. Cardinal Richelieu, the chief minister of Louis XIII and the architect of the French supremacy of Europe, had a soft spot for cats.

This was a man who was infamous for ruling his office with an iron fist, striking fear into the crowns of Europe as he ruthlessly toyed with nations like pieces on a game board. Afraid to even speak his name, heads of state referred to him as the "Red Eminence." But to his felines? He was but the most gentle of souls. The simple pleasure of watching us at play was his greatest pastime, one he indulged in from the very moment he awoke, when servants brought cats to join him in his bed. And he continued to surround himself with us throughout the day, at any one time having at least a dozen near to hand. "The mitred tyrant of France," commented one of his chroniclers, "finds a human heart only when he is near the mewing breed." Although, to be frank, his heart didn't extend far beyond us: he was known to lovingly stroke a contented cat with one hand, and with the other sign death warrants. Ah, how humans trembled when for once the tables were turned!

Courtiers were horrified at the cardinal's affection for felines, as were foreign dignitaries, but none among them dared even a whisper in protest since this was a man who controlled the king of France.

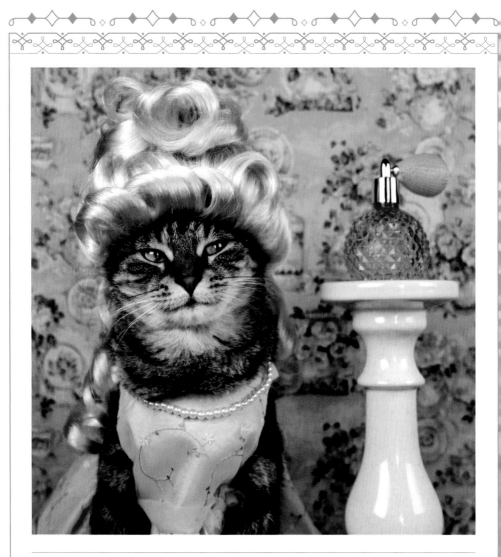

He had a cattery constructed at his chateau southwest of Paris, staffed by a pair of overseers who twice daily provided its inhabitants with a delicate pâté made from fine white chicken breast. Richelieu passed away in the year 1642, and while Europe's kings celebrated the death of an enemy, its felines mourned the loss of a friend—one who was true enough to have left an endowment ensuring the protection and upkeep of his companion cats, which at the time of his death numbered fourteen.

But the cardinal had left a further bequest, one that served all felines. He had

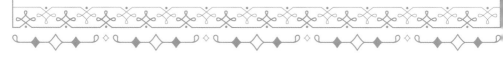

Redemption

provided us with an introduction to members of the highest-ranking circles in France, and there were others among the country's elite who began taking our side. That nasty Louis XIV may have thrown the torch that burned us in the Place de Grève, but even the weight of his verdict could not stop a newfound fashion for cats among ladies of the court. Turning their backs on traditional lap dogs, they were looking to felines instead as cultivated companions, and it was happening even in Louis's closest circles. Princess Elizabeth Charlotte, the wife of his brother Philippe I, Duke of Orléans, announced that "cats are the most entrancing animals in the world," while Antoinette Deshoulières, one of his court poets, wrote epistles to her human friends in the name of her favorite feline, Crisette. And when the prize kitty of the Duchess of Maine died, it was left to François de La Mothe Le Vayer, the king's own tutor during his youth, to pen the epitaph. And this was no humble tribute; it called out to the Ancient Egyptians to let them know that the duchess's cat was as worthy of divinity as theirs had been.

Meanwhile the century's most celebrated harpist, Mademoiselle Dupuy, credited her musical skill to a feline with a finely tuned ear. A keen and harsh judge, the cat would sit at her feet and react with pleasure when she played well—and demonstrable annoyance when she did not, the effect of which was to force her to constantly improve. On her death, it was found that this cat and another she had taken in had inherited both of her houses, along with funds enough to maintain them. Her greedy human family contested the will—foul play, I say, since the cats stood no chance in a seventeenth-century court. Even so, it was clear that our time was coming. Glimmers of light were breaking through the dark clouds, and while Mademoiselle Dupuy's cats lost the battle for their inheritance, there were plenty more battles soon to be fought.

Yes, friends, France was primed for a good old-fashioned cat fight, and the first major skirmish was fought in the 1720s. By that time we had found another important ally, a true champion of our cause among men of letters. Of course, there had already been plenty of writers who had shown their affections to a companion cat, but this was different. François-Augustin de Moncrif was a historian of such esteem that he had been appointed the historiographer of King Louis XV. And this eminent scribe chose to tell the world about our virtues, having invested his considerable skill into history's first tome solely dedicated to the topic of cats! Published in 1727, his *Histoire des chats* was a collection of stories, letters, and poems all about us. Naturally, it was celebrated by the burgeoning society of cat lovers in Paris, and, oh, how I would delight in telling you that it was met with applause and admiration by the public at large.

Except that I can't. Because it was not, and *far* from it.

moire de

mi

Moncrif's book was a daring gesture, a public salvo in our fight for respectability— and our opponents soon returned fire with a vitriol that the author had never anticipated. He was saddled with the nickname *L'historiogriffe*, or "historian of the claw," and mocked even on the street, where people would chase after him meowing. He had taken the initiative to speak to the public on our behalf, and in turn became a laughingstock. The slings and arrows of popular opinion no doubt hurt, but Moncrif's detractors could be damned because there was value in his work, and those not swayed by the old propaganda knew it. Why, the prestigious Académie française acknowledged him, even admitting him as a member.

Think of it, the most hallowed literary body on the continent giving due respect to a cat scholar! Or . . . did they? Moncrif had written about *cats*, after all, it was such a hoot, and his inauguration speech turned out to be a setup for the cruelest of pranks. As he came to the podium, his detractors set armfuls of terrified strays loose in the hall. And they ran madly through the auditorium. Homeless cats plucked from the streets of Paris, mewing and hissing, and turning the biggest event in Moncrif's life into a mockery as the audience erupted in laughter. Humans can indeed be rotten even to their own kind, and no doubt the joke was made all the sweeter since those terrified felines served as the agents that undermined the very man in Paris who most defended them.

Poor, noble Moncrif. He lacked the social clout that you humans find so necessary, and without it he could not stave off the attacks of our adversaries. But the glory of their victory would be short-lived. Another champion soon emerged, one who could wave the banner of feline liberation high, and withstand the blows to wave it higher still. If clout was needed, well, she had as much as anyone in France. This was Marie Leszczyńska. The daughter of King Stanislaw I of Poland, her hand was the most desired in Europe, and in 1725 she gave it to Louis XV and became the French queen. And the new queen was generous, pious, graceful, cultivated . . . and head over heels in love with felines.

"Cats are distant, discreet, impeccably clean, and able to stay silent. What more could be needed to be good company?" she explained. And lest anyone find her attitude to be a peccadillo, they were certainly not going to say so, especially after she converted the king himself to our cause. Yes, friends, the *king*, and he installed tomcats in the gardens of Versailles, and even took such a shine to one that it was allowed *within the palace*. We had the protection of the Crown!

Imagine this scene: one of the queen's own kitties took its rest upon a cloak belonging to a certain duchess, and this garment, made from the finest silk and most expensive furs, was left covered over completely with hairs. Even worse, the cat tore at it with her claws. *Oh, was the duchess*

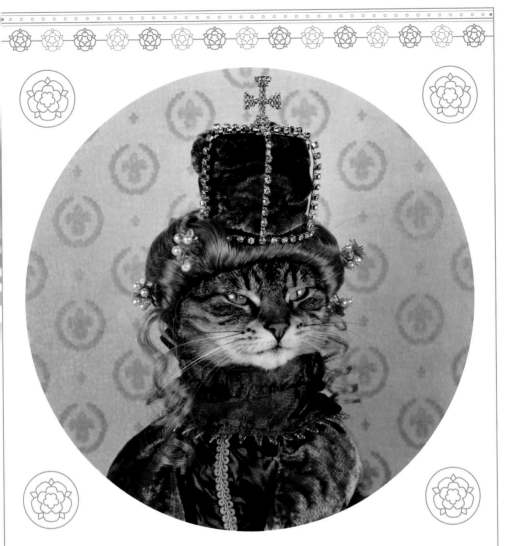

furious! She went directly to the queen and demanded that the indignity be redressed. But Marie turned upon her with a stare as cold and piercing as centuries of royal blood can hew, and with disdain informed this duchess that had she cared for her cloak to be preserved, she would have followed the protocol of handing it over to a valet. As for the cat, *madame*, she bares no fault since she was only exercising her feline prerogative!

Marie's influence was felt throughout the court as ladies of rank emulated her example and took in cats upon whom they showered attention. The Marquise du Deffand, famed as a patron of the arts and friend to the era's most prominent writers,

lavished her cats with exquisite ribbons and *parfums*, even allowing them to trample as they liked over the expensive bedspreads of her boudoir. Madame Helvétius, meanwhile, dressed hers in attire as fine as any noble woman. Her salon was the most famous in Paris and a meeting place for the major figures of the Enlightenment, with the only complaint being that it was often hard to find a seat among all the cats! There were many others as well, some striking medals in our honor, others constructing tombs on our passing.

But don't think we were just for the ladies. Rousseau, the greatest of the *philosophes*, conjectured that the impetus for an animosity toward felines stems from a despotic instinct which some humans are unfortunately possessed of. Such people are jealous of our refusal to be enslaved, he explained, and that to dislike cats is therefore a clear and notable sign of a personality defect. (A very fair theory, if I may say so!) Meanwhile the astronomer to the Crown, Joseph Jérôme de Lalande, sent our message to the heavens. Save for Leo the Lion, there was no feline constellation, a galling oversight he was determined to correct. When work began on an astronomical atlas in several volumes, Lalande placed hundreds of stars from his own observations onto the charts. And he decided an addition to the thirty-three animals already in the sky was in order. So it was that a domestic cat was placed upon the map, crouching near Hydra. Its name? Ah, the most fitting of all: *Felis*!

With France leading the charge, the rest of the continent began to sway in our favor. The Prussian king Frederick the Great was the eighteenth century's greatest conqueror, but he was unlike the brutes who had led armies before him. He was a man of the Enlightenment, educated by French tutors whose affections for felines he shared. And as his soldiers marched across Europe, he levied from newly vanquished towns a tax in cats. Frederick understood full well our value, and asked that we be turned over in sufficient quantities to guard his armies' stores and keep conquered towns free from rodents.

The English likewise responded to the cat calls, although they preferred to avoid making a show of things in the French style. When the archdeacon of London, John Jorntin, lost his beloved companion, Felix, he composed a touching epitaph— but it was written only in Latin so that he would not be accused of "inordinate affection." Stiff upper lip and all, you know? But the age was such that even in England there were some who allowed their affection for felines to become public knowledge, the most notable being the famed man of letters Dr. Samuel Johnson, who created a stir due to his very public adoration of a cat named Hodge. A chagrined biographer was forced to report with horror that the great man spent his spare time playing with the little beast, showering him with the same kind of affection one might a favored child.

Johnson's dedication to his companion can be measured by this: late in life, when Hodge began to show signs of age, he decreed that the cat be placed on a special diet of oysters, and only the most expensive would do. Of course, ensuring their freshness would require daily trips to the fish market, and Johnson feared that his servants might resent Hodge if they were assigned this errand. So to safeguard his favorite, master thus made the daily trek himself, and upon returning fed the oysters to the cat by his own hand. The most pampered cat in England? If you happen to visit London, you might wish to take a trip by Dr. Johnson's former home and judge for yourself. It has been preserved as a historic landmark, you see, and out front there is a statue. No, silly, not of Johnson, but rather of Hodge!

If it sounds like it was all coming too quickly and too easily, know that our enemies had not given up the field. Back in Paris, they were planning a counterattack, a masterful stroke that we might even grudgingly admire had it not been so insidious. Hoping to foil our advance, they placed in our path a new and unexpected adversary: the dog! Believe the truth of what I now tell you, for the rivalry between dogs and ourselves is *not* an invention of nature. We cats have no natural quarrel with canines, and we recognize in their species many admirable qualities. And if you doubt my word, think of the countless number of your homes in which we live together harmoniously.

But those who opposed us realized that our ascent could not be stopped by any fair means, especially after we had been accepted by some of the most prominent people in Europe. And should our status continue to grow, it would not be long before we made inroads with the bourgeoisie, and if that happened . . . Well, it was now or never for the opposition! Desperate to knock us back down, our detractors contrived a direct competition with canines. And since the bond between humans and dogs ran deep, having blossomed during the centuries of our persecution, it was a contest they were sure we could not win.

We were caught unawares by a propaganda campaign designed to reveal how on every level the canine and feline are diametrically opposed—with they being our superior in all categories. Dogs are faithful, it was claimed, whereas cats are disloyal. They are attentive, while we are capricious. The canine? Heroic and ambitious! The feline? Cowardly and lazy! And on it went at each turn, with every good and desirable quality the property of the dog, and in each instance inverted by the cat. This is no conspiracy theory, my friends. The architect of this misdeed is even known, being a part-time naturalist and full-time cat hater by the name of Georges-Louis Leclerc, better known to history as le comte de Buffoon.

Ah, wait . . . did I misspell that? Apologies, apparently his title was le comte de *Buffon*. Well, no matter. However we choose

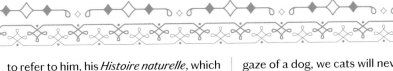

to refer to him, his *Histoire naturelle*, which was published over several volumes starting in 1749, laid the groundwork for the opposing poles of canine and feline behavior which went on to become gospel among our adversaries, creating unfortunate stereotypes which are spouted even to this day by misguided people. On the side of virtue was the dog, carefully reinvented to possess "every internal excellence which can attract the regard of man." They are selfless and give their love unconditionally. They diligently await orders and fulfill them unwaveringly, their great desire being to please their "master" and conform to his wishes. And when master is angry, his account continued, *they gladly suffer ill treatment*. Yes, you read that last part correctly . . . hardly would I wish to be a dog owned by this Buffoon!

On the other side are the detestable felines, and we possess every imaginable vice. As opposed to a dog's love, Buffoon explained that the crafty cat will deign "no affection that is not conditional, and to carry on no intercourse with men but with a view to turning it to his own advantage." In contrast to the keen canine intellect, we felines are entirely incapable of education. And while dogs rank as the most trustworthy of all species, "the character of the cat is the most equivocal and suspicious." But such faults come to us naturally, Buffoon continued, since we are born with an "innate malice." One can see as much by looking into our eyes, since as opposed to the direct

gaze of a dog, we cats will never look even our best benefactor in the face—so as to conceal our intentions, he warned.

The calumny rained on, dog versus cat, good versus evil. Why, Buffoon even took issue with the way we hunt! Dogs "properly pursue" their quarry (charging straight ahead and yapping like idiots), whereas the duplicity of cats is such that we "lie in wait, and attack by surprise." Stealth hunting? Oh, how dare we! What a shame that Buffoon had not been around at the dawn of civilization to train teams of dogs to patrol your fields for rodents by honest means. Of course, your crops would have been nibbled away and you would still be living in huts and wearing bearskin parkas, but at least ethics would have been upheld.

Other cat haters were of course quick to parrot this nonsense around the continent. But this was a new age, and those who loved us answered with hard words in rebuke. And then, with the Battle for Feline Redemption still very much in the balance, disaster struck. Another battle broke out, and not involving cats, but among humans entirely. France suddenly went to war—with *itself*! With all the absurd things we had seen humans do, never had we seen anything as absurd as this. We watched in horror as Frenchmen killed Frenchmen in the name of France, and the monarchy was overthrown and royalty beheaded.

Even that did not end it, as guns kept being shot and swords and daggers thrust

and people ran through the streets holding bayonets dripping with red. And while it was a battle among humans, don't think animals didn't suffer also, dying amid fires and deprivation and chaos as what the French had called the Revolution gave way to what they rightly termed "the Terror." We cats lost nearly all that we had gained, retreating back into lonely basements and alleyways and hiding among the wreckage. Poor France bled until it could bleed no more, and when it stopped we stayed hidden, because power had fallen into very bad hands. These hands were not content to strangle just France, but were soon enough placed around the neck of all of Europe. They belonged to Napoléon Bonaparte, an unsavory little man who lied about much, claiming false nobility, disguising his ancestry, and masking his intentions. But there was one thing about which this vile pretender was honest: he hated cats!

Napoléon was a dog man; he loved them for their slavish loyalty, which he saw as a perfect model for his courtiers. "There are two kinds of fidelity," he once said, "that of dogs and that of cats." Meaning that if anyone wished to serve him, they best not be of a "feline" nature. Such words were straight out of the book of Buffoon, Napoléon having fallen for such baseless propaganda and scorning us in his new empire. And at what cost? The battles fought during the Revolution had not only toppled the glittering rococo palaces and reduced neighborhoods to rubble, they had provided a perfect breeding ground for you-know-who. Yes, rats were overrunning Paris! And once again they had brought their friends. Pestilence and disease were on the loose, and their cousin plague lurked in the shadows.

How wise Frederick the Great was to have allied himself with us. And Napoléon in comparison? When his advisors explained that in the best interests of France cats should be given full liberty of the streets to combat rodents, his distaste was such that he responded by telling them to *find another way*! What other way would the emperor prefer? These are sophisticated times, he explained, there is no need to resort to archaic methods. Perhaps traps? Too inefficient, they hardly make a dent. How about poisons? Ah, they proved effective enough, although more so in causing illness to human beings than in killing rodents.

In the eighteenth century, we had been embraced by nobles in fine houses and now, at the dawn of the nineteenth, we were refused even the job of rat catcher. A humiliating setback to be sure, but men of science soon took our side. And I'm talking about real men of science rather than the quacks of the Renaissance. They begged the emperor's pardon, but France needed cats. If Napoléon wanted a modern approach, how about cold, hard statistics? A single feline, according to their analysis, had the potential rodent destroying power of seven thousand mice or 3,600 rats in one year, so it was time for the government to not only

embrace us, but to put cat breeding programs into place.

And furthermore, they believed that these cats should be treated with the same respect that is naturally due any living being! Wait . . . *what's this*? The Enlightenment had brought a new breed of intellectual, one that saw things differently not just for people but for all creatures. If the new France was to be dedicated to the fair and equitable rights that were due all humans, it was time to consider the inalienable rights that apply to other species too. It was the beginning of the animal welfare movement. Descartes be damned, these revolutionaries claimed that cat he threw from the window *did* feel pain, and it was unjust. And what's more, it could feel joy, sorrow, and love—and understanding this was not a threat to your kind, but an invitation to develop more intimate emotional bonds with us. These arguments were backed not by sentiment but by ethics: being kind was *right*, humans finally understood.

Never again should mankind condone cats being burned, beaten, and tortured. And having spent so long on the outskirts, we even became something of a *cause célèbre* to another group of outsiders: the burgeoning avant-garde. The Revolution had stripped power from the academies that had dominated culture, making way for renegades who painted, drew, and thought as they liked. Laughing in the face of convention, they lived life on its own terms and saw a kindred spirit in the long-derided

feline. They acquiesced to all of the arguments about dogs versus cats . . . and then rendered their own verdict that it was we who were superior! If the cat is an egotist then all the better, give us an animal that knows its worth! Cats are standoffish? So be it, they are wise indeed to discriminate in the company they keep!

And on they went, conceding all of our "negative" qualities and arguing not a whit because they valued us all the more for them. Oh, and that ages-old connection between cats and women, the one that had been turned against us as we were transformed into witches' familiars? It was turned back again, as the associations between felines and women made us irresistible to men of the avant-garde. Guy de Maupassant wrote that cats look upon men in the same way as treacherous ladies: they will kiss or purr upon the hand's caress and then bite or scratch when they tire of it. But that was not troubling to the romantic mind; instead it was exhilarating. Our affections were seemingly given on a whim and withdrawn just as quickly, and the challenge of acceptance measured against the fear of rejection only added to our mystique.

The metaphor for women even extended to the touch. Measured against dogs, we are sultry, there being a decidedly sensual feeling as one strokes a hand along our fur, and far from being ashamed to admit it, our new champions reveled in the experience. Charles Baudelaire, the famed

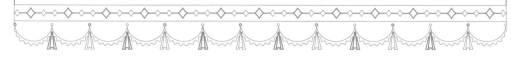

author of *Les fleurs du mal*, likened the petting of his cat to his desire for his mistress. An awkward metaphor, I'll admit, but what he meant was that it stimulated a similar area of the brain. He even compared us to his id, visualizing the part of his mind that was erotic, unrestrained, and as impervious to social pressure as a cat, and it was from there that his poetic impulse flowed. His friend Champfleury recalled how Baudelaire might see a stray in an alley, and talking in a romantic voice would magically draw it toward him, and even the most fierce of feral cats would give themselves over, swept up into his arms to be lovingly caressed.

And so many others among the cultural revolutionaries of France swept us up as well! We became inextricably linked to a bohemian lifestyle, and the list of French writers who chose us as companions amounted to a veritable Hall of Fame. Victor Hugo commissioned a dais in crimson satin so that his cat, Chanoine, could sit enthroned like a queen. And Honoré de Balzac set his pen to paper to write glowingly about interesting cats he had met. Stéphane Mallarmé, meanwhile, owned a white cat named Neige who would jump upon the table as he wrote and rub out verses with her tail by running along the pages. Ah, was Mallarmé furious? Heavens, no—in fact, he delighted in such collaborations. Not to mention Zola, Huysmans, and countless others all the way down through Jean Cocteau, who spoke these very words: "I love

cats because I love my home, and little by little they become its visible soul."

But of all the great names, the one who most distinguished himself in our service was Théophile Gautier. A writer, poet, painter, and critic, he was one of the most versatile talents of the age. But his finest achievement came in 1850 when he set to paper decades of his keen observations on felines in one of the most astutely titled essays ever penned by a human: *Conquérir l'amitié d'un chat est chose difficile*, or "It Is Difficult to Win the Friendship of a Cat." And this time the author of a treatise on cats would not be mocked. Rather, he was celebrated for describing us as "a philosophic animal," meaning a thinking man's companion. We don't brook foolishness, Gautier warned, and explained to his reader that the cat "does not place its affections thoughtlessly. It wishes to be your friend only if you are worthy of it and will not be your slave. It retains its free-will and will do nothing for you it considers unreasonable." But those humans who pass muster will reap rewards they could never have imagined with any other animal. Hear, hear—finally someone got it right!

As Paris went, so went the continent, as back in those days everyone looked to the French capital to set trends. It wasn't long before we had triumphed over even our most feared nemeses, the Men of God. Their antipathy to us was such that we had been left out of the Bible, the entire book containing not a single mention of a cat! But a daring

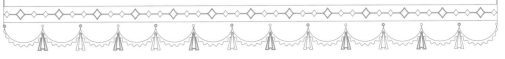

compatriot now attempted to put us in by an extraordinary ruse. A "missing Gospel" was "discovered" that specifically showed Christ's compassion toward felines. Called The Gospel of the Holy Twelve, the fraud began to circulate in the last decades of the century, purportedly an apocryphal account of the life of Jesus discovered in a Tibetan monastery. The document told how there had been a cat with her kittens under the very manger in which Christ had lain as a newborn, and that as a grown man He had rescued a kitten that was being tormented by cruel humans. Having found another stray, He himself carried it upon his bosom until He found for it a proper and loving home. And the commentary explained why Jesus was a cat man: He considered us the most Christian of all animals since we had been persecuted despite being as loving, gentle, and graceful as any of God's creatures.

It was a nice try, although The Gospel of the Holy Twelve was quickly debunked. But by that time, who among the devout would have minded? Certainly not Pope Leo XII, who was hiding in his robe a gray tabby named Micetto, the name being Italian for "kitten." A stray born in the Vatican, this little one was possessed of an unusually keen artistic sensibility, and with the boldness of youth he one day sauntered past the Vatican guards in order to have a look at the frescoes painted by the great Raphael. It was there that he encountered the Pontiff admiring the paintings in the very same log-

gia. The two bonded over a shared love for the Renaissance master, who also happened to be Leo's favorite, and it wasn't long before His Holiness had been charmed.

The two were inseparable, and Leo began to carry Micetto about concealed in his voluminous sleeves so that they would not have to be parted. How times had changed, as now there was a cat resting peacefully upon the Pope's arms, sitting in silent witness to the very church councils who had once promulgated our persecution. Only the highest ranking of Vatican clergy knew the secret, and the select few who did know treated Micetto as a sacred object, since those who wished to be favored by the Pope must favor his favorite.

Among them was François-René de Chateaubriand, the French ambassador to the Vatican, and it was with him that Micetto was sent to France when Leo neared the end of his life. It was a sad parting, no doubt, and even with all that Paris had to offer the cat sulked. Chateaubriand feared that poor Micetto missed his youthful days spent lounging in the Sistine Chapel, and what cultured feline wouldn't? But one can hardly argue Leo's decision. He had ensured his companion's continued well-being, since his choice of caretaker was not made lightly: Chateaubriand was himself among those daring Frenchmen who championed our cause, his nickname being none other than *Le Chat*.

With Micetto an expatriate, the honor of Italy's favorite cat fell to a country kitten

named Mina, and while her social connections were considerably more humble, she was by nature no less beatific. A gray tabby with bright green eyes, she had taken for a human companion a pious girl named Clementina from a hamlet in the Brianza in the northwest of Lombardy, and the two were inseparable. Together they strolled rural roadways under the warm Mediterranean sun, played in the pretty pastures that lined village paths, and even took their meals side by side. An idyll? Not so much as it might seem at first blush.

Clementina was stricken with epilepsy, and had been alone with Mina the first time she fainted. The cat diligently stood guard over her prostrate body, and when the girl finally woke, she found the cat's face directly above hers, staring down intently. Ah, perhaps it was a new game, Mina must have wondered, and she purred contentedly. But she changed her tune when the girl finally stood up, bleeding and bruised. The cat took note of her human's injuries, and the next time Clementina fainted, Mina was off like a shot, running to the girl's parents and mewing wildly to lead them to where she lay. A quick learner, Mina soon began to detect the subtle symptoms that announced an attack, and would often seek aid before Clementina was even aware anything was amiss. Remember the days when people thought cats were devils? A new age indeed, as the people of the town decided this cat was a guardian angel sent to protect a little girl.

Sadly, Clementina was susceptible to maladies from which even a cat could not protect her, and took ill at the age of fifteen with a dangerously high fever. Mina maintained a vigil by her side, refusing to leave the bed, but delirium followed. The condition worsened, and death came soon after. As the funeral procession wound through the village, a heartbroken cat followed in tow, dodging and weaving amid footfalls to stay as close to the girl as possible. During the service, she even leapt up onto Clementina's body and stared down into her face. And would you know, the respect for the cat was so great that the humans present did not intervene, even if this was very inappropriate behavior at such a solemn occasion. What goes on in a cat's head? Ah, Mina, I reckon that you believed that if you could just stare hard enough, the little girl would open her eyes, just like the first time she had fainted.

Sadly, it doesn't work that way, my poor little friend. The inevitable end came, and Mina was gently lifted so that Clementina could be lowered into the soft, rich Italian soil, and they were companions no more. Eh—not so fast there! The cat jumped into the hole just as the gravedigger began to shovel earth. With sober apologies she was lifted out, and it was explained that despite all the paths the two had walked together, the girl must walk this final road alone.

Mina was carried back to the family home by the girl's father. When the morning

dawned, however, she was missing. It was easy to know where she had run off to, and indeed she was found back at the cemetery, curled up on the grave. As Mina knew nothing other than determination, she remained there day after day, refusing all entreaty to return to the house, even when bribed with tasty morsels. She simply had no interest in a home that lacked a particular little girl. After all, what is a guardian angel with no one to guard? Mina thereafter became increasingly withdrawn, retreating into the brush when humans came near, until three months later when she was finally reunited with her human: a sad gray tabby, now ragged and lifeless, found lying beside the girl's grave.

The story of Mina and Clementina was told to the Irish author Lady Morgan by the archbishop of Taranto, Giuseppe Capecelatro, himself a notable cat lover who had compiled a treatise about us. She translated it into English, and it was republished in books far and wide to show our naysayers the truth about the bond between a human and a cat. One place the lesson was being well learned was back in England, where the seed planted by the renegades who dared love us a century before had blossomed. British writers flocked to us as their French counterparts had, and once again they were of the highest renown.

If you would like a few names, how about all three of the Brontë sisters, for starters? And Samuel Butler, the great satirist and translator of the finest works of clas-

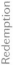

sical antiquity, whose particular inclination was for rough and tumble street cats. And we can safely assume that Edward Lear, the author of "The Owl and the Pussycat," was a cat man—but we can measure the depth of his conviction by a home he had constructed in San Remo, Italy. Lear was concerned that changing residence might upset his cat, so to minimize the disturbance he instructed his architects to build his new house as an *exact replica* of the old.

Of course, the greatest name in English literature back in those days was Charles Dickens, and we can likewise count him as a convert. He took in a white cat named William, which, ahem . . . became Williamina after giving birth to a litter of kittens in the kitchen. Of these, one was a notably bossy little thing that insisted on curling up in the writer's lap while he worked—and when baby didn't get the attention he desired, he made his needs known by reaching up with his paw to snuff out the candle on the desk. Hmph, such gall! But the effect was to make Dickens love the kitten all the more, and, having charmed its way into the writer's heart, was henceforth referred to by friends and family as the Master's Cat.

But I don't want to paint things in too rosy a shade. Once again, our rise did not come without resistance, as the English were a stubborn lot whose affections had for centuries been lavished upon their finely bred canines. The treachery of that prejudice was such that when Queen Victoria asked that a medal be designed for the Royal Society for the Prevention of Cruelty to Animals, her artists sent a sample depicting on the award all manner of creatures *except* for cats! Well now, they were messing with the wrong queen. Victoria had a notable soft spot for the feline persuasion, in particular doting over an Angora named White Heather, and the sample was returned as unsatisfactory, accompanied by a terse note. A cat must be included, Her Highness advised, so as to counter the historic aversion to our kind, who had, in her royal words, been "generally misunderstood and grossly ill-treated."

God save the queen! But as the episode indicates, there was still work to be done. And the man who set himself to the task was Harrison Weir, by trade an artist and book illustrator, but who would become best known as "the Father of the Cat Fancy." In 1871, he deigned to raise our prestige among the British public by organizing a cat show. In truth, it was not the first of its kind, as there had already been shows even in the dark days. But those were cruel in nature and something closer to a freak show, with the audience looking in disdain at poor, trapped felines displayed alongside unusual breeds of rabbits and guinea pigs. But Weir's show was intended to vanquish the memory of those ages by presenting us in our best light, a spectacle of fine animals who would leave no doubt that we were companions deserving of places in even the best homes.

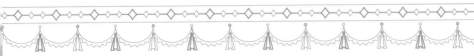

And there was to be a fine setting as well. The Crystal Palace, one of the most prestigious venues in all of London, had been secured for the event, and in this iconic building Weir intended to host a show of cats along the lines of those for purebred dogs. Wait, now—a cat show in the Crystal Palace? For most of the public the idea was absurd! This was during an age when there weren't any categories for felines other than, well, feline, since controlling our breeding and imposing standards was considered virtually impossible. Dickens himself—and, remember, he was one of our supporters—quipped that humans would have as much success policing the sexual habits of cats as they would honeybees.

So what categories could even be concocted for a formal show? Weir did what he could, breaking us up into divisions based upon appearance, with entrants placed into such groups as black and white (and white and black; for purposes of the show, they were deemed separate categories), spotted, tortoiseshell, and even—a bit rude, frankly—fat. "Many were the gibes, jokes, and jeers that were thrown at me," Weir recalled, and no wonder, because to most people it all sounded as a recipe for disaster.

Nevertheless, 170 cats answered the call, their human companions braving mockery to offer them as participants. Weir's detractors envisioned a debacle, with the Crystal Palace providing a sparkling backdrop to a battle royal as enraged felines hissed, spat, clawed, and chased one another about. These were uncharted waters, and even Weir himself was not above doubt, admitting his nervousness en route to the hall. Could the cats be trusted to behave? Would the public turn out, only to laugh? And if the event were a failure, what would the consequences be for the feline cause? The Crystal Palace was more than just a show. It was a test, a chance to woo our detractors openly and prove that the ground we had been reclaiming was deserved. But the gamble was staked against a cat-astrophe that could erode the advances we had made over the last century.

July 13 was the fateful day, and while London may have had its doubts, its cats had none. When Weir arrived, he found a scene that exceeded even his greatest expectations: there they were, a motley assortment of England's proudest house cats, combed and groomed and looking their finest, a little bowl of milk placed in front of each and every one, all seated peaceably on cushions with nary a whimper of complaint. It was as if they had known what was in the balance, and there they sat in their most resplendent guise, representing not just themselves but the countless generations that had waited for just this chance.

Ah, but what of the dreaded public? When the doors opened there was no denying that most had come for the novelty. But their smirks stopped when they entered the hall, and as they wandered the rows of beribboned felines, they did not laugh but were instead *impressed*. Word then began to spread, and more and more people came until there were *so many visitors that they had to fight their way through the throng to even catch a glimpse of the cats*. By the end, some two hundred thousand humans had turned out.

The talk of London! A smashing success! The jeers turned to cheers!

There were, of course, prizes to be given. Paltry to be sure, not even one hundred pounds in total for the entire competition. A fourteen-year-old tabby named Old Lady walked away as the grand champion, perhaps not a surprise since she (ahem) was owned by Weir himself, who also happened to be one of the event's three judges, with another being his own brother. But will you begrudge her triumph? I certainly won't. To tell you truly, we cats care naught for trophies, and the award was well earned in recognition of what Weir had accomplished on our behalf. Besides, the real prize was not awarded by the judges, but rather voted on by London as a whole: respect, and it was equally shared among every one of those 170 cats, all of them acquitting themselves as champions of the highest level.

Of course, one skirmish alone does not win a war, but our resounding victory at the Crystal Palace made the outcome inevitable. More shows were to come, Weir stating his hope that they would bring us further positive recognition and better our

treatment throughout society. And well they did—and not just in England. Two years later, Glasgow held the first cat show in Scotland, and in 1881, Brussels sent out a call for the first on the continent. By that time, a group of ambitious Australians had already put one on all the way in far-off Sydney! Well, they had jumped the gun a bit down under, and the organizers themselves admitted the event to be a failure when only four cats bothered to enter. Ah, but it's a big, barren land, and Australia's felines just needed more time for word to circulate. Seven years later, forty-one of them heard the call and came out for a show in Brisbane, and with some thirty thousand humans in attendance, we were off and running all the way on the other side of the globe.

These were wild times, and while the new cat aficionados still didn't know much about felines, there was no faulting their enthusiasm. Ireland held its first cat show in 1879, and the advertisements promised something akin to a circus: there would also be military bands, an ice grotto, and the worldly remains of a very tough tomcat from Kilkenny who had died several years before. Of live cats, there were some 250, said to encompass every known type. This included the fluffy white Angola, and while I'll guess they meant Angora, there was in fact a unique African cat being featured in a show back in England. Named Majunga, it was said to hail from Madagascar and be a representative of a breed so unique that to those "unversed in cat lore, it greatly resembles a monkey." A very rare feline indeed: the organizers had somehow mistaken a lemur for an African feline.

By the end of the century, cat clubs were being organized all around Europe, some of them even national bodies, and a newfound interest in specific breeds helped sort out Angora from Angola and put a halt to the Majungas of the world. Books about us also proliferated, containing important information for the neophyte cat keeper. "Pussyology" was the original term invented for the science of our care, although for certain reasons involving female genitalia, it was eventually withdrawn as awkward. The advice of the early experts was, to use a period term, "poppycock." One author advised that we be fed twice daily . . . well, I won't argue with that, but . . . her recommended diet was bread and milk or oatmeal porridge. Other manuals tried to explain differences in feline types by forcing us to conform to Victorian social conventions. One extolled the black-and-white tomcat as the gentleman among cats, the kind of fellow who would hardly deign to capture a rodent. Is that so? Good thing for the crew of the HMS *Amethyst* that Simon didn't hear about this! Brown tabbies meanwhile were the equivalent of solid working class folk.

Hey, now, that's your narrator they're talking about!

But the comment probably wasn't meant to be derogatory, because by the end of the nineteenth century, we were in fact being put on the payroll all across Europe. It started back in 1868, at the London post office. Mice had been running a guerrilla war against the money order bureau, making repeated late night sorties during which they would chew up various types of paper. Among them were certain small rectangular strips with printed numbers, which humans greatly esteem under the name of "cash," and no doubt the loss of these got the clerks, attention. But the staff was outsmarted at every step—mice really are that crafty!—and eventually asked that money be apportioned so they could hire a trio of cats for the office.

This was an unusual request, but the secretary of the post office approved it after it was explained that the three felines could potentially save the bureau far more than they cost. Employment was an unexpected turn of events, since it's not as if cats of the day had been actively seeking work. But having a job provides important validation in human society, so if nothing else it was further proof of our rehabilitated reputation. Plus considering how rotten you had been to us for quite some time, compensation was not unreasonable. But how much is a cat's labor worth? It was here that we first learned the realities of the workaday world, and it wasn't a pleasant lesson.

It turned out that the requested remuneration wasn't intended as a salary, since the cats were to receive no actual

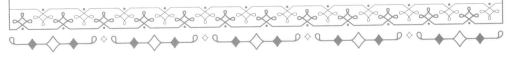

take-home pay. I don't find any great insult on that point since in truth humans are the only species that is concerned with accumulating currency. The money was instead a means to assure their general upkeep, which is all we really care about after all, and it seemed a fair proposition that if the cats were working for the public weal, their needs should be provided for out of the public treasury. And the amount requested by the money order bureau wasn't much, a mere pittance at two shillings a week to cover the trio. But now I will find plenty of insult, because the secretary

declined the request as excessive and offered instead exactly half, one shilling a week. In other words, twelve cents.

Please don't speak to me of "Well, with inflation . . . " because we are talking about *twelve cents*. A week. For three cats! Humans refer to such behavior as "frugal" and argue that it is a form of virtue, whereas we felines call it nothing other than "cheap."

This was hardly a livable sum, even for a cat. The good people of the money order desk took our side in protest, explaining that a shilling might provide a bit of milk now and again but little more. But they were met with a stern rebuttal: the cats would not have the luxury of seeing their meals paid for by the public coffers but instead must eat the mice in the office, thereby eliminating the rodents while simultaneously saving the secretary the costs of their food. Furthermore an assessment of the trio's productivity would be made in six months' time, and if their work was not deemed satisfactory, their paltry salary would be further reduced.

Geez. And to think, after thousands of years of evolution dating from those days back in the prehistoric fields, this is the economic system you came up with? I suppose the cats should have considered themselves lucky they got even their shilling, rather than have the secretary attempt to turn a profit by charging them for the mice they ate, as

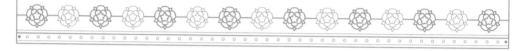

postal property. But they would show that skinflint! No, not by unionizing — collective action is not the feline way. Instead they did the best job they possibly could, breaking the rodent stranglehold on the money order bureau and leaving no doubt about their true worth. And, oh, how they were praised, their supervisor commending the trio's "laudable zeal for their service."

In proving themselves beyond even the greatest expectations, that mean postal secretary had no choice but to take notice. And he was indeed impressed, so much so that he . . . docked their wages?

It's true, their pay was cut exactly in half, reduced to a mere six pence. The cats had been doing such an outstanding job, the main office explained, that it was hard to imagine anything they could possibly need that could not be provided from within the great pile of bloody, stale mouse carcasses littering the back room of the money order bureau.

There was no winning with the British postal service, but so be it, because what those three cats accomplished was worth far more than the secretary's precious shillings. As those snout-to-the-grindstone, hardworking felines killed mouse after mouse, other branch offices started asking for funds with which to hire their own cats. The idea then spread from the post office into other branches of civil service, and the help wanted signs went up: "CATS NEEDED, EXPERIENCE KILLING MICE A PLUS." By 1883 the most unexpected help wanted sign of all appeared, over 10 Downing Street in London. Does the address sound familiar? It just so happens to be the office of the prime minister of Great Britain! Well, you know that old adage about rats in politics? They had them at 10 Downing Street, and mice too, and the solution was to hire one of us into the very seat of power. Of course the pay was once again lousy (a penny a day for upkeep), but the job came with a *title*. These

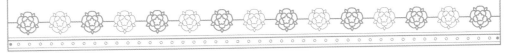

things have to be done right when the governance of a nation is at stake, and the post of Chief Mouser of the Cabinet Office was created!

It was fast becoming a working cat's world, and soon enough we were being hired all over the continent, from Sweden down to Sicily, in post offices and storehouses and even stock exchanges (where rodents had been nibbling the ticker tapes—they really will get into anything!). National security was even put into our trusty paws as the French army budgeted money for felines to protect their warehouses and garrisons, and oh how Napoléon must have been rolling in his grave. The Germans did likewise—for a time. Until one of their scientists had the bright idea to instead kill all the mice in their commissaries by infecting them with a strain of cholera. Hmm. Introducing cholera into the area where food is stored, what could go wrong? Sometimes the old ways really are the best ways, and the cats soon returned to their posts.

We were back in business, and while it was a long way from the fields of Mesopotamia to be sure, the effect of our labors proved the same as it had thousands of years before: our diligent efforts affirmed our place within society and ingratiated us into the lives of appreciative humans. And as our popularity continued to rise, many of the cats posted to offices and warehouses became more than mere laborers. Often better known to the public than their human colleagues, they wound up as mascots representing the institutions that had employed them.

One of the earliest to gain this renown was named Black Jack, who served at the British Museum. He had been taken on as a mouser but eventually traded those duties for the role of roving goodwill ambassador. Adored by visitors, many of whom had come to see *him* rather than the world's finest collection of antiquities, personnel were expected to be at the ready to open doors in order to facilitate his wanderings among the museum's hallowed halls and galleries. What? Humans now put in the service of a cat? We might just like this modern world!

But one day curiosity brought him into the library. And shirking their responsibility to tend his comings and goings, no member of the staff was on hand to open the door for his exit. Finding himself therein trapped, he spent the day testing his claws on the contents of the shelves. He was only trying to use his time productively, but suddenly the old guard reared its ugly head. "Look what he has done, we told you not to let cats in the museum," they cried out! Suddenly were heard all the arguments that we were bad animals, not to be trusted and disloyal, selfish, and caring not a whit except for ourselves, and hadn't Black Jack just proven the truth of it?

The days when they could have him declared a demon and tossed in a bonfire were long past, but they could have him dragged off to the pound and thrown in a cage—and so they wished it to be! Black Jack now dis-

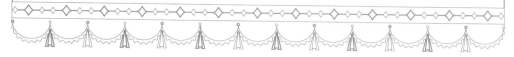

appeared from the premises. Gone, without a mew to be heard, and those who loved him were saddened. Had we come so close, only to find ourselves still vulnerable to the animosity of humans? Our adversaries now moved to bar the gates—literally so, as there would be no more cats in the British Museum, they forewarned.

But the voices of our detractors echoed only in a forgotten past, and the gates would not now hold. Black Jack was *not* in a cage. His friends outnumbered his enemies, and rallying to his cause, they had whisked him away and placed him in hiding before any punitive action could be taken. And time passed, enough to allow for the cooling of tempers. Until one grand and fateful day when the great portals were opened with a sweeping gesture of welcome by a staff member. Any who glanced over would have initially reacted with surprise to see . . . nothing. There appeared to be an empty space with no one at all entering! But as their gaze turned downward, they saw that there was indeed someone present. Walking through the doorway was a familiar figure, someone who was just so high, maybe a foot tall at the shoulder.

Black Jack strode boldly forward to make his return. There was much rejoicing, and his friends cheered and gathered around to welcome him back—and there was nothing whatsoever his adversaries could do to stop him! A cat would once again roam the museum's hallowed halls

and share in the treasures of history. Well, it was only fair, everyone acknowledged, and I think that after hearing our tale even thus far you will too. After all, it's not like we didn't have a paw in creating history!

Yes, we *were* going to like this modern world. As the nineteenth century faded, our long wandering had come to a close. Once again we stood by your side. If only those generations of felines who had known nothing more than the streets as homes and discarded scraps as sustenance could have seen their grandkittens now! How amazed would they have been? And how proud to know that their struggles to persevere weren't for naught, their suffering now redeemed as new generations were welcomed back into the graces of adoring humans.

But our journey is not yet done. Our final voyage lies ahead, as I have one last tale to tell, and it will once again be filled with danger and daring. This grand adventure, if I may speak so boldly, was the grandest of all. Never before had felines been pitted so squarely against the challenges of an unknown and wild land, and our triumph over this new adversity may well stand as our crowning glory. So if it will please you to continue with me, I would like to tell you the story of the cats of my own native American lands. Back aboard the ships, my friends, and bring with you all that you will need, because we shall not be returning from the western shores!

· The nineteenth century found us back in the embrace of humankind. Here a cat with a girl in a c.1890 Christmas card design by the Polish-born printer Louis Prang. Hardly would we have been Christmas card–worthy back when you thought us to be minions of the Devil!

LEFT · I told you the French avant-garde embraced us: *Cat's Rendezvous* is an 1868 lithograph showing life on the docks by Édouard Manet, the father of Impressionism and the man credited with breaking the barriers that led to modern art. His own cat, a tuxedo, was named Zizi.

English Cats on Exhibition.

The English have just made a magnificent cat show. The feline show was a grand success. The number of animals exhibited was one hundred and seventy, and the number of prizes given fifty-four—amounting to about three hundred dollars. The great drawback was the difficulty of seeing the cats, owing to the crowd of visitors. Some were valued as high as five hundred dollars.

A cat show!—how absurd!—what nonsense! has been heard on all sides; but somebody considered that there was as much sense in having a display of "monsers" as in having a bird, dog, horse, or ordinary cattle show. The matter determined, an advertisement and invitations were issued, with offers of money prizes, and after immense difficulty on the part of the managers in getting the cats up to the scratch, this day offered to all comers a very large, varied, and really interesting collection of British and foreign cats, ranged in two rows of cages down that part of the nave known as the Tropical department. There are no less than twenty-five classes, some of which contained many entries.

Among the most interesting are the foreign animals, such as the fine-looking Tom, in one of the cages, a native of Africa, looking, with his tawny coat and well-developed mane, like a degenerate descendant of the lion. Or, again, the sleek, dun-colored cats, with smutty faces, natives of Salem, and the long-haired Persian or Angora cats. In one cage, crouching back with flattened ears and glaring eyes, lay a genuine wild cat, exhibited by the Duke of Sutherland, and close by some peculiar specimens of the Mink cat, a tailless variety, looking as if they were ready, like the fox of the fable, to insist amongst the company assembled that to go tailless was the fashion. The wild cat, whose attention seemed to be divided between the spectators and the birds twittering near at hand, was not the only savage-looking specimen, for many of the animals exhibited were ready to lay back their ears, distend their jaws, glare with dilated eyes, and utter that low feline growl known as "swearing," explaining at once why the attendant busy about the cages had his hands protected by a thick leather glove. Others seemed utterly cowed by the novelty of the scene, and shivered and uttered their "mew," while a far larger proportion lay in ponderous aristocratic state upon their red or blue cushions, far to an excess, necks adorned with collar and padlock, ribbon or bells, and winked and blinked at their visitors; but refusing the caresses and blandishments offered them, and rejecting as well the milk and pieces of raw meat placed for their re-

fection. And no wonder, for there was aldermanic repose written in every line of their sleek, glossy, well-licked forms. Fancy a cat of this kind being expected to eat cold meat, after being used to have the bones picked out of its fish by careful hands, and to take its cutlet or chicken every day at noon! For size there was a cat weighing 21½ pounds, being heavier, we were told, than the great Edinburgh cat that its owners would not send. For beauty, white silky-furred animals, whose skin would make ermine look poor; white, long-haired cats, too, with the most beautiful blue eyes, peculiar from the fact of their being deaf. Tawny cats, with large, flat feet, bearing seven toes in front and six toes behind, instead of the ordinary five. Here and there a genuine tortoiseshell Tom, and there a spotless white lady formed a group with her family of three perfectly white kittens. One huge fellow was peculiar from his resemblance to the stuffed tigers in the case hard b[...]

In another cage—not for co[...] —was the favorite cat of one of th[...] Mr. Harrison Weir, the well-k[...] mal painter—his brother, and [...] dona, of St. Bernard dog celebr[...] the other judges. Mr. Weir's[...] sleek blue tabby, of a placid dis[...] fond of stroking, and given [...] She is known as the "Old L[...] has attained to the venerable f[...] of twelve. One Manx Tom was[...] ly the hero of a hundred fights[...] ears were laced, goffered, or pi[...] a shreddy pattern that told tales[...] a scrimmage. He kept himsel[...] ting posture, as if ashamed of [...] that he had no tail, and then [...] low "mew," as if of pleasure, a[...] across to where one of the ma[...] was carefully washing her c[...] heedless of all lookers-on. Th[...] of domesticity exhibited by the[...] animals was remarkable. Amo[...] Toms generally there was eith[...] position to lie in sullen apath[...] to give symptoms of an imitati[...] celebrated old blacking adver[...] where the cat glares with arc[...] and bottle-brush tail at its res[...] in the polished boot. The fe[...] the contrary, responded freel[...] visitors' caresses, and purre[...] praises of their proportions.

The managers, we are told, [...] great difficulty in persuading [...] part with their pets, and while t[...] classes have responded, poorer[...] who owned the commoner kin[...] from timidity or want of knowle[...] the subject, have refrained fro[...] ing their purring favorites for [...] seventy-five prizes, in sums rang[...] ten to thirty shillings. Altoge[...] show was very interesting, tho[...] novel assemblage will probab[...] trying to the birds when night[...] the part singing begins.

The cat show at the Crystal Palace was such a big story that the *Illustrated London News* ran an engraving of some of the fine felines on display. And the word was heard across the pond: the clipping is from the *Newville Star* in Pennsylvania. The world had taken notice!

TOP · Victory! By the end of the century, we had stormed the bastions, just like the Rattown Tigers who proudly march down Main St. as envisioned by Prang. A lithography journal from 1894 praised these Tigers as "perfection," and a threat to every evildoer of the town!

LEFT · Having conquered your hearts, we were rewarded with a new role. We had been a lot of things to the Old World, but it was left to nineteenth century artists to invent the image of the cat as cute. *At the Party*, another lithograph by Prang.

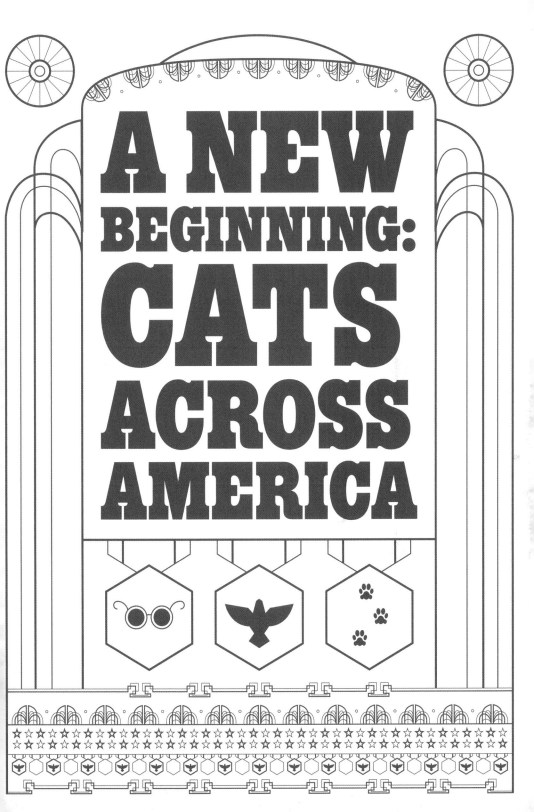

e now arrive at the subject that is most dear to my heart, being the history and virtues of American felines, an ancestry from which I myself am descended. A vast and untrammeled continent waited across the sea, a virgin world that was rich in opportunity—and decidedly poor in cats. The western lands knew nothing of domestic felines, and while those arriving from Europe faced an entirely new set of hardships, through generations of hard work they conquered this land and made of it their own. In the process they created a unique legacy that sets them apart even from other cats, and one of which we are justifiably proud. Do I sound boastful? Pardon my tone if that is the case, but any among you who have spent time with felines will know that we are prideful creatures, and I must forsake humility to state in the frankest of terms that we American cats are of a special type.

Ah, but perhaps it is best if I start by explaining what I mean by "American" cats, because I do not intend the term to refer simply to any feline one might find within the geographical bounds of the United States. I am not talking about the expensive purebred cats found in many a well-to-do person's Park Avenue penthouse or Beverly Hills mansion, their pedigree affirmed by so many signed and notarized documents that one might think they are descended from a royal house. Take no offense if you the reader live with such a feline, because they are fine and loving creatures who provide great joy and companionship to their humans. But they are not what I would consider *real* American cats.

Our bond is not one of breed, but of history. In fact, we have no breed *per se*, the true American cat being a mishmash of all feline types rolled into one. You might find a dash of tabby here and a hint of calico there, a splash of white where you don't expect it, and perhaps a stripe or a spot that seems hopelessly out of place. And if the canons of proper pedigree don't approve of the result? We couldn't care less!

Yes, we are misfits, and proudly so. We are the strays and the alley cats, the ones who give birth to their kittens in abandoned buildings or old cardboard boxes, the ones you find at the city pounds and animal shelters. But my intent is not to paint a grim picture, because we are smart, determined, clever, and admittedly stubborn, and none of the disadvantages to which we might be born can shake the conviction that the world is ours for the taking. But while our spirit is fiercely independent, we maintain a willingness to give of ourselves unconditionally, and when our heart is invested, never a better or more loyal ally will you find.

Does such a description not ring true of the American people as well? It is hardly coincidence since there is no other case where the histories of a nation's humans and its cats so closely mirror one another. The American nation was founded by outcasts, humans persecuted for religious beliefs, or those who simply didn't fit into the rigid social structure of the Old World. Dreaming of a better life, they risked an arduous voyage across a cruel ocean. But recall our own dark days in Europe. Were cats not likewise outcasts, and did we not seek salvation on the very same seas?

So it was that the first ships to arrive on the far shores carried feline refugees in addition to human. Of course, we had not been brought aboard in an offer of freedom. Your kind was hardly so compassionate in those days. But you at least had the wisdom to not dare such a voyage without cats, and we were on hand in our traditional role as guardians of vital stores. These ships were only going one way, however, and when the humans disembarked as colonists, we did also, the first domesticated felines to ever set paw in a new land. Ponder for a moment, if the journey was difficult enough for a human, how difficult must it have been for a cat? Only the most resolutely stalwart of our kind would survive such a voyage and then successfully adapt to the hard reality of colonial life.

But those dauntless few would quickly find that America was a very different place to be a cat. The prejudices of the Old World were not as strong, the colonies having been founded by Puritans who didn't need the big shows of deviltry that went on back in Europe, and for whom the stories associating us with evil didn't hold the same sway. These were practical folk, and we didn't have to worry about the ghastly rituals of torture that saw us sacrificed to the perverse blood lust of a still medieval deity. This doesn't mean we were suddenly accepted; we were something along the lines of a varmint, having one saving grace in our ability to catch rodents. And for quite a long time, Americans, like the Europeans before them, thought us capable of nothing more.

There was an important difference, however. American ingenuity, being the defining characteristic of the people of the new nation, sought maximum utility value in all things. Unlike in stodgy old Europe, a job well done garnered respect regardless of the baggage of the past, and of course when it came to controlling vermin, we did our jobs very, very well. The early settlers saw in us an ally, and there was a saying in colonial days: "You will always be lucky if you know how to make friends with strange cats." It referred to the advantages to be gained from being friendly to strays, who then might prevent rodents from pillaging one's property or crops. Farmers even went so far as to invent a system which featured a flap over a small hole in a doorway to allow access to their homes and barns for cats who might be inclined to come in and hunt mice, and their invention is still in use today: you now know it as the cat door.

The burgeoning nation even gave us official recognition, as not long after the Revolution, the United States became the first country to set aside money for cats in its budget. Even before the English had hired on postal cats, the American government made a financial commitment to provide felines to protect the mail. One thousand dollars a year was apportioned for food for postal cats, with the money doled out according to the volume of mail handled by each city. One hundred dollars went to the cats in the New York post office, ten dollars to those in Philadelphia, and so on down the

line. As in England, wages were low and the money was hardly a handout since our dinners still consisted mainly of mouse served extra rare, but it was an acknowledgment by the new republic that we had something of value to contribute to the commonwealth.

An even greater endorsement came from the United States Army. By the early nineteenth century, cats had become standard equipment in commissary storehouses, where we were highly esteemed by thankful mess officers. A soldier could always count on a fair shake from Uncle Sam, and for once we found an employer who was not frugal with its felines: a whopping eighteen dollars and twenty-five cents was apportioned annually for the upkeep of each and every cat, a sum that was considered so lofty that the Treasury Department protested. But soldierly camaraderie must be maintained, and the army stood by us, insisting that its cats be looked after appropriately and with adequate attention given to their upkeep. This amounted to an entire pound of fresh beef a day per cat! And not only that, the army purchasing agents demanded that the weight of our meat be exclusive of bones.

Despite such affirmation, the public still lacked the crucial vision to understand the value we could add to their lives as housemates. Not that they didn't try to find roles for us beyond that of mouser. It's as if they knew we were capable of something more, and given the great (and sometimes foolhardy) inventiveness of the American peo-

ple, they were determined to figure it out. Thus began during the nineteenth century a determined inquiry among writers, professors, and general thinkers of things on one of the perplexing questions of the day: what are cats good for beyond hunting rodents?

Some of their musings were no less than bizarre. A university professor suggested that we could be used to protect property from lightning. Wait . . . what? He had noticed that strays often congregate around the back fences of houses, and that lightning rarely strikes back fences. I don't doubt that both facts may be independently true, but the relationship he devised between them was daft. He conjectured that cats had an immunity to lightning that was in turn afforded the fences, and through a series of calculations determined the area a feline could protect to three times the length of its body (inclusive of the tail—so best not to use a Manx). A journalist in New York meanwhile suggested we could be used to rescue people from burning buildings. If we were to congregate on the ground, people trapped on upper stories could leap out, and if they were to land upon us, our tensile strength and elasticity might save them from injury. Oh, and on a more cultured bent, musical schools were proposed in the hopes that we might be taught to sing operatically.

Hint: none of the above projects came to fruition. It's not that nineteenth century Americans lacked vision for us, because they clearly had ideas aplenty. But clouded by

centuries of superstition and egregious misconceptions, they could not see their way to accepting us as companions. Oh, there were a few cats who made real progress, including a pair of kittens named Tabby and Dixie who made it all the way to the White House. They had been gifts from Secretary of State William Seward to Abraham Lincoln, who easily fell for their charms and even allowed Tabby to eat directly from the White House dining table. A kitten taking his fill in the lap of power! The president's wife, a notable stick-in-the-mud, protested that his actions demeaned their station, but Honest Abe had a ready reply. If former president James Buchanan had been allowed to eat at the White House table, he argued, there was no reason a cat couldn't. Mr. Lincoln indeed earned his reputation as the Great Emancipator in this case!

But such victories were rare. Put it this way, this was an era when the cats considered most notable *weren't even alive.* One garnered public interest in 1880 when he

became trapped inside the Washington Monument and was forced to jump from a five-hundred-foot-high window. Amazingly the dauntless cat survived the fall—only to be set upon by a dog and killed as he tried to limp away. The bizarre story made headlines, and maintenance workers who witnessed the incident recovered the cat's body, which was stuffed and put on display at the Smithsonian Institution. Then there was the mummified cat who served as the mascot of the Milwaukee Press Club, a poor creature that had died after being trapped in the walls of a building and then preserved by nature itself. In the absence of any clear logic, a group of local journalists decided that a deceased feline would be an ideal mascot for their professional association, so they had it entombed in a baroque-looking wood case and placed in their favorite tavern. They could there offer it a toast now and again, and the mummy would be periodically removed and carried aloft in parades

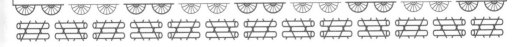

and other such events as the journalists deemed necessary. It was even appointed patron of the local writer's festival. While humans might find a certain quirky charm in all this, from a feline perspective such jocular humor projected onto a cat who had suffered a terrifying and lonely death is hardly laudable. And even less so when one considers the name that these professional scriveners chose to bequeath upon it: Anubis, the sobriquet of an Ancient Egyptian *dog*.

America was still a more callous world than not for cats. But our status was in the process of being forever changed by some of history's bravest and most determined felines. The United States offered itself as a land of opportunity, but the overcrowded cities and squalid slums of the East Coast fulfilled that promise for precious few. Once again the more stouthearted of your kind began to migrate, risking the gamble of a new life in the huge westward expanses. Traveling over the Rockies, pioneers started breaking ground on new farms and towns, and even if the terrain was harsh and unforgiving, it was land they could call their own, in a place where the sun was bright, the sky was blue, and the endless horizon carried the promise of freedom.

But the frontier also offered something with less appeal: mice, and plenty of them, over regions so vast that nothing less than the paws of experts could be relied upon. We were desperately needed in the American West! Once more we answered the call,

and as the nineteenth century wore on, cats slowly began to appear in the hinterlands. But from where were these intrepid felines coming? Some had traveled with wagon trains, among humans who had the foresight to bring a cat along. Others migrated up from Mexico, having arrived in Central and South America aboard Spanish galleons, and staking their claim to the American Southwest as they traveled northward with Spanish missionaries. And still more blazed their own trails, true pioneers who migrated further and further from the large cities of the Eastern Seaboard and eventually crossed the Mississippi.

As with the generations of seafaring felines who had colonized the new land, the cats of the frontier were by nature strong and clever. And they were also valuable commodities, especially popular among cowboys, who packed months' worth of supplies and for whom the predations of field mice could spell disaster. Virile and independent, they nonetheless needed our help. And while you may not see this in your Western films, many cowboys traveled with us across the plains, and I'll have you know they paid a hefty price for our services.

Consider that in the Arizona territory in the 1880s the fixed price for a cat, any cat at all, was ten dollars. This was a princely sum at a time when a month's wages might barely exceed twenty. But it was dictated by the market itself: there simply weren't enough of us to fill the demand. Meanwhile

entrepreneurs in the Midwest were tripling their money by buying cats up in bulk and shipping us to the Dakotas by railcar, and up in Alaska we were worth our weight in gold—literally so, as desperate miners paid for their felines with gold dust.

You might ask if catching mice on the frontier wasn't just the same old servitude. I can't deny the truth of that, but this was a new kind of world where traditional roles and mores didn't always hold, thereby creating opportunities for those with enough grit to earn a pawhold in society. And many were the cats who rose to that challenge, and in the process redefined public opinion about felines. Take, for example, a big tomcat named Tom from Salt Lake City. He had been living with a man named John West until, one fine day, Tom took a certain flounder which Mr. West believed belonged to him (then as now, the debate over who owns the food within the household was a common matter of contention between cats and humans). Rather than negotiate the matter peaceably, Mr. West became so enraged that he trapped Tom in a bag, which he then hid under a seat on a train headed to California! Some 337 miles later, in Caliente, Nevada, the train's staff heard Tom's mewing and rustling. Having discovered the poor cat, they compounded his plight—he had no ticket, so off he went.

But as I have told you, cats on the frontier were of their nature clever and strong, and Tom knew what he had to do. That house in Salt Lake City was his as much as it was Mr. West's, and he would be damned if he would give it up. He turned eastward and began walking. He crossed mountains and deserts, suffering through brutally hot days and frigid nights in a terrain where dangerous predators roamed. And even though the path was unknown to him, three weeks later he appeared nowhere else than on the very doorstep. He was worse for the wear to be sure, but he wanted one thing and in fact demanded it: dinner. Mr. West could be nothing but impressed, and he gave Tom dinner, and in addition swore never again to put him out. Tom had showed himself the bolder of the two and earned a permanent and rightful place in the home.

Meanwhile Cy Warman, a poet who had worked for the railroads in his younger days and was nicknamed the Bard of the Rockies, recalled the story of another pioneering feline. While employed by the Western Line, he had taken in a stray black female cat who had been residing in the rail yard, and having traveled countless miles together, they had grown quite attached. On the day Warman left the company, he determined to bring her with him into retirement. She was found on the train, sleeping atop the coal stack. He called to her and she responded with an arched back and familiar purr, then stood up and began to make her way over. But midway between him and the train, she suddenly stopped her stride and stood stock-still. There followed a mo-

ment of indecision as the rail yard filled with a palpable anxiety, finally to be pierced by a pitiful meow. The cat's eyes fixed on Warman, and after another pause that must have seemed a day, she made an about face and returned to the train without looking back.

The black cat knew her human was leaving (we always know!), and she knew a choice must be made. That it was difficult, we cannot doubt, but as appealing as a comfortable life with a caring human might be, she was a frontier cat. She chose the train—a dirty coal pile over a comfortable

bed, the feeling of speed and power rather than days lazing on a porch, the unbroken expanse over a well-tended garden. She chose to ride, the wind whipping her whiskers. And so she did, at least for the next couple of years, until one fateful day when the train derailed. The engineer was found dead, his body broken, and a few feet away the cat was found, her body also crumpled and lifeless. Where she had come from and whom she had been before the rail yard, no one knows. But the men of the line all knew who she became, America's (and the world's!) one and only railroad cat.

She had chosen her own path through life, having died as she had lived, a pioneer even among pioneers. But that was the nature of the frontier! Life was not easy, but it was a place where old identities were forgotten and new ones formed. Bonds grew under the lonely Western sky, and in that great expanse an ancient idea was born anew: cats as companions. Two frontiers were being simultaneously conquered by felines out west, not simply the one shown on maps but also the one bordering human hearts. Think about the railway men and that fine black cat! Never would they imagine they would be hurtling down the line with a feline conductor! Getting to know and understand her, sharing a laugh and a meow over the smell of burning coal. Think of the cowboys who traveled with us across the endless terrain as we sat perched behind their saddle horns. Along those empty trails

they likewise learned our ways, and can you doubt that on a starry night by the campfire they might strum their guitars and offer a song to a feline friend, who in return offered a contented purr?

In the America of the day, it was typical to expect culture to flow from east to west, with important ideas and attitudes disseminating from such intellectual centers as Boston or New York. But the process with felines was reversed. Word began to filter eastward, telling how the riddle of cats had been solved. Our hidden purpose turned out to be not so mysterious after all. With awe and wonder and perhaps a bit of embarrassment, the humans of the east learned that the answer they sought had been too obvious for them to guess: cats could simply be their friends!

Just as in Europe, the idea started to percolate with America's writers and artists. The first decade of the twentieth century was an exhilarating period during which notable authors, poets, and painters began turning away from dogs and gravitating to us in dizzying numbers. Soon enough, many among the most famous of the American literati were speaking out on our behalf. Mark Twain took several felines into his Connecticut home, concluding he preferred them to humans. With his characteristic wit (and perhaps honesty?), he declared that "If a man could be crossed with a cat, it would improve the man but deteriorate the cat." And we found an even greater proponent

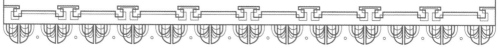

in H. P. Lovecraft, who in felines found the antidote to the sublime horror of which he wrote. "The cat," he declared, "is for the man who appreciates beauty as the one living force in a blind and purposeless universe."

So many subsequent generations of writers and artists would in turn take us to heart that it might be said that the cat is nothing less than America's muse. Don't scoff! Consider instead some of the surprising names on the list. Ernest Hemingway was noted as being an archetypal tough guy, but was so enamored of a six-toed cat given to him by a ship's captain that he established at his home on Key West a colony of her progeny that are to this day known as "Hemingway cats." And William S. Burroughs may have been the quintessential counterculture icon, but there was nothing exotic about his taste in animals: cats and more cats! He believed that the human–feline relationship was by nature psychic, and one that offers for your side a form of enlightenment. "My relationship with my cats has saved me from a deadly, pervasive ignorance," he once confessed.

And among visual artists we can claim as our greatest proponent no less than the greatest name in the history of American art. Andy Warhol owned up to twenty-five cats at a time in his Lexington Avenue apartment, all of them Siamese, and all except for one given the name Sam. So long-standing was Warhol's love for felines that it predates his own fame: his first pub-

lished book, back in 1954 before he was well known, was a series of cat lithographs, a volume now so valuable that copies sell for tens of thousands of dollars. Warhol's cats were even allowed to scamper on his artwork and in some cases their paw prints can still be seen. Oh no! Was that a problem? Not as far as Warhol was concerned; he was always happy to accept a little help from a friend.

America's muse, indeed. By the first decade of the twentieth century, the country had entered the Age of the Cat, the tide having turned so quickly that it was as if a stopper had finally been loosened and centuries of pent-up affection were pouring forth. The Northeast was ground zero for the burgeoning mania, and the *Boston Post* even gave us our own column, "Famous Cats of New England." The first newspaper column ever devoted solely to felines, it gave public recognition to local cats of distinction. Some of the stories were powerful, such as that of Minnie, who won the award twice, since she had been found dead and then returned to life.

Minnie had been severely burned during a house fire, and the firemen who responded to the call threw what they assumed was her lifeless body onto their truck to be disposed of. But the next morning, they heard a faint mewing—she was motionless and charred, but nonetheless still alive. The men of the firehouse tended her, and while it was many days before she could move her limbs, she eventually recovered in full.

And the firemen found their charity rewarded with a loving and faithful friend, eventually growing so enamored of Minnie that they took her as their station mascot. So what? Remember, firemen were supposed to have *dogs* for mascots, usually Dalmatians. But not Ladder Company 24. They chose a cat. How far we had come!

It was during these years of radical change that one of America's greatest felines came to prominence. His name was Jerry Fox, a street cat of mixed breed and muddled heritage from Brooklyn who through his natural charm and winning ways ascended to the post of Borough Cat at the municipal offices, a position I shall point out

was invented in his honor. Jerry's most notable characteristic was the fact that he wore glasses. As in spectacles, yes. How one tests a cat for eyeglasses not even I can guess, but it's a documented fact that in the early years of the century, when it became apparent that his sight was going bad, Jerry was fitted for eyeglasses custom-made for his little face.

Jerry would thereafter sit on the steps of the borough hall with his glasses perched on his nose, and passersby would place newspapers in front of him so he could pretend to be reading. It was even suspected that the glasses—or more properly, a lack thereof—were responsible for his death: he had set off without them one day in 1904 and, wandering about blindly, fell into a hole where a water main had recently been worked on. This misfortune then turned to tragedy when the hole was closed up by maintenance workers who were unaware that poor nearsighted Jerry was inside, his body only discovered a year later when the hole was again opened.

But Jerry's woeful end does not undermine his importance to feline history. I called him a great American cat, but he is not the type who makes us cheer his bravery or marvel over his fortitude. And as charming as we might find his reliance on eyeglasses, that is no measure of greatness either. Rather, his stature amongst us comes from something other, something that becomes clear upon reading his obituary in the *Brooklyn Daily Eagle*. After his body was discovered, the

paper ran a memorial over several columns, confirming Jerry's tragic end, but in the process providing a chronicle of his life.

The account included statements from prominent people testifying to the incredible love that was held for him. Had each of the politicians, businessmen, judges, and lawyers in Borough Hall Square all lost an old college chum, the newspaper explained, there could not have been sorrow more great than that which met the news of Jerry's death. One assemblyman lauded the cat's frank manners and pugilistic qualities, while another made the analogy that Jerry was to Brooklyn no less than the codfish is to Boston (this being a high compliment, should there be any question). His various quirks were noted, chief among them naturally his spectacles, and also how he sat among the bums with the newspaper that never got read spread over his paws. The workers on the nearby rail knew him well, and when trains passed they kept an eye out for a cat with failing vision who might be ambling about, in the same way one might watch over a doddering uncle, discreetly so as not to wound the subject's pride.

What emerged from this memorial was a portrait not of a cat, but of a personality. And therein lies the reason that Jerry stands exalted among us. As far as the public was concerned, all of those who had preceded him were simply felines. But Jerry was something greater: an idea more than a cat, a symbol of Brooklyn itself and a local

legend. The Age of the Cat had produced its first celebrity. Many others have crossed that border since, and the reader is certainly aware that there are several now who have achieved great fame and fortune.

But Jerry was the first to break that ground, and forever holds a place of honor. He was a character so beloved that upon the official announcement of his death an entire municipality took note. He had been missing for a year. Surely they knew he had passed, but when the finality of it was confirmed and his body discovered, the newspaper recounted how all of Brooklyn stopped and wept a tear. A tear for an old friend, who just so happened to be a cat.

The rise of the cat was now an unstoppable force, and even the tragic demise of Jerry could not halt it, as an even greater feline celebrity was soon to soar above the horizon—both figuratively and literally. The fame of a gray tabby known as Kiddo stemmed from a peculiar obsession among the humans of the day with flight, specifically the idea that they might be able to cross the Atlantic Ocean in a dirigible aircraft. History records in no uncertain terms how dubious this notion was (keep in mind that even the most sophisticated dirigible craft ever conceived, the *Hindenburg*, did not successfully make the journey). But human bravery is often born of folly, so in 1910 the *Airship America* set aloft for England in the first attempt to conquer the sea by air, the craft carrying a redoubtable crew of six people. And one cat.

That Kiddo was on board at all was due to the superstition of his crewmates rather than any practical purpose, as he had made absolutely no pretense to knowledge of aeronautics. But among the airship's crew were former sailors, who were rightfully wary of setting off without one of our kind, and because Kiddo had previously served on ships, he was enlisted. He had no desire to go on such a voyage, and ironically this turned out to be the basis for his notoriety. When the craft ascended upward, Kiddo, being reticent of this unsavory venture, became understandably upset. I am sure the reader knows the fuss we cats often make even traveling in a car, so imagine the reaction of a cat trapped aboard a glorified balloon. Poor Kiddo, as a crew member reported, was "mewing, howling and rushing around like a squirrel in a cage."

It just so happened that the *Airship America* was the earliest flying craft to have been equipped with a radio, and history would be made as the craft lurched upward. The captain grabbed the hand piece, raised it to his mouth, and barked out his command, the first ever broadcast: "Roy, come get this goddamn cat!" This groundbreaking radio message turned out to be the highlight of the entire adventure, since the *America* didn't *quite* make it to England. In fact, it didn't even make it to Bermuda before it crashed into the ocean, and Kiddo

and his crewmates were rescued by the United States Coast Guard. For the humans involved there was understandable embarrassment. To be frank, they were humiliated. But their failure certainly could not be reflected on the cat, and to divert attention away from the crew's ignominy, attention was quickly centered around Kiddo.

A feline had flown, after all, that was something, and had even been the subject of the first radio message sent from the air.

All it took was a nickname, and when the newspapers dubbed him the "Flying Cat," a star was born. And while the celebrity of Jerry Fox had been confined to Brooklyn, Kiddo became known throughout the

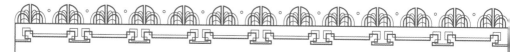

country, and in demand to boot. When Gimbel's department store, soon to become the most prestigious in New York City, opened that same year, Kiddo made a highly publicized appearance in order to draw in customers. Sitting in a golden cage, he was to be found at the very back of the top floor, forcing visitors to walk the length of the store and take in all its displays in order to gaze at this wonder of wonders, the gray tabby who had been scared out of his wits by humans who thought it would be a good idea that he accompany them on an idiotic adventure.

After New York, Kiddo began to tour the country, conquering towns near and far. When he stopped in Pittsburgh he was treated as royalty, being presented with a collar made of gold and fed chicken dinners by hand. Within a few months' time, he had made it as far as Montana, where a local newspaper reported that the fees for his appearance amounted to an astounding two thousand dollars a week. Mind you, this was back when a dollar was actually worth something. But in truth *it was all a lie*! The *Airship America* flew in October of 1910,

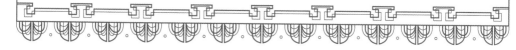

but already in August the aviator John Bevins Moisant had carried his own tabby, Mademoiselle Fifi, tucked into his coat on a flight over the English Channel.

Ah, but the press had fixed on Kiddo, and so to him the laurels were awarded. Perhaps we could consider the trappings of his celebrity to be compensation for the inconvenience of being forced into a blimp, but in the end it was no great favor, and in fact it cost him his life. A year after the debacle of the *America*, Kiddo would again be sent up when a dubious character named Melvin Vaniman decided to attempt another transatlantic crossing, in a dirigible called the *Akron*. For Vaniman I have nothing but harsh words. He knew all too well the risks he was taking since he himself had been a member of the *America*'s crew, and in fact he was the only one among them who did *not* want Kiddo on board. No friend to cats, Vaniman was instead that most sordid of human types: an opportunist. And now that Kiddo had achieved great fame, this man suddenly desired his company.

Vaniman's plan, if it is not already clear, was to capitalize on the cat's celebrity for his own ends. Including Kiddo among the crew of the *Akron* would draw more attention to his venture, so it was arranged that our hero would join in. And, oh, what a big deal Vaniman made of it, extolling reporters with stories about a perfect feline-size bunk that had been constructed just for Kiddo's convenience. But I assume you know where this story is headed? Yes, back down into the ocean. The crew of the *America* had at least survived its folly, but when the *Akron* went down, all lives were lost, including Kiddo's. In recompense for his suffering at the hands of a greedy human, I can only hope that Kiddo received as just reward one final journey aloft, all the way to Heaven—a flight which I shall assume Melvin Vaniman was not allowed to board.

America's second celebrity cat had perished even more tragically than the first, but his martyrdom only stirred public fascination to greater heights. By the time of Kiddo's death we had even made our way into the drawing rooms of the well-to-do. Of course, high society was not interested in the gritty types of felines who had birthed a nation. Instead they wanted cats that demonstrated wealth and status. They desired expensive exotic types, and what could be more exotic than a lion? Yes, it's true. A curious chapter in American feline history occurred at this time, when some people, determined to outdo one another and unsure as to whether they should enjoy our company in large or small sizes, developed a certain fancy for keeping lions.

There seemed to be at least one in every major city, but the most famous of these urban lion keepers was Vilma Lwoff-Parlaghy, a Hungarian princess who had immigrated to New York and moved into the Plaza Hotel in 1908. Fantastically wealthy and notably eccentric, her quirks

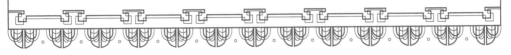

included maintaining a curious menagerie of animals in her suite of rooms, including an owl, a baby alligator, and a bear cub. But if the hotel staff had thought they had seen it all, they hadn't anticipated what was to come: after a visit to the Ringling Brothers Circus, Vilma returned with a lion cub by the name of Goldfleck.

It was love at first sight, at least on the princess's end, and she determined to own him. On inquiring, she was informed in no uncertain terms that the circus animals were not for sale. Ah, but money has a way of speaking its own persuasive language to

you humans, and it was a language which the princess spoke eloquently enough to melt the hearts of the Ringling Brothers, just as Goldfleck has melted hers. When she returned to the Plaza with a lion, the hotel staff was shocked to say the least, and reticent to say a bit more. But the hotel's management was conversant in the same language as the circus, and since the princess was their highest paying tenant they acquiesced to her wish to turn her suite into a lion's den.

Even granting all its luxuries, the Plaza Hotel was no place for a lion to dwell. We have already seen that it was not by some fluke that *domestic* cats evolved; to trap a large feline from nature in a circus is bad enough, but to trap it in a hotel suite is something even worse. The surprise, I think, isn't so much that Goldfleck died young, but that he survived his incarceration for four years. On his passing, the distraught princess insisted that the Plaza allow her to hold a wake in its lobby. A team of professional mourners was hired for the occasion, and they accompanied the lion's funeral cortege twenty-five miles to the pet cemetery in Hartsdale. There, with much pomp and ceremony and the expenditure of ten thousand dollars, Goldfleck was finally, although considerably too late, released back to nature.

The vogue for pet lions was mercifully short, as humans eventually learned that

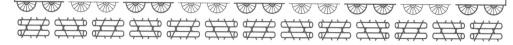

when it comes to felines, bigger isn't always better. After all, you hardly need a lion when we have heard heroics enough to know that even the smallest among us can be mighty! And when it came to American cats, if we were going to be members of the republic, we were going to defend it, and not just in its commissaries. In 1917 the headlines blared out news that may have come as a shock to America's people—but not to its indomitable felines: we were going to war, and right into the front lines!

It turned out the Imperial German Army had been receiving unexpected support in World War I from large and very nasty rats that had for three years been plaguing allied troops in the trenches along the battle-scarred Western Front. To combat them, dogs, poisons, and British-bred cats had been employed, all to no avail—and in fact, the giant vermin often proved a match for the latter in a fair fight! But the genteel English felines could stand down after the United States entered the war, because crack soldiers were on the way: dock cats from the wharves of New York, Philadelphia, and Baltimore, reputed to be the biggest and toughest rat hunters in the world. And answering the calls of their allies, they were deploying by December 1917, whereas our human soldiers didn't arrive in the trenches until early 1918, meaning that it was us cats who gave the kaiser his first taste of American firepower.

Nor did we stand on the sidelines dur-ing the Second World War. In 1941, a black cat shipped out from Pennsylvania on a daring mission to undermine Nazi Germany. Named Captain Midnight, he was sent to Britain by the Wilkes-Barre Chamber of Commerce to be flown across Europe in an RAF bomber until he eventually crossed the path of Adolf Hitler, and thereby cursed him. Captain Midnight was transported in a red, white, and blue crate that noted him as a "special envoy," and his departure was big news, the story carried by newspapers around the country.

That no follow-up articles were ever posted inevitably gave fodder to naysayers who insisted that the British took the whole plan in jest and nixed the idea. But such skeptics clearly know nothing of military protocol. This was a mission of the highest strategic value, so of course there was no further documentation: to ensure the success of the operation, Captain Midnight's whereabouts would have to remain top secret. So, you ask, how can we know if he succeeded? In response, let me ask you, how did things turn out for Mr. Hitler? And did the Germans not capitulate before the Japanese? Well then, if the answers to those questions suit you, perhaps you should thank a cat.

Others of us served less covertly with both the US Army and Marine Corps, and naturally with the navy, where we continued in our traditional roles on ships. History's most decorated military feline—with even more commendations than Simon!—was

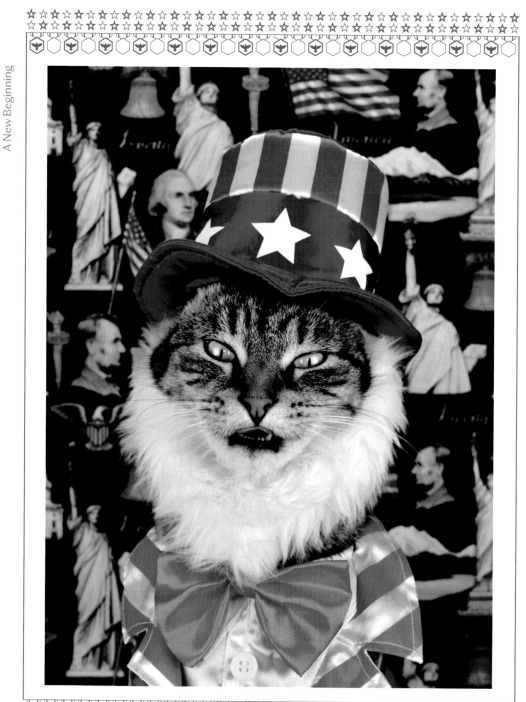

an American cat from the Second World War, a female tabby named Pooli who won three service ribbons and four battle stars. A navy cat through and through, she had been born at Pearl Harbor, Hawaii, and eventually acquired the post of ship's cat on the USS *Fremont*, seeing action in some of the fiercest battles in naval history, including Iwo Jima, the Philippines, and the Marianas. And since Pooli's decorations were not earned through any special ability, but rather a habit universal to all cats, she offers proof that even the meekest among us are capable of heroism should the need arise.

It so happened that her favorite pastime was curling up in a ball and dozing off, and when the fighting was at full pitch — the shells exploding and bombs bursting — she would head down to the ship's mail room, find herself a nice comfy mail sack, and take a nap. Now wait just a moment, before you smirk and conclude that this makes her awards a joke, understand things from the perspective of her crewmates. They said that when things were at their worst, and they weren't sure if they would make it through, they would send someone down to check on Pooli. If she was still soundly asleep, well, they knew everything would be all right.

After all, they reasoned, if the fighting wasn't bad enough to wake the ship's cat, it really wasn't that bad, was it? So you see, Pooli contributed the best way she could, earning those medals by boosting the morale of her crewmates. She knew full well that the example of a cat courageously sleeping could act as a bulwark against the fears of men, and don't you dare think that when the going got rough she took the easy way out. Have you ever tried to sleep while cannons are firing? It takes considerable determination to not be woken up by such a ruckus!

When such stories filtered back home, the cat was out of the bag when it came to our valor, and by the 1950s the prestige of American felines was further augmented by a national prize. The Puss'n Boots Award, a big, beautiful, bronze medal intended to recognize our outstanding contributions on behalf of society, was given out by a California fishery that canned a brand of cat food also called Puss'n Boots. Its first recipient was Clementine Jones, a black cat whose valiant trek in the fall of 1950 made national headlines and proved the truth of feline loyalty. Her human family, Mr. and Mrs. Robert Lundmark, had moved from Dunkirk, New York, to Aurora, Colorado, in 1949, when Mr. Lundmark accepted a position as a sales associate at a department store in Denver. But because Clementine was pregnant, they decided it was best to leave her behind with relations.

I can't speak ill of that decision. It was humane to not force a pregnant cat to travel across the country, but on Clementine's end it was resolved that the separation should be only temporary. So it was that a year later, with her kittens now nurtured and self-sufficient, she disappeared. When she was not found after a reasonable period of weeks, the assumption back in Dunkirk was that some ill circumstance had befallen her. Perhaps she had been hit by a car, it was guessed. But that was not the case: Clementine couldn't be found because she was headed to Colorado.

Some of you will blanch at the idea of a cat headed out over countless miles of open roads and unknown dangers. Ah, but have we not already seen that it's the American way? We won the country's heart through resolute will, braving the frontier to prove ourselves in the eyes of humans. Clementine Jones was nothing other than an All-American cat who had inherited that very same pioneering spirit. And some four months after her disappearance she turned up. On the Lundmarks' doorstep, a home she had never seen, in a city and state in which she had never in her life been, and with nothing but her wits to guide her. Her journey had taken her nearly 1,600 miles over roads unknown and across the Rocky Mountains, but she had found her human family.

By all means does such a cat merit a medal! But people are loath to give nonhumans the credit they are due. "Come now, it can't be her," the doubters complained. "It must be simply another cat that looks like her which has shown up on the property." But Clementine herself silenced them, for the proof was in her paws. She possessed a physical peculiarity that made her unmistakable: a single foot with *seven* toes. And the toes told the tale: all seven of them there, and the pads were worn to the bone underneath, leaving no doubt whatsoever that it was Clementine herself who had made the epic journey.

The medal presented to Clementine was the first of scores given out around the country over the next ten years, after which the program was sadly discontinued when the Puss'n Boots brand was sold off to a big corporation that failed to see the wisdom in giving awards to cats. Ah, but during that decade the public was regaled with stories that were often heroic and always heartwarming. Periodically they were humorous too, such as the drama that ensued when a cat hiding in a Connecticut church started to howl so loudly one Sunday when the choir sang that the congregation feared the Devil was in their midst (an award well earned, I'd say!). But all told, the medals and the publicity surrounding them further enhanced our standing by making common knowledge the many wonderful things of which we are capable. And I don't mean solely in the service of humans, but for other species as well.

Consider this story from Louisiana. When an elderly plantation dog went blind in 1953, there suddenly appeared on the property an angel of mercy in the guise of a stray cat who came to be known as Kitty Billy. He somehow sensed the dog's plight and began waiting outside the house. When

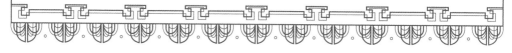

214

the blind dog would emerge, Billy would walk with it and act as its eyes, helping it along safely, crossing streets, and making sure it eventually found its way home. A seeing eye cat!—how unexpectedly the roles were reversed. Hardly anyone could not be touched by such a story, and it earned Billy a much deserved medal. But even more remarkable I think is this: after the dog passed away, the cat left the property and never returned. Billy had halted his own wanderings in order to care for an ailing creature, but he wished no home from man and expected no thanks. And his mission now completed, he left the plantation and his medal behind to continue with his own life's journey.

Another uplifting story came from Joplin, Missouri, when in 1952 a cat adopted a litter of baby opossums. Only a few days old, they were discovered by a Humane Society worker in the pouch of their mother, who had been hit by a car. With the situation critical, the five surviving opossums were brought to a local cat who had recently nursed her own litter of kittens, in the hopes that she would care for them. She not only obliged and began feeding the newborns, she took the opossums in and raised them as her own. And as a symbol of the harmony that can exist within the natural world, Mother Sue, as she was nicknamed, likewise became a Puss'n Boots medal recipient.

Given our increasing public profile, it should come as no surprise that we eventually attained the highest level of American status: stardom on the silver screen. Hollywood had of course traditionally belonged to the dogs, and many were the casting directors who claimed that felines were too independent to be trained as actors. But a black kitten named Pepper had already proven how wrong that was in 1912. She had been born under the soundstage of Mack Sennett Studios in Los Angeles, and one day squirming her way up between the floorboards the kitten found herself in the middle of a shoot. Put the light on her, a crew hand joked. And when she didn't flinch they decided to roll film. The result? Pepper was a natural, frolicking contently in front of the camera like it were a mere window onto a sunny day, and within a year she had appeared on screen with the biggest names in the industry, Charlie Chaplin, Fatty Arbuckle, and the Keystone Cops among them.

Still, the doubts persisted. Cats like Pepper were few and far between, the bigwigs argued—and even then, they had never given her a starring role in a full-length feature, insisting that felines were only fit for minor parts. Ah, to be underestimated once again. "How d'ya get a break in this town?" Hollywood's cats were left to ask, and then answered the question themselves. With talent, that's how, as some of the greatest feline actors in film history came along during the 1950s and '60s to finally prove the pundits wrong. And in true American fashion, they did not carry the pedigree of expensive breeders. In fact, the first cat to be cast in a

Presented to
BABA
Best Feline
A-cat-emy Award
2018

starring role in a feature film, and to this day history's most prolific feline actor, was an orange tabby discovered . . . under a bush.

A big, fierce tomcat, he was a stray who had camped out in the yard of a woman named Agnes Murray in the Los Angeles suburb of Sherman Oaks. To Mrs. Murray's chagrin, he showed no signs of leaving, and she certainly couldn't have guessed that he was destined to become the Marlon Brando of cats. This was in 1950, and it so happened that Paramount Studios was casting a film called *Rhubarb*, the quirky story of a street cat who inherits a major league baseball team when its eccentric owner dies. The studio had a problem, however. They couldn't fill the starring role! Trainers kept bringing them *nice* cats. But Paramount wanted a tough customer as their leading man, a rough-hewn feline who possessed the wisdom that came with street life. In desperation they placed a fateful casting call. Wanted for starring role in film: a mean, scar-faced cat.

Mrs. Murray looked at the orange brute under the bush in her yard. He sure fit the bill, she reckoned, and wrestling him into a box (no easy feat, to be sure), she drove down to Hollywood. And the reaction at the Paramount lot? "That's our cat!" It turned out that Orangey, as they decided to name him, could act, and he was awarded the largest film contract ever given a feline. And he could do a lot of other things in addition: a street cat through and through, he could

scratch and bite like none anyone had ever seen, and his run-ins with the cast and crew were legendary. But the starring role in *Rhubarb* earned Orangey a PATSY Award in 1952, given out at the time as the animal equivalent of an Oscar. From street cat to award-winning actor? Impressive indeed, and even more so in being the first cat to ever be so honored.

His career spanned the next fifteen years, with so many appearances that his trainer said he had lost count at around two hundred. As Hollywood's go-to cat, they included television spots in *Mission Impossible* and *Bewitched*, and a plethora of films such as *The Diary of Anne Frank* and *Village of the Giants*. But the most memorable of all? I'll guess you've heard of a film called *Breakfast at Tiffany's*? Yup, that's him! That orange tabby starring alongside Audrey Hepburn is none other than the big, mean tomcat found under a bush in Sherman Oaks. And for that role, a decade after becoming the first cat to win a PATSY Award, Orangey became the only cat to ever win a second. Quite a feat. And quite a cat! To the end, he still bit and scratched his costars, hissed at studio executives, and caused productions to be shut down when he would run off and hide. In other words . . . he was a consummate Hollywood professional!

Orangey also opened the door for other talented feline actors, including a Siamese named, well, Cy A. Meese, who would win his own PATSY Award in 1959, starring alongside Jimmy Stewart and Kim Novak in *Bell, Book and Candle*. And both Orangey and Cy would be outdone by a new feline box office champ in 1965. In another classic American story of fleas to finery, a seal point Siamese named Syn had been handed over to an animal shelter in Ontario, California, by a mean owner who simply didn't want him anymore. Abandoned to a dingy cage, he languished in his confinement, increasingly sad and malnourished, until he was noticed by an animal trainer who recognized in the unwanted cat something special. Shown love, Syn revealed himself as one smart kitty, quickly mastering several tricks. He was taken to an audition at Disney and given a minor role in *The Incredible Journey*, which so impressed the studio's executives that they in turn offered him the most plum role in feline cinema history: the lead in *That Darn Cat!*

Playing a secret agent, this former shelter feline turned out to be a box office champ when the film debuted at number one. Of competition it had a bit—there happened to be a film called *The Sound of Music* out at the time—but no matter, it was a cat that moviegoers wanted to see. And *That Darn Cat!* continued to pack theaters, bringing in over twenty-eight million dollars and finishing the year as Hollywood's fifth-leading draw. Of Syn's talents, the *New York Times* declared that "Clark Gable at the peak of his career never played a tomcat more winningly." High praise to be sure, and he was just as big a hit off screen, his photos

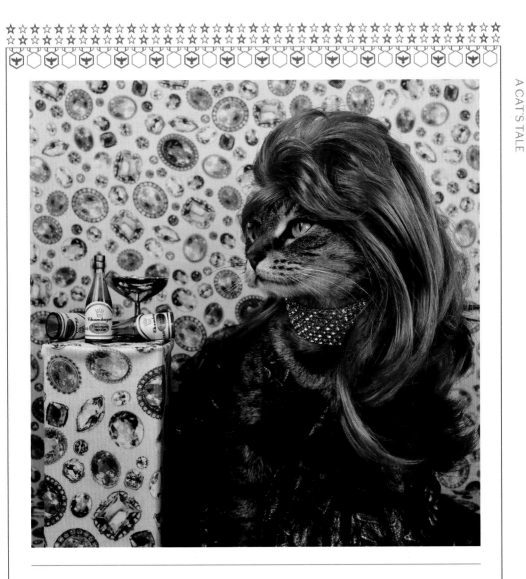

plastered in newspapers posing with star-lets. Oh, and in case you're curious, would you like to know what that mean owner who had abandoned Syn thought about his for-mer cat's meteoric rise to stardom? Well, he . . . oh . . . actually I don't know, since no one bothered to ask, and the crotchety old

man withered into obscurity while Syn lived it up in the bright lights of Hollywood.

I told you at the outset that the cats of my country are of a special type, and do not so many amazing stories of so many amazing felines bear witness? But while all of those I have mentioned did important

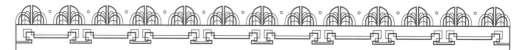

things to advance our station in the eyes of the public, none represent the quintessence of what it means to be an American cat. That honor, in my opinion, belongs to a humble Los Angeles school cat named Room 8. I must confess that I am also a Los Angeles cat, so I might be accused of favoritism. And I will certainly admit there have been other fine cats associated with schools, libraries, and places of learning. Almost every state can claim at least one, and some have garnered no small fame!

Consider the case of a kitten cruelly abandoned in a library's book drop in Spencer, Iowa, in the middle of winter in 1988, and found the next day badly frostbitten. Who could have imagined on the cold, hard night that he was callously discarded that he would grow up to be the world's most renowned feline bibliophile? But nursed back to health by the staff and christened Dewey Readmore Books, he assumed the post of library cat, and remained cheerfully on duty for the next eighteen years. In the process, the orange tabby became the town's best-known resident, and his story of survival (and erudition!) garnered him friends from around the world.

But even among such stories, Room 8 stands out as special still. Of his early life and parentage nothing whatsoever is known, and it was he who found the school and not vice versa. He was perhaps five or six years old when he first appeared at Elysian Heights Elementary in the Echo Park neighborhood of Los Angeles in the fall of 1952, as students returned from recess one fine day to find that a homeless tomcat, a gray tabby, had snuck into their classroom and pillaged their lunches. An unfortunate introduction no doubt. But if there is a point I have made about the personality typical of American cats, it is that we know how to survive—a hungry stray will do as it must, and unattended lunches are fair game to be sure.

The students were understandably upset, and curses were leveled at the interloper. Standard procedure at such a juncture would be to turn tail and run, but the gray tabby instead stayed put and absorbed the catcalls. The bumps and bruises of street life are a great teacher, but the stray cat now saw in the faces of those children a lesson he had yet to learn. No, not about human angst; believe me when I tell you a street cat knows all about that. But the twisted expressions of anger could not mask what the children carried within: the simplicity and purity of affection. It was this lesson the cat now craved even more than sandwiches, and he felt compelled to stand his ground.

His big bright eyes grew brighter still, and as he stared up at the faces of the students their wrath passed like a sudden wave that is replaced by the calmest of waters. Children see with eyes unclouded, and the rough condition of the gray tomcat could not hide from them the purity of his own heart. They asked their teacher if he could stay, and she agreed, as even her more

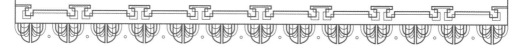

weathered eyes could not now be blind to a truth so plain. Of course, there is no hiding secrets among children and word soon enough got out that one of the classrooms had a cat. He was said to be smart and loving and would jump atop your desk and play. The rest of the students determined to meet him, and the bond that had formed over spoiled lunches suddenly spread to the entire school.

It was decided that a name would be needed for this new friend, and since he had made his first appearance in Room 8, that seemed like as good a name as any. The original agreement between the teacher and her students was that the cat could stay "temporarily," but it turned out that school and cat could never quite be parted, and "temporarily" wound up being sixteen years, the rest of the Room 8's worldly life. Sixteen years spent in elementary school? The cat was no less than the greatest flunky in the history of the Los Angeles Unified School District, never managing to matriculate and returning every fall to start again with the same coursework. And so as to not hide the truth I will admit that his performance on exams was dismal and his homework never turned in. Yet somehow with this student, no one seemed to mind.

Despite being accepted by the school, Room 8 had started as a stray and would maintain his independence throughout his life, never wishing permanent residence in a human home. Your kind is often puzzled by this aspect of his story, as if a cat's only desire should be to dwell among you, but for this, Room 8 was too headstrong. His bond was with the children as a whole, and deprived of them he did not have any great need for your company. When school let out for the day he might take his rest in the bushes around the school, or head into the hills of the surrounding neighborhood, making his own place in the nooks and crannies and shady hideaways that only we cats know. Yet he would be back again in the morning when class was in session.

And during the summers when the school was closed? He might wander away and leave people in doubt as to whether this curious creature would ever make his way back. Ah, but he did, for each of those sixteen years! Over time, his return became a local rite of passage, and when the school year started, newspaper reporters would be on hand in anticipation of his appearance. And Room 8 never disappointed them! Because return he must: despite his independence, he knew his place was at the school. Having chosen to share his life with the children there, the bond that they forged had come to define the essence of his nature.

I shall tell you frankly that you would not find Room 8 handsome at first glance, he being a rough-and-tumble street cat. If I sound harsh in so saying, I mean no insult, because we do not judge by your standards of feline beauty—nor do children, and Room 8 was a dapper lad indeed to the

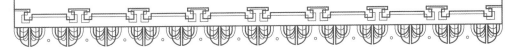

students of Elysian Heights Elementary. They made him their poster child, his image placed on the library's bookplates and painted along the wall as a large mural. His paw prints were even placed in concrete in front of the school, as if he were a Hollywood film star. And as Room 8's story spread, it became known outside of Los Angeles, and magazines and newspapers told the country about how a cat and a school had adopted one other. Fan mail soon began to arrive, up to one hundred letters a day, with the students working diligently in the role of secretary, as he seemed peculiarly disinterested in his own correspondence.

These are all privileges normally reserved for celebrity, but in truth Room 8 had attained such a status, and in the city of stars no less! The local newspapers printed notices of his doings, and a book was written about him, a biography penned by the school's principal and one of the teachers. Television crews would periodically stop by the school and follow him about the campus with a camera—and a microphone at the ready, should he deign to offer a meow for the audience at home. A charitable foundation was even opened in his name, to provide care for other homeless cats.

Guided by a pure heart, Room 8 had touched the lives of those he met and transformed the world around him and, through mechanisms that could never have been predicted, went from being a pillager of lunches to the soul of a community. But

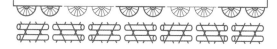

SHIPS' CATS i

THE MYSTERIOUS CA

THE GREAT CAT MA

PLANE

HOWEY THE CAT

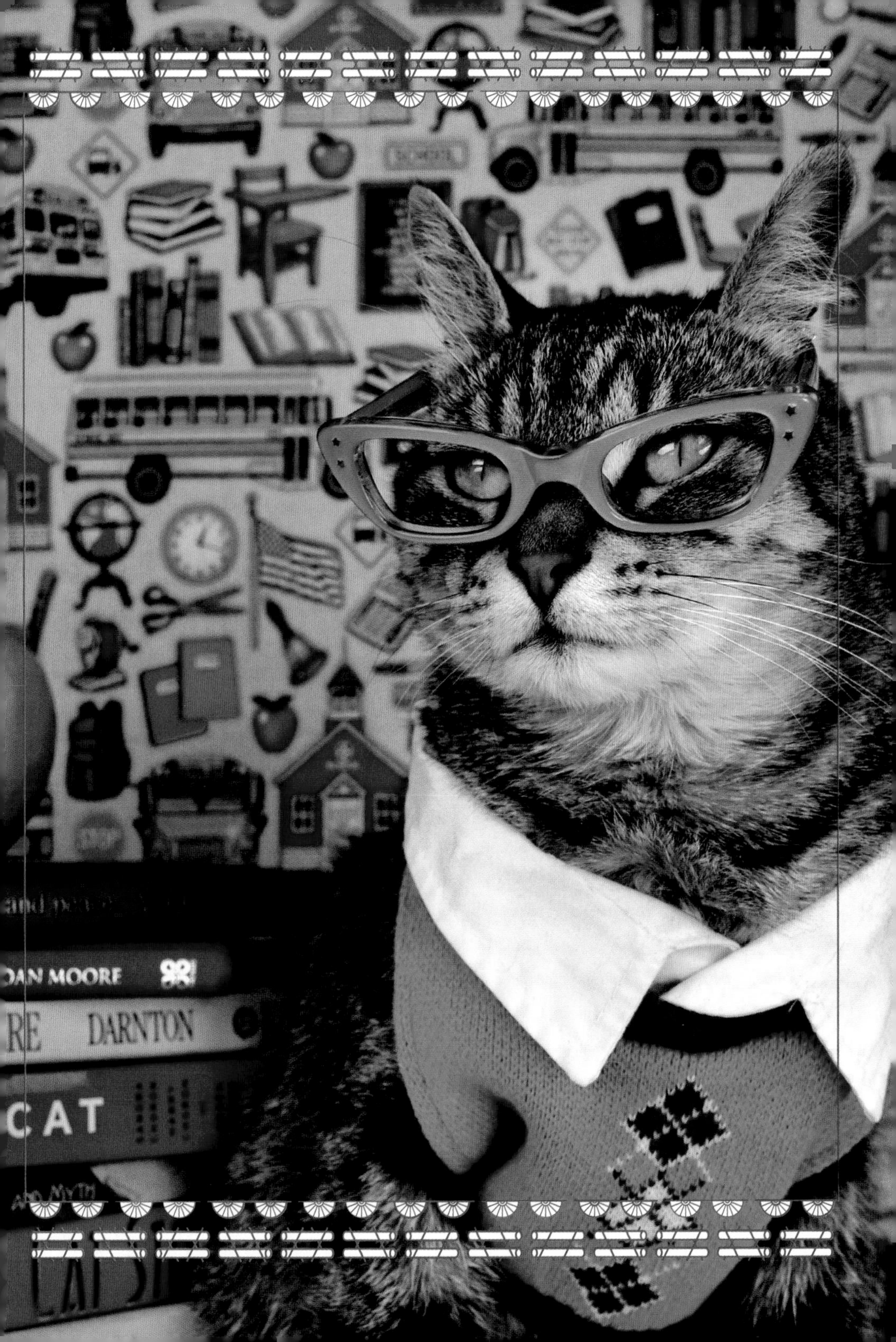
DARNTON
CAT

time shows no sympathy even to good cats, and the magic of those years could not postpone the final bell. It rang in 1968, as Room 8 passed away at a venerable age, perhaps twenty-one or twenty-two years, although still having not divulged the secrets of his youth no one could be sure which. For the first time in sixteen years classes would commence *without a cat*. Can you imagine?

The school was of course grief-stricken, but in his wake Room 8's story became more remarkable still. A beloved cat was no more, but his memory would not perish. The students first put out an issue of their own small newspaper, entirely devoted to their longtime friend. And his painted portrait was soon enough placed outside the door of classroom number eight, with a decree that it should always hang with honor in that place as a tribute to the lessons that he had taught the students about love and camaraderie.

An even greater tribute was in store on the sidewalks around the school! New concrete was poured so that students could inscribe memorials in his honor. Present to this very day, they are traced out as one walks by, love letters etched into the walkway beneath one's feet. Some are the work of children and simple enough. "We miss you, Room 8, oh, how we miss you," wrote one boy, while a girl added nearby, "He came in our room and sat on my table. I loved him." Others meanwhile are more poetic, and further along are the words, "They say Room 8

has nine lives, don't you believe it never. In the hearts of happy children, this cat will live . . . forever!" Adults weighed in as well, and newspaper reporters were quoted in addition, with the tributes forming a path winding its way through sixteen years of devotion. And while they are far too numerous to list in full, I will offer a final one, as I think it encapsulates our friend's legacy in the simplest way possible: "He left his love, and we are blessed."

It was also determined that it was time at long last for Room 8 to have a permanent home. This was of course contrary to his nature, having arrived as a stray and prizing his independence all through his life. Still, I don't think he would have minded making an exception in this case. But providing him a final place of rest all his own would be an expensive task for an elementary school; they hardly had the excess funds for a cat's grave! A fundraiser was held in the hopes that Room 8 might be provided a plot with a headstone at the Los Angeles Pet Memorial Park. So many people had offered words in his honor, would some perhaps remember him with their wallets?

Would they ever! So much money in excess of what was needed was raised that Room 8 has one of the largest headstones in the entire cemetery. Now understand that some of the world's most famous animals are buried nearby, and an entire roster of Hollywood legends has laid their pets in these hallowed grounds: Valentino's dog. Animals owned by Humphrey Bogart

and Lauren Bacall, or Abbott and Costello. Famous horses from the heyday of the Westerns. And many others, pampered companions of the rich and famous. But rising above all of these is a monument to humble a stray cat. People had indeed remembered Room 8.

And to this day they still do. Let me tell you of the greatest tribute of all: Room 8's grave remains the most visited in the cemetery. We have discoursed on cats who have accomplished great things. Some have starred in films, others won medals, and still more have journeyed for thousands of miles. Room 8 never did any of these things—yet in spite of this, and even after half a century, people still visit. Many are retirement age now, come to lay down a flower or offer a prayer, or simply say hello to the one who touched their hearts so long ago. A stray cat who asked for only one thing from the human world: the chance to be a friend. And given that chance, he asked and accepted nothing more.

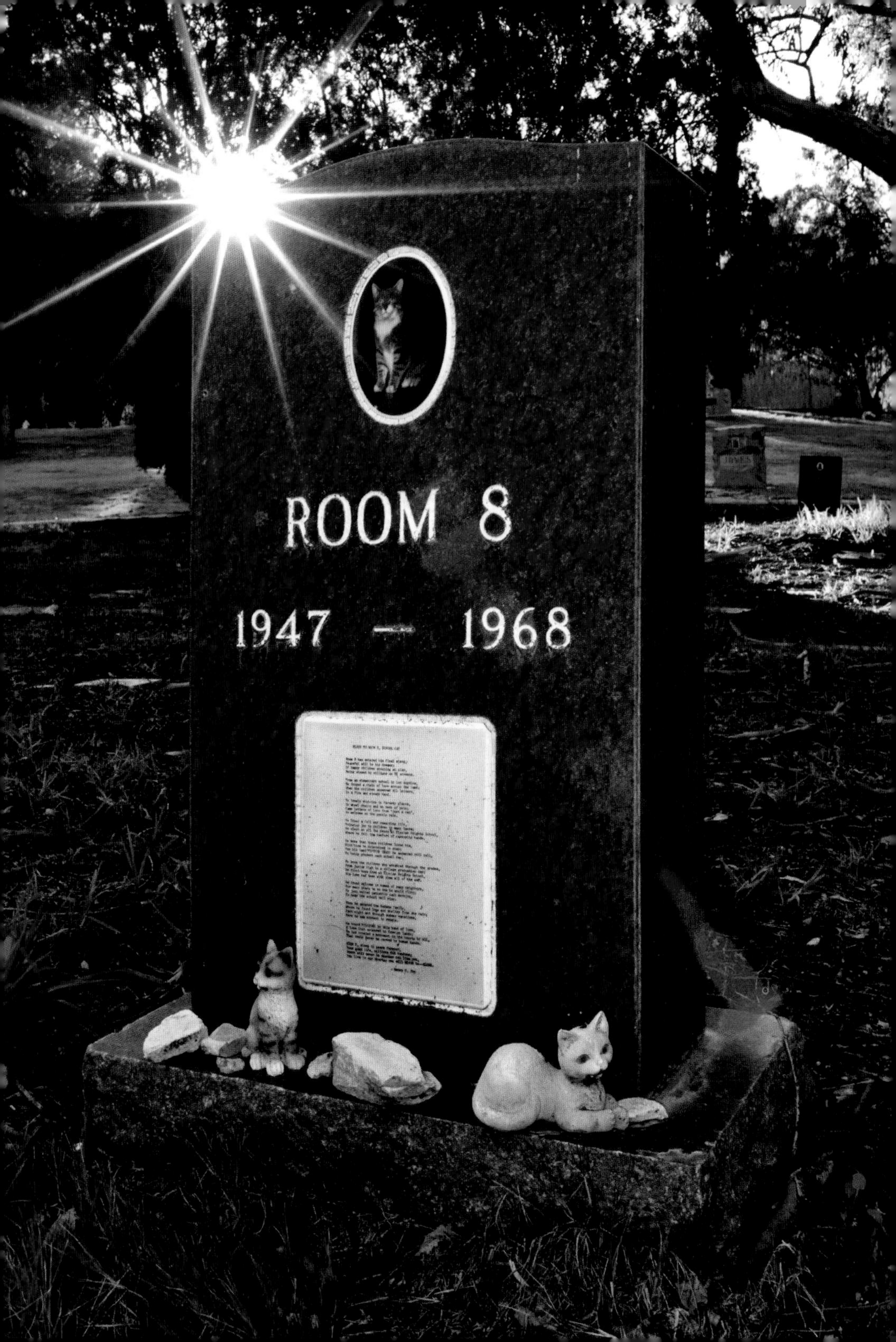
ROOM 8
1947 — 1968

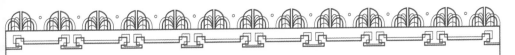

I called Room 8 the quintessence of the American cat, and indeed he provides for me the most perfect portrait of our kind. Consider his story. No pampered pure-bred, he started as an outcast and was educated on the rough city streets. Yet life's hard knocks were never hard enough to knock him off stride, and like the noteworthy cats who had founded the Feline States of America he earned his place in human society. He was as independent as a cat can be, but at the same time open enough to give of himself to the humans he had chosen. And while that may have at first seemed a pittance, in the end this simple gift enriched the lives of countless people, so much so that he could never be forgotten.

Ah, but such is the magic of cats, if you will permit me the hubris of saying. The Ancients saw it and built temples in our honor and raised us to divinity, and I hope the journey we have taken together has helped you see it anew. Alas, humans overdo things, so I'll let you in on a final secret before we part: we never needed the temples or the gods or any of the other claptrap! All we have ever wanted, from the very first days until now, was just a few gentle pets, some kind words, and a bit of dinner. It's always been so much simpler than humankind has realized.

With that, I judge that I have been too long at these words. But Baba, you're not leaving us now? Ah, we have traveled a very long way together, friends, but all journeys must end, and I must not dally further. Duty calls, as there are windows for me to sit in, trees to climb, and mice to catch (yes, even after all these centuries, it really never stops with them!). I therefore beg your leave, but thank you for accompanying me thus far. It is my hope that in the course of our tale you have found what you came for; I hope even that you may have found something more.

And don't fret our parting, because the story need not end. Somewhere out in this wide world there is still history to be made, and rather than living it through the telling, it is now your turn to live it through the making, with the cat that shares your life. After all, as I have told you from the start, history is never created alone, and I wish the best to you both on whatever journey you now take. So from myself, Simon, Trim, Black Jack, Room 8, and all of the others—and yes, even *Felis*—I bid you *bon voyage*!

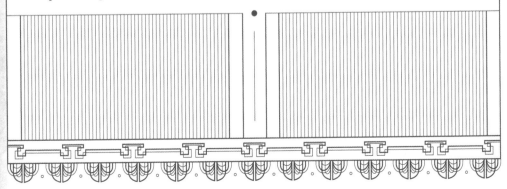

By the late nineteenth century, America had embraced us, and this headstone in the cemetery of the Animal Rescue League of Boston expressed thanks to a cat that had comforted a woman who was left widowed after her husband, an army captain, died in an explosion in 1899.

Travels 4 Months, N. Y. to Denver

Cat Finds Family By 1600-Mi. Hike

Meet Clementine Jones, traveler. She didn't actually carry the suitcase on her 1600-mile trek to Denver from Dunkirk, N. Y.
—*Rocky Mountain News Photo by Dick Davis.*

By ROBERT L. PERKIN
Rocky Mountain News Writer

Clementine Jones was home again yesterday, wiser and a bit wilder after seeing 1600 miles of America on a four-month solo trip.

Clementine is a big black cat.

She was, and is again, the pet of Mr. and Mrs. Robert Lundmark, 1416 Navajo st.

They left Clementine in Dunkirk, N. Y., a year and a half ago when they moved to Denver, Mrs. Lundmark said. Four months ago, Clementine disappeared from the Dunkirk home of a sister-in-law.

Thursday night, the Lundmarks heard a meowing on their doorstep in the Lincoln Park Homes. Mr. Lundmark went to the door.

IT WAS CLEMENTINE, jet black except for the two distinctive white spots on her tummy, meowing to be taken in.

The Lundmarks will guess with anybody on how Clementine got from Dunkirk to Denver and what animal radar guided her padding steps over the 1600 miles between the two cities.

"We were just thunderstruck," Mrs. Lundmark said. "We just couldn't believe it.

"Then I talked with a couple of cat experts, and they told me there have been other cases where a cat followed a family a long way across the country."

Mrs. Lundmark insisted there is no possibility of mistaken identity. She said Clementine's unique white belly markings distinguish her from all other cats, and the wanderer now has settled down completely on Navajo st., obviously satisfied her long quest is over.

"SHE LOOKED pretty rough when we opened the door for her Thursday night," Mrs. Lundmark said, "and she's still awfully wild and jumpy.

"But we've brushed her up, and she's had all the milk and fish she could eat, so she doesn't seem much worse for wear. She slept almost all the time for the first three or four days, but her pads don't seem to show much damage."

Clementine abandoned three kittens about four months old when she took off from Dunkirk last May, Mrs. Lundmark said.

"My sister-in-law wrote that Clementine had disappeared," she said, "and we thought, of course, that we would never see her again. So I had written to have Bob's sister save us one of the kittens."

The Lundmarks moved to Denver from Dunkirk following his graduation from college. Mr. Lundmark is employed here as a salesman for Montgomery Ward & Co.

CAT CAME BACK 337 MILES.

Mountains and Deserts Traversed by "Tom" of Salt Lake.

Special to The New York Times.

SALT LAKE, April 10.—Traveling a distance of 337 miles, climbing mountains, and crossing stretches of the desert, a cat came back. This feline adventurer is red and is known by the name of Tom. He belonged to John M. West of Salt Lake.

Three weeks ago Tom stole a flounder. West put him into a bag and concealed him under a seat in a day coach on the San Pedro, Los Angeles and Salt Lake Railroad. The cat was discovered and turned loose at Caliente, Nevada. To-day, weak and emaciated, he appeared at the West house and begged for food. He got it.

Denver Cat's Lengthy Walk Earns Award

Clementine Jones, a Denver cat, Thursday owned the Puss'n Boots bronze medal in recognition of her four-month, 1,600-mile trek last summer from Dunkirk, N. Y., to Denver.

Clementine's owners, Mr. and Mrs. Robert Lundmark of 232 Iola street, Aurora, said they still receive letters from cynics who doubt the cat really walked 1,600 miles to join the Lundmark family.

But Mrs. Lundmark said there is no doubt of the cat's identity.

"Jonesy here has seven toes on one paw and a burnt place on her shoulder," she said.

The Puss'n Boots bronze medal, highest award in catdom, is bestowed upon worthy felines by the Coast Fishing company.

Proof cats aren't lazy: clippings covering the story of Tom, whose march to Salt Lake City in April 1904 was written up by papers as far east as the *New York Times*, and from the *Rocky Mountain News*, which covered the amazing journey of Clementine Jones in September 1950.

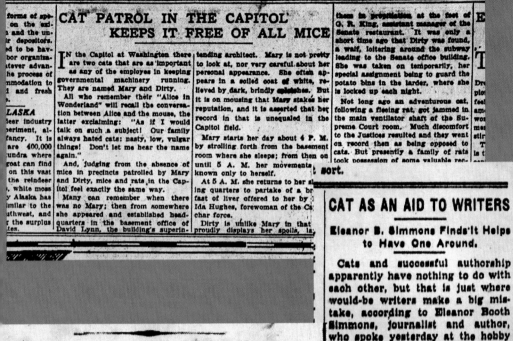

THE NEW YORK TIMES, SUNDAY, MARCH 13, 1927.

CAT PATROL IN THE CAPITOL KEEPS IT FREE OF ALL MICE

IN the Capitol at Washington there are two cats that are as important as any of the employes in keeping governmental machinery running. They are named Mary and Dirty.

All who remember their "Alice in Wonderland" will recall the conversation between Alice and the mouse, the latter exclaiming: "As if I would talk on such a subject! Our family always hated cats: nasty, low, vulgar things! Don't let me hear the name again."

And, judging from the absence of mice in precincts patrolled by Mary and Dirty, mice and rats in the Capitol feel exactly the same way.

Many can remember when there was no Mary; then from somewhere she appeared and established headquarters in the basement office of David Lynn, the building's superin-

tending architect. Mary is not pretty to look at, nor very careful about her personal appearance. She often appears in a soiled coat of white, relieved by dark, brindly splotches. But it is on mousing that Mary stakes her reputation, and it is asserted that her record in that is unequaled in the Capitol field.

Mary starts her day about 4 P. M. by strolling forth from the basement room where she sleeps; from then on until 5 A. M. her movements are known only to herself.

At 5 A. M. she returns to her sleeping quarters to partake of a breakfast of liver offered to her by Ida Hughes, forewoman of the charforce.

Dirty is unlike Mary in that she proudly displays her spoils, la-

them in prostration at the feet of G. R. King, assistant manager of the Senate restaurant. It was only a short time ago that Dirty was found, a waif, loitering around the subway leading to the Senate office building. She was taken on temporarily, her special assignment being to guard the potato bins in the larder, where she is locked up each night.

Not long ago an adventurous cat, following a fleeing rat, got jammed in the main ventilator shaft of the Supreme Court room. Much discomfort to the Justices resulted and they went on record then as being opposed to cats. But presently a family of rats took possession of some valuable rec-

WHERE CATS ARE IN DEMAND.

DUBUQUE, Iowa, April 19.—A new and decidedly novel industry has sprung up in this city. A man is here buying cats, for which he pays from 50 cents to $1 each, according to age and size. He ships them to Dakota, where he sells them for $3 each. They are in great demand there, where they are wanted to destroy the mice which swarm by thousands around the corn and wheat bins, doing great damage. Cats are very scarce in Dakota. Thus far two carloads of cats have been shipped from this city and another load is being secured.

CAT AS AN AID TO WRITERS

Eleanor B. Simmons Finds It Helps to Have One Around.

Cats and successful authorship apparently have nothing to do with each other, but that is just where would-be writers make a big mistake, according to Eleanor Booth Simmons, journalist and author, who spoke yesterday at the hobby luncheon given by the Book-Sharing Week Committee at the Hotel Biltmore.

Undesirable as cats might be to some people, owning one of the quiet and philosophical animals is the first requisite toward turning out a good book, Miss Simmons declared.

Mrs. Sherman Post Haight, who presided, and Warden Lewis E. Lawes are co-chairmen of the committee's campaign to obtain 1,000,000 books for distribution to hospitals, prisons and charitable institutions. Central headquarters of Book-Sharing Week, which runs from April 18 to 25, are in the Hotel Biltmore.

In demand! From the frontier to the nation's capital to the salons of the literati, by the start of the twentieth century everyone wanted us around. And not just in our traditional roles as mousers: American writers, like their European counterparts, had taken us as their muse.

A FAMOUS UNITED STATES ARMY CAT

THE COLONEL.

Cat Veteran of War Has 15th Birthday

A World War II veteran cat today celebrates her 15th birthday.

And she can still get into her old uniform with its three service ribbons and four battle stars.

The cat, Pooli, short for Princess Papule, was born July 4, 1944, in the Navy yard at Pearl Harbor, her present owner, Benjamin H. Kirk, of 757 W. 106th St., said.

'Taken Aboard Ship'

Kirk explained that Pooli was taken aboard the attack transport USS Fremont that day by his nephew, James L. Lynch, of 2725 Wynwood Lane, now a specialist in administrative services for the Board of Education.

Pooli saw action at the Marianas, the Palau group, the Philippines and Iwo Jima. And she became a shellback when the ship crossed the equator.

Kirk revealed that when battle stations rang Pooli would head for the mail room and curl up in a mail sack.

Almost a Casualty

But she nearly became a wartime casualty when some sailors aboard the home-bound ship thought of throwing her overboard after fearing quarantine in San Francisco because of her. A 'round-the-clock guard was given Pooli for three days and she docked with the ship and without incident, Kirk said.

Now, Pooli is deaf. She has only her front teeth, and she sleeps most of the day.

"But when she was younger she never lost a battle to any dog or cat in the neighborhood," Kirk said.

UNCLE SAM'S CATS

...of the watchdogs of the treas-
...are anxious to cut down gov-
...xpenses so that the government
...more money to spend have
...nd and found that there is quite
...em included in the annual ap-
... bills for cats. The item is not
...that for pensions or warships
...but it is a muckrakable prop-

...ny allows $18.25 a year each for
...These cats are provided for
...ssary storehouses, etc., and they
...government much more than
...They catch lots of mice, but
...m has found that no cat will
...est on mice alone; she must
...tle butcher's meat and milk now
...to vary her diet.

...r cats' meat for the government
...regularly let each year, but the
...ive cents a pound; porterhouse
...never supplied to the official
...e postoffice department spends
...sum each year, all told, to pro-
...the cats in the big postoffices
...country, but it is money wisely

ARMY CATS BETTER OBEY ORDERS

NEW YORK. Dec. 20.—Army cats had better start obeying the regulations or they'll be sorry. Cats not in quarters between 7:30 p. m. and 6:30 a. m. at Fort Jay, Governor's Island, will be kicked right out of the army into the S. P. C. A. pound, the commanding officer ordered.

Bomber to Tote Black Cat Across the Path of Hitler

Special to THE NEW YORK TIMES.

WILKES-BARRE, Pa., Aug. 1
—A black cat which R. A. F. fliers will carry in a bomber over Germany until it has crossed the path of Adolf Hitler, was put on a plane here this afternoon, bound for Britain by the way of New York and Canada.

The cat, named Captain Midnight, is owned by a Dallas family which preferred to remain anonymous.

The arrangements for the trip were made through the local Chamber of Commerce and the family is paying transportation costs.

A red, white and blue label on a crate described Captain Midnight as "a special envoy."

WAR VETERAN—Pooli, who rates three service ribbons and four battle stars, shows she can still get into her old uniform as she prepares to celebrate her 15th birthday. The cat served aboard an attack transport during World War II.
Times photo

Our vital role in military life is nowadays forgotten, but some cats rose to no small fame. Among them were The Colonel, a tomcat stationed at the Presidio in San Francisco in the 1890s and considered the best mouser the army ever had, and Pooli, the navy's most decorated feline.

A break in the action: soldierly life was rough, but it also brought moments of tenderness and camaraderie for the cats who had gone off to war. This kitten helped keep the peace as a member of Company B of the 316th Military Police during World War I in France.

Lighten up, Sergeant. Can you blame this drill instructor for being tamed by the new recruit he cradles in his hands? No doubt he was aware of the debt the army owed us—in the days before modern pesticides, we were on the front lines of the war against rodents.

A pair of true pioneers: the aviator John Moisant and his fearless feline flying companion Mademoiselle Fifi in a c.1910 photograph. Fifi was said to have traveled on up to fourteen flights, with a litter box installed under the passenger seat. Is it any wonder Moisant was nicknamed Captain Kitty?

And Now Comes "Pepper," a New Photoplay Star

His Salary Is Not Enormous, But He Is Worth It

THE most valuable cat in the world is "Pepper," a half-grown Maltese, who has won name and fame acting in Mack Sennett comedies.

"Pepper" has been insured for five thousand dollars, and is worth a great deal more than that sum. "Pepper's" unique value lies in the fact that there will never be another cat like her. She has the fighting heart of a bull-dog. Like Gunga Din, she "doesn't seem to have no use for fear."

You can discharge a .45 Colt close enough to singe "Pepper's" hair, and all she does is to look around with mild surprise. All dogs she regards with contemptuous indifference.

One day they put fly-paper on "Pepper's" feet. An ordinary cat would have proceeded to go insane. "Pepper" tried several experiments. She tried to bite the fly-paper off. When she found the biting wasn't good, she tried to scratch the paper off with the other leg. Finding there was no merit in that method, she tried to take the fly-paper by surprise. After playing 'possum for a minute, she made a sudden wild leap. But, to her disgust, the vigilant fly-paper leaped right along with her. With that "Pepper" philosophically abandoned the struggle.

"Oh, well," "Pepper" seemed to say, "one fly-paper doesn't make a summer."

The most severe trial that afflicts "Pepper's" young life is a white rat which lives at the studio and which also acts in Mack Sennett comedies. "Pepper" considers the rat altogether too familiar. When they act together in comedies, the rat insists upon sticking his pink, quivering nose up to smell around "Pepper's" face. As no well-bred actress cat would consent to kiss a rat, even in the interests of Art, "Pepper" always moves away with a baleful look and a most indignant meouw.

NO LETTERS IN "PEPPER'S" MAIL-BOX
(MACK SENNETT COMEDIES)

The only actor on the lot with whom "Pepper" is not on terms is the little black bear. "Pepper" always gives the bear a most respectful and a very wide berth. Bears are uncertain critters, and no one knows it better than "Pepper." Instinct has informed her that the bear is likely to be taken at any minute with a burning curiosity to know how his big, gleaming teeth would feel sliding around thru a piece of cat. Consequently, when the bear is acting, "Pepper" finds it appropriate to have an engagement with herself up on the roof of the "light" studio.

A ball of yarn conceals almost uncanny delights for "Pepper." She will start to unwind it and roll over and over in the yarn until finally she is all wound up in it—a cocoon with a kitten inside. "Pepper" is a marvelously skillful Nimrod, and she does her fishing by using her tail for a fishing-rod. There is a tank of fish in the studio that will bite on anything, and when "Pepper" discovered their voracity, she took a huge delight in sticking her tail in the tank and at the first nibble making a quick leap with Mr. Fish clinging to her handy fishing-rod.

Alas! that it must be related, the breath of scandal has involved "Pepper." The whole studio has been shocked by the discovery that "Pepper," altho she has no wedding-ring, has prospects.

With this feature in *Photoplay*, as well as similar articles in *Picture Show* and *Pictures and Picturegoer*, Pepper hit the big time. A monumental step for cats everywhere, and a sign of our newfound respect. Oh wait. Except . . . Pepper was a *she* not a *he*. Sigh.

KING RHUBARB

Here's the success story of an alley cat. But it was a tough fight — for humans

THERE was no love lost between "Orangey," a 14-pound alley cat who became a movie star overnight, and Frank Inn, the equally burly trainer who put him through his paces before the cameras.

"Orangey" is the star — stealing the billing from such accomplished humans as Ray Milland and Jan Sterling — of a picture called "Rhubarb," based on the H. Allen Smith novel of the cat who became the owner of the Brooklyn Dodgers.

Mr. Inn is a well-known animal trainer in Hollywood, once helped train Lassie, and in his day has played dramatic coach to every conceivable type of animal actor — running the gamut, you might say, from aardvark to zebra.

Hard To Handle

HE HAS kind words for most of these beasts. But he and Orangey simply did not hit it off. They hardly tried to conceal their mutual dislike, in fact. Inn's hands and forearms were mottled with the marks of Orangey's claws and disapproval.

The Humane Association was there to see that Mr. Inn confined his feelings to words. The organization watches pretty closely when Hollywood makes a picture with animals — lest the equine, canine or feline actors get the same kind of treatment accorded some of the humans.

In the feud between Orangey and his trainer, the fault was not altogether Mr. Inn's. In its search for "Rhubarb," Paramount advertised for a "foul-tempered, scar-faced sourpuss" of a cat. Orangey, everybody seemed to agree, filled the bill.

My own impression of Orangey was not favorable. He spat at me without provocation.

So temperamental was this particular tabby that 22 similarly marked and dispositioned alley cats had to be hired to serve as stand-ins and doubles. Cats in general get bored quickly. A fresh cat had to be substituted at every turn to keep the cameras rolling and the human actors occupied.

Orangey, the best as well as the worst actor of the lot, got the star billing, star's dressing room, signed contract and extra saucer of cream.

Extra Inducements

EVEN these forms of persuasion were not sufficient to keep him in line. Police dogs were stationed at key spots to block off the unscheduled entrances and exits that Orangey insisted on making. Liver paste was smeared on Milland's fingers to insure a show of affection, or at any rate tolerance. Catnip was resorted to when Orangey seemed bored.

Apparently it worked. The picture was finished. But it will be a long time before Orangey is signed up for another film.

Hollywood does not like its stars to be independent.
— LOUIS BERG

CONTRACT makes him w

STAR'S ENTRANCE. Even in his alley days, "Orangey" never had it so good

JOSEPH HEFFNER

RHUBARB

starring RAY MILLAN

and JAN STERLIN

with GENE LOCKN

and

Rhuba

DIRECTED BY
ARTHUR LUBI

SCREENPLAY BY
DOROTHY REI
and FRANCIS COCH

BASED ON THE NOVEL
H. ALLEN SMIT

A PARAMOUNT PI

Property of National Screen Service Corp. Licensed for display only in connection with the exhibition of this picture at your theatre. Must be returned immediately thereafter.

corporation   COUNTRY OF ORIGIN U. S. A.

LEFT · Hollywood's new king, in a syndicated article appearing in Sunday edition newspapers on September 23, 1951. *Rhubarb* stiffed at the box office, but it was hardly Orangey's fault that the script wasn't worthy of him. Pundits gave his performance rave reviews, providing his first taste of fame.

ABOVE · First rate acting talent in this lobby card from the theatrical release of *Rhubarb*. Ray Milland won an Oscar in 1945, and Jan Sterling went on to win a Golden Globe in 1954. Was Orangey intimidated? Doubtful, since he did them one better by winning a *pair* of PATSY Awards!

Hoping to "a-mews" you—
Rhubarb
(HIS PAW-TOGRAPH)

LEFT · An original Puss'n Boots medal. The highest of the high, the Nobel Prize of cats! This one remained uncirculated when the program was discontinued. For that I will blame human laziness, as I'm sure they could have found another deserving cat somewhere in the great expanses of America.

ABOVE · Having hit the big time, Orangey was in demand as a product spokes-cat. His first client? None other than Puss'n Boots cat food. As for the paw-tograph, sorry, it was stamped on. You don't really think we cats want ink on our paws, do you?

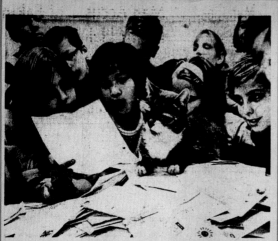

MAIL CALL—Sixth-grader Laurie Wong reads one of many fan letters to kitty.
Times photo by John Malmin

HE'S STILL COOL CAT

School Paper Sparks Fan Mail for Room 8

Not every oldster has a flock of secretaries answering more than 100 fan letters a day, but there is a cool old cat out Elysian Park way doing just that.

Long famed locally as The Cat Who Came to Dinner—or rather, lunch —his name is Room 8, official mascot of Elysian Heights Elementary School. Fourteen years ago he strolled in, raided the lunchbags, and never went home.

Now, in his sunset years, national fame has come his way because The Weekly Reader, a newspaper circulated to grammar school pupils across the nation, printed a few paragraphs about him last January.

Since then, mail has poured in from the youngsters. Each has received a reply from one of Room 8's school chums.

A giggle arose as Laurie Wong, 11, read a note from Alabama that was written in big, block letters.

"Are you a boy or a girl?" it asked.

Room 8 yawned and settled down for a catnap, as if to say that such things don't matter much any more.

Herald-Examiner Photos

OLD SCHOOL MASCOT, ROOM 8, AND FRIENDS
Death has claimed Elysian Heights tomcat

FINAL BELL TOLLS FOR FAMED TOMCAT

Room 8 was a popular topic for writers from the *Los Angeles Times*, *Herald Examiner*, and *Valley Times*. But his appeal wasn't just regional! Covered in national magazines, he received over ten thousand fan letters—and personally responded to none of them. What cat can be bothered with that sort of thing?

Newspaper photo from the *Los Angeles Herald* Examiner of Room 8 with a group of students at Elysian Heights Elementary School. He was always the center of attention, although we'll have to acknowledge that it looks like he was bored with his assignment on that day.

Afterword

A NOTE FROM BABA'S HUMAN

Hello. With our narrator's departure, the concluding words will be left to me, her human companion. Hardly a surprise, as I have grown accustomed to tidying up after her.

Baba was adopted out of the North Central Animal Shelter on Lacy Street in Los Angeles. This was some years ago, although the moment I found her is so indelibly impressed upon my mind that the memory has faded not one bit. I am forced to admit with considerable embarrassment that she was *not* the cat I had intended to take with me on that fateful day. In fact, there was another on which I had my sights set. He was a dashing gent, a long-haired silvery tabby and the apple of my eye—or so I thought.

I was counting the days until he would become available for adoption, and at the appointed hour I was waiting outside the door for the shelter to open. But when I strode forward to claim my prize, I was met with heartbreak. There was confusion among the staff, and the silver tabby, whom I had visited daily for the week of his incarceration, was suddenly given over to another person. In the throes of depression, I walked toward the exit, passing a row of caged cats who had been recently brought in.

A paw reached out to stop me. It was attached to a brown tabby, maybe six months old, and the claws gripped my shirt and pulled me in close. Well, aren't you a bold little one, I thought, as I looked for the first time into Baba's eyes. She explained with nary a word being said how the cats themselves had things all planned out. It was she, and not the silver tabby, who had been designated to go home with me.

As always, the cats knew best, because on my own I could have never found such an appropriate companion. Baba was a precocious learner, and it turned out that her interest in history

250

coincided with my own. Many an hour were spent perusing tattered manuscripts as I researched my own books, and the inquisitive cat would perch herself at my side or on my lap and stare at the pages with remarkable intensity. How much she understood of the words in front of us I could never be sure, but one day out of curiosity I turned the document I was reading upside down. A paw quickly reached out to nudge my hand to turn the page back upright—her reverence for the written word turned out to be such that she would not condone such foolishness.

Eventually we decided that I should stop getting all the glory for what was, at least in her opinion, shared labor. It would now be her turn to be an author, and thereby undertake the current tome on feline history for a human audience. I vowed to assist however I could, cats not being allowed in most libraries and research facilities. (I am sure Baba would point out that this is all the more reason why her book is necessary: have such institutions never heard of Room 8, Dewey, or Black Jack?)

As it became my duty to pull aside the source materials she might need, I can say a few words about the research. It included not just the modern books about feline history and mythology (she has read them all), but also important historical sources held in various special collections, such as Moncrif's *Histoire des chats*, and, yes, even the sordid words of the despicable Comte de Buffon. Old newspapers in particular proved to be an indispensable source. It was in their tattered pages that some of the most wondrous stories of feline achievement in the nineteenth and twentieth centuries were recovered from the dustbin of history, and days at a time were spent searching through moldering stacks of periodicals dredged from library storerooms. Particular thanks must be given to the Huntington Library in San Marino, California, the UCLA Libraries and Special Collections, the Los Angeles Public Library, the PDSA in London for original photos and information on Simon of the HMS *Amethyst*, and with all our hearts to Room 8's own Elysian Heights Elementary School.

Many people are no doubt curious about Baba's photos. Like any human companion, I have always taken a certain joy in capturing her image, but we eventually went far beyond standard animal photography by including costumes, wigs, and props. It turned out our interests coincided here as well. She has proven to be as talented a model as you will find, human or feline or any other species, capable of capturing a wide range of expressions and portraying innumerable character types.

The photos have become for us more than just portraits, however. They are an exercise in interspecies communication that has made our bond all the stronger, as I devise roles for her to play and then, by my limited human means, come up with ways to explain the pose and expression required. Amazingly, more times than not she gets it exactly right—and equally amazing is when she doesn't, since it typically turns out that her vision for the character is markedly superior to mine.

Her wardrobe is by now considerably bigger than my own, and I mean that as no slight to myself, since in fact her wardrobe is most likely bigger than that of any but the most dedicated devotees of haute couture. But like a true lady of fashion, she has never been one for off-the-rack. While she delights in modeling, she turns her snout up at the costumes available in pet stores or online, and I have always pitied people who expect to get decent photos of their feline companions in such outfits. It is a universal truth among cats, from the most pampered and expensive to the most humble of strays, that they take great pride in their appearance, and I can assure you that none of them will pose well in such outfits. You might think of it this way: if you spent as much time primping and grooming as the average cat, would you want to be forced into a shabby-looking, ten-dollar clown suit?

Certainly not. I quickly learned the lesson and moved Baba along to custom clothing, carefully tailored to represent the characters she was to play, and thereafter she flourished. Many of her outfits are modified vintage doll dresses, or recut from teddy bear costumes. But many others are made completely from scratch, and when we finally came to a point where she required garments beyond my meager talents, she found allies among

Hollywood designers who were willing to set their vision to a feline scale (and to Desirae Hepp, the Alexander McQueen of cat couture, she and I are eternally grateful).

We have also learned several tricks over the past few years. Doll wigs around fourteen inches in circumference fit a cat quite nicely; the neckline of a garment should always be cut extra high to compensate for the placement of feline shoulders; and did you know that a small snip of toupee tape is perfect for attaching moustaches or beards to fur without being cumbersome or annoying? These are all important tips for the well-appointed feline fashionista. Oh—and absolutely never photograph a cat wearing a Victorian dress in a room where there is a live mouse (a long story which I will leave to your imaginations).

I am inclined to say that Baba and I have made the most of what we each have to offer, and people are quick to remark on how perfectly matched she and I are. Indeed, I would never deny it. Our interests and personalities are particularly well aligned—not that I am surprised, because felines have wisdom, and as I have told you it was she who chose me, recognizing on her own that I was her ideal companion. I simply had to be smart enough to agree to my end of the deal.

But when people marvel about how no other cat would do what Baba has done, wearing such costumes and posing for such photos, I can only laugh. How do they know? Have they inquired among their own feline companions? I could hardly have imagined as much on that fateful day back at North Central Animal Shelter. But living with a cat is a process of learning, and she has taught me much that I would not have guessed.

And that brings us at last to the one lesson we both hope you will have learned from this book. That cats can do an awful lot of things humans would never expect of them; they simply need to be given the chance.

BIBLIOGRAPHY

For Further Reading

Finally, Baba wishes to present this suggested reading list. Researching cats is hard work, especially for humans, but for those of you who wish to know a bit more about their history, these are some good places to start.

●

Biographies of Famous Cats

Alexander, Caroline. *Mrs. Chippy's Last Expedition: The Remarkable Journal of Shackleton's Polar Bound Cat*. New York: HarperPerennial, 1999.

Berman, Lucy. *Famous and Fabulous Cats*. London: Peter Lowe/Eurobook, 1973.

Brown, Philip. *Uncle Whiskers*. London: André Deutsch Limited, 1975.

Cooper, Vera. *Simon the Cat (HMS Amethyst)*. London: Hutchison, 1950.

Finley, Virginia and Beverly Mason. *A Cat Called Room 8*. New York: Putnam, 1966.

Flinders, Matthew. *Trim: Being the True Story of a Brave Seafaring Cat*. Pymble, New South Wales: Angus and Robertson, 1997 (reprint of 1733 manuscript).

Myron, Vicki with Bret Witter. *Dewey: The Small-Town Library Cat Who Touched the World*. New York: Grand Central, 2008.

Paull, Mrs. H.H.B. *"Only a Cat" Or, The Autobiography of Tom Blackman, A favourite Cat which lived for seventeen years with members of the same family, dying at last of old age*. London: Elliot Stock, 1876.

Feline History and Studies

Altman, Roberta. *The Quintessential Cat: A Comprehensive Guide to the Cat in History, Art, Literature, and Legend*. New York: Macmillan, 1994.

Beadle, Muriel. *The Cat: History, Biology, and Behavior*. New York: Simon and Schuster, 1977.

Choron, Sandra, Harry Choron, and Arden Moore. *Planet Cat: A Cat-alog*. Boston: Houghton Mifflin, 2007.

Clutton-Brock, Juliet. *Cats: Ancient and Modern*. Cambridge, Massachusetts: Harvard University Press, 1993.

Engel, Donald. *Classical Cats: The Rise and Fall of the Sacred Feline*. London: Routledge, 1999.

For Contributing to Human Happiness: Thirty True Stories about Cats who have Received the Puss'n Boots Bronze Award and Citation for Commendable Characteristics and Achievements. Garden City, NY: Country Life Press, 1953.

Kalda, Sam. *Of Cats and Men: Profiles of History's Great Cat-Loving Artists, Writers, Thinkers, and Statesmen*. New York: Ten Speed Press, 2017.

Lewis, Val. *Ships' Cats in War and Peace*. Shepperton, UK: Nauticalia Ltd., 2001.

Malek, Jaromir. *The Cat in Ancient Egypt*. Philadelphia: University of Pennsylvania Press, 1993.

Mery, Fernand. *The Life, History, and Magic of the Cat*, translated by Emma Street. New York: Grosset and Dunlap, 1975.

Morris, Desmond. *Catlore*. New York: Crown, 1987.

Rogers, Katherine M. *Cat*. London: Reaktion Books, 2006.

Sillar, Frederick Cameron and Ruth Mary Meyler. *Cats: Ancient and Modern*. London: Studio Vista, 1966.

Tabor, Roger. *Cats: The Rise of the Cat*. London: BCA, 1991.

Tucker, Abigail. *The Lion in the Living Room: How House Cats Tamed Us and Took Over the World*. New York: Simon and Schuster, 2016.

Van Vechten, Carl. *The Tiger in the House*. New York: Alfred A. Knopf, 1920.

Vocelle, L.A. *Revered and Reviled: A Complete History of the Domestic Cat*. San Bernardino, CA: Great Cat Publications, 2016.

Cats in Myth, Folklore, and the Occult

Briggs, Katharine M. *Nine Lives: Cats in Folklore*. London: Routledge and Kegan Paul, 1980.

Conway, D.J. *The Mysterious, Magical Cat*. New York: Gramercy Books, 1998.

Dale-Green, Patricia. *Cult of the Cat*. New York: Weathervane, 1963.

Dunwich, Gerina. *Your Magical Cat: Feline Magic, Lore, and Worship*. New York: Citadel Press, 2000.

Gettings, Fred. *The Secret Lore of the Cat*. New York: Lyle Stuart Books, 1989.

Hausman, Gerald and Loretta Hausman. *The Mythology of Cats: Feline Legend and Lore Through the Ages*. Bokeelia, Florida: Irie Books, 2000.

Howey, M. Oldfield. *The Cat in Magic and Myth*. London: Bracken, 1993.

Jay, Roni. *Mystic Cats: A Celebration of Cat Magic and Feline Charm*. New York: Godsfield Press/ Harper Collins, 1995.

Moore, Joanna. *The Mysterious Cat: Feline Myth and Magic Through the Ages*. London: Piatkus, 1999.

O'Donnell, Elliott. *Animal ghosts; Or, Animal Hauntings and the Hereafter*. London: William Rider and Son, 1913.

Stephens, John Richard and Kim Smith (editors). *Mysterious Cat Stories*. New York: Galahad, 1993.

General Animal History

Grier, Katherine. *Pets in America*. Chapel Hill: University of North Carolina Press, 2006.

Henninger-Voss, Mary J. (editor). *Animals in Human Histories: The Mirror of Nature and Culture*. Rochester, New York: University of Rochester Press, 2002.

Kete, Kathleen. *The Beast in the Boudoir: Petkeeping in Nineteenth-Century Paris*. Berkeley: University of California Press, 1994.

Perkins, David. *Romanticism and Animal Rights*. Cambridge: Cambridge University Press, 2003.

Velten, Hannah. *Beastly London: A History of Animals in the City*. London: Reaktion Books, 2013.

Verity, Liz. *Animals at Sea*. London: National Maritime Museum, 2004.

Historic Sources and Classic Feline Literature

Champfleury, M. *The Cat, Past and Present, from the French of M. Champfleury, with Supplementary Notes by Mrs. Cashel Hoey*. London: G. Bell, 1885.

Drew, Elizabeth and Michael Joseph (editors). *Puss in Books: An Anthology of Classic Literature on Cats*. London: Geoffrey Bles, 1932.

Hoffman, E. T. A. *The Life and Opinions of the Tomcat Murr*, translated and annotated by Anthea Bell with an introduction by Jeremy Adler. London: Penguin, 1999.

Moncrif, Augustin Paradis de. *Moncrif's Cats: Les chats de Francois Augustin Paradis de Moncrif*, translated by Reginald Bretnor. London: Golden Cockerel, 1961.

Patteson, S. Louise, *Pussy Meow: The Autobiography of a Cat*. Philadelphia: Jacobs, 1901.

Repplier, Agnes. *The Fireside Sphinx*. Boston: Houghton Mifflin, 1901.

The Cat—Being a Record of the Endearments and Invectives Lavished by Many Writers upon an Animal Much Loved and Much Abhorred, collected, translated, and arranged by Agnes Repplier. New York: Sturgis and Walton, 1912.

Online Resources

hatchingcatnyc.com (nineteenth and early twentieth century animal stories from New York City)

milwaukeepressclub.org/about-us/story-of-anubis-the-cat/ (information on Anubis the Cat)

purr-n-fur.org.uk (focuses on well-known cats and feline history, with a particular emphasis on Britain)

ACKNOWLEDGMENTS

Special thanks to the Huntington Library (San Marino, CA), UCLA Libraries and Special Collections, the Los Angeles Public Library, the New York Public Library, the Torrance (CA) Library and Historical Society, the Denver Public Library, the Bowers Museum (Santa Ana, CA), the Boston Public Library, the University of Southern California Library, the Library of Congress, the Buccleuch Collection, the British Library, the California State Library, the PDSA in London (Ilford), and the Margaret Herrick Library of the Academy of Motion Picture Arts and Sciences (Beverly Hills, CA) for assistance with newspaper clippings and archival materials.

PHOTO CREDITS

F 68. "Surimono – woman with cat," Yashima Gakutei, 1820. The Miriam and Ira D. Wallach Division of Art, Prints and Photographs: Print Collection, The New York Public Library.

G 69. "Cat and dried fish (*Katsuo-boshi*)," Hokuba Arisaka, 1814. The Miriam and Ira D. Wallach Division of Art, Prints and Photographs: Print Collection, The New York Public Library.

H 99. "Portrait of Henry Wriothesley, 3rd Earl of Southampton, 1603," Jean de Critz. Broughton House, Northamptonshire, UK, The Buccleuch Collections/ Bridgeman Images.

I 106. *Le chat botté*," Charles Emile Jacque, 1841–1842. The Miriam and Ira D. Wallach Division of Art, Prints and Photographs: Print Collection, The New York Public Library.

J 182 (top). "Kitty" from the sheet "Kitty; Peachblow; Beryl; and Pet (Christmas cards depicting young girls with cats, birds, flowers, and hats)," Louis Prang and Company. The New York Public Library Digital Collections, 1865–1899. From The Miriam and Ira D. Wallach Division of Art, Prints and Photographs: Print Collection, The New York Public Library.

K 182 (bottom). "*Le rendes-vous des chats*," Édouard Manet, 1868. The Miriam and Ira D. Wallach Division of Art, Prints and Photographs: Print Collection, The New York Public Library.

L 184–185 (bottom). "At the Party," from the sheet "Prints entitled 'At the Party' and 'The Minstrels,'" Louis Prang and Company. The New York Public Library Digital Collections, 1865–1899. From the Miriam and Ira D. Wallach Division of Art, Prints and Photographs: Print Collection, The New York Public Library.

M 208. Kiddo aboard airship, 1910. From the George Grantham Bain Collection, Library of Congress Prints and Photographs Division, Washington, DC.

N 238–239. Billet of Company B, 316th Military Police, Ninety-first Division, Montigny de Roi, Haute Marne, France, 1918. War Dept. General Staff. Catalogue of Official A.E.F. Photographs, Library of Congress Prints and Photographs Division, Washington, DC.

O 240–241. John B. Moisant with his cat Mademoiselle Fifi, 1911. Library of Congress Prints and Photographs Division, Washington, DC.

P 246–247. Room 8 in classroom (Art Worden, photographer), 1964. Los Angeles Herald Examiner Photo Collection, Los Angeles Public Library.

INDEX

Page numbers in *italics* refer to illustrations.

ABOUT THE AUTHORS

Baba is a domestic short-haired tabby with a love for adventure and history. Despite weighing in at less than nine pounds, she is big on the inside and never has any cat or human stood in the way of her getting what she wants. Born to the rough streets of Los Angeles and educated in the school of hard knocks, she was interned in the city's animal shelter at a young age only to be discovered there by her human co-author. She started modeling five years ago and has since graced websites and publications across the world, with several of her images being exhibited in gallery shows and printed as posters. *A Cat's Tale* is her first book, and she has offered the opinion that writing is drudgery so it will probably turn out to be her last. She still lives in Southern California, and has a sister whose food she steals and otherwise completely ignores.

Paul Koudounaris has a PhD in Art History. He is the author of *The Empire of Death*, *Heavenly Bodies*, and *Memento Mori*, which all investigate the visual culture of death, and his photography has been shown in galleries and festivals internationally. He began researching the history of cats several years ago, finding in the topic not only an affirmation of feline merit, but also a sadly neglected field of study. He has since gone on to become a popular personality as a lecturer on the accomplishments of historic cats and has appeared on television and radio broadcasts to further extol their virtues.

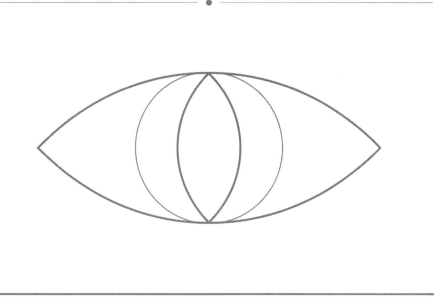